The Heresy of History

Alexander S. Holub., Ph.D.

Alexander S. Holub, Ph.D.

Copyright © 2004

For permissions, or serializations, condensations, adaptations, or for
our catalog of other publications, write the Publisher at the address
below.

Library of Congress Cataloging-in-Publication Data
Holub, Alexander S. (Alexander Steven), 1943-
    The Gospel truth: the heresy of history / Alexander S. Holub.
        p. cm.
    Includes bibliographical references

    ISBN 1-893157-11-3 (pbk.)

    1. Bible--Criticism, interpretation, etc. 2. Christianity--
Controversial literature. 3. Jesus Christ--New Age movement
interpretations. I Title.

    BS533.H59 2004
    220.6--dc22   2004057018

Published by
BRIDGER HOUSE PUBLISHERS, INC
P.O. Box 2208, Carson City, NV 89702, 1-800-729-4131

Cover design and text by TheRightTypeGraphics.com
Printed in the United States of America
10 9 8 7 6 5 4 3 2 1

Table of Contents

Alexander S. Holub, Ph.D.

FOREWORD

History is written by the winner. It does not matter whether the history is political, cultural or religious; history *is* written by the winner. What comes to you, the reader or re*searcher* is an extremely biased perspective of a particular period, incident, or series of incidents. To find the facts you need to go outside of the prevailing historical viewpoint and to confront other perspectives. In this way you can begin to piece together the available history to get a better idea of what actually occurred. By looking at other sides of the same event you can get different views of it. This must be done in an objective, unbiased way. Only by not having a pre-disposed mind-set can the facts be openly presented, digested, and understood as they approach more precisely what had transpired.

The true re*searcher* is one who seeks to objectively examine, to understand, and to know the facts, as well as possible, and to express those facts as clearly as they can be presented. To do this, it is necessary to not go into any research with a preconceived notion and/or biased point to prove. You can research *critically* examining every point and issue available *before* coming to a decision. To research properly, you will follow a systematized pattern or process leading toward an understanding of the subject. This process comprises an active attempt to understand and evaluate the available information and make a wholly unbiased decision as to its meaning. That decision is not looked on as the *whole* truth, but only *provisional* truth. This is so because there could be some information which may come later that could affect the outcome based on the present information.

It is of utmost importance to use critical thinking when considering all of the information which you find. All too often researchers want to fit what they find into what is currently *accepted*. In this way they do not have to deal with it in the context in which it was discovered nor in reference to other information from outside of *a* specific source. Many times academic researchers will "adjust" the information they find so that it can be published. For quite often publishers will take only the data that fits the current beliefs and theories. The reason being that only that which is "politically correct" will be accepted and sell.

This often happens with history. In reality, this has been going on since the first histories were written down. History was made to fit into the accepted *legends* and *myths* rather than to objectively express what has occurred. Then as time goes on, the tales became accepted and "adjusted" to fit the current belief structure promoted by those in charge to fit the prevailing practices.

Critical thinking is an active process. It involves delving deeply into as much information as is available. Only by doing this will you find what actually occurred and the meaning of the specific occurrence. Critical thinking is a step-by-step process; a systematized way of making sense out of information. It is not the acceptance of something just because someone said it or because it is written in some book. It does not involve one point of view but considers many points of view and arguments. Only then can a clear, unbiased perspective be seen. Hence, it is necessary to understand what the arguments pro and con are as well as the evaluation of the validity of those arguments. An important aspect of thinking critically is that of questioning those claiming to be an authority. The mark of a true science is that it can be wrong so that it can be adjusted in order to more approximate the "real world." Finally, the process of critical thinking involves experimentation. This means it is necessary to take the theories that have been postulated and put them up to find *empirical evidence* that can prove their correctness. If an idea, theory, or concept cannot be proven empirically it is relegated to the realm of belief. Beliefs, you will find, do not have to have facts backing them up. They are held simply because they seem to fit a particular frame of reference.

Remember the old proverb: "In truth we know nothing, for truth lies in the mystery." (Democritis c. 410 - c. 400 BCE) Beginning from the point of not knowing you can start to learn by searching with an open mind desirous of knowing the truth.[1]

There is no single right way to understand and evaluate what can be found. There is no guarantee that the material that you find is absolutely correct. It is the wise individual who does not accept a single point of view or interpretation of anything . . . especially history.

As examples of the convoluted history that are found in United States history books, we will consider first what the legends are and what we are told and then what actually occurred.

1. The Puritans (fanatical followers of John Calvin) came to the North American continent in order to escape religious persecution.

    The Facts: The Puritans themselves were actually persecuting other religions. The English government forced them to leave England for that reason. After settling down in the "New World" they proceeded to persecute other religions and other Christian sects. Also, after the "first Thanksgiving" that they spent (thanks to the local friendly natives) they proceeded to attack and murder part of the tribe.

2. The founding fathers of the United States were good, upstanding, orthodox Christians.

    The Facts: The founding fathers of the United States were by and large *Freemasons* (occultists) whose main religious affiliation was Unitarian. They had very little patience for religious sects like the Anabaptists, Calvinists or other sects that forced obedience through fear and ignorance. This can

---

1   It is an interesting point that western religion is always talking about truth and the search for truth. Unfortunately, when they are presented with the truth they do not want to hear it. The truth is "of the devil" as far as they're concerned.

be seen in the writings of Thomas Jefferson and Thomas Paine for example. The fact of the matter is that the founding fathers were not very devout church-goers either. As far as their belief in God was concerned, essentially, they were deists, not theists. A theist believes in God and that God directly influences and controls individual lives. Deists believe in God as well. The difference is that God does not exert power over individual lives.

3. After the Declaration of Independence of the United States was read its signers stood in line to affix their signatures to the document.

    The Facts: After John Hancock and Charles Thomsen signed the Declaration of Independence there was another month wait until anyone else signed it. Altogether it took more than five years before all of the signatures were finally placed on the document. This was well after the Revolutionary War had ended.

4. The American Revolution was a popular movement through-out the thirteen colonies.

    The Facts: The American Revolution was taken up by only a small minority of individuals in the colonies. It was backed mainly by the wealthy, some of the merchants, and some of the farmers. It was not a popular idea at all. In fact, one reason that it took five years to sign the Declaration of Independence was because there were still many who felt that breaking from England was not in the best interests of the colonies.

5. The Emancipation Proclamation was eagerly signed by Abraham Lincoln and it freed all of the slaves.

    The Facts: Lincoln originally was not sure he wanted to sign the Emancipation Proclamation, even though it was his idea. He was maneuvered into doing so for several reasons: 1) The

American Civil War began as a war to reunite the country. This was an unconstitutional act. The Constitution grants the states the right to secede. Forcing states back into the Union directly violated state's rights and the Constitution. After a year or so of the war, the abolitionists began to gain more power and the thrust of the war became that of freeing the slaves; 2) He was told that either he would sign the Emancipation Proclamation or he would not be reelected for a second term; 3) The signing of the document would be an excellent way to keep any European intervention (British and French especially) out of the war. Even though cotton from the South was needed in Europe the Emancipation Proclamation would effectively limit trade with the South. Slavery had been abolished throughout Europe for quite some time and no European country would want to be known as one which was approving of slavery by trading with a slave-based economy; and 4) Lincoln himself owned slaves and the Emancipation Proclamation did nothing for the slaves that were already owned or below the Mason-Dixon Line, where the Proclamation did not have any jurisdiction.

6. The assassination of archduke Francis Ferdinand of Austria was one of the important events which led to the beginning of World War I.

    The Facts: Archduke Francis Ferdinand was greatly despised throughout Europe. His murder was actually welcomed by many. Few countries sent their ambassadors to his funeral. The assassination was later used as an excuse to begin the war.

7. Once Ho Chi Min gained power he immediately embraced Communism.

    The Facts: When Ho Chi Min gained power in Vietnam (then known as Indo-China) he declared independence for his country. Several United States Senators were in the audience when the Declaration of Independence was read. The

Declaration of Independence of Indo-China was modeled after that of the United States and Ho Chi Min sent a request that his country become a United States protectorate. Either the request was never received or it was shelved because Indo-China was not considered an important area. With no response from the United States, Ho Chi Min turned to China.

8.   Sun Yat-Sen led his people in the famous 1911 revolution that brought down the Manchu dynasty.

The Facts: Sun Yat-Sen was in the United States, in Denver, Colorado specifically, at the time of the rebellion and read about it in the paper. He was given credit for starting the revolution only because he convinced people that he did start it. The fact of the matter was that some years before the beginning of the revolution he was locked up in the Chinese legation prison in London, England. He was locked up because he was a fugitive from Chinese justice and had walked into the Embassy. It was from his prison cell that he orchestrated a newspaper campaign on his own behalf. So powerful was this campaign the Chinese legation was forced to release him. He then came to the United States.

As you can see by these few facts (and I am sure that you could find many others if you would search), history is not what we are taught to believe. To find the facts you must research and sift through volumes and volumes of material—something you most likely do not want to do.[2] It is much easier to listen to what someone who sets himself up as an authority tells you and accept that without reservation.

By accepting what you have been told, you risk being manipulated and controlled by others. When the true facts are presented,

---

2   Two rather good books to start with are both by Richard Shenkman: *Legends, Lies & Cherished Myths of American History*, Wm. Morrow & Co., 1988 and *Legends, Lies & Cherished Myths of World History*, HarperCollins, 1993.

you will refuse to even consider them for they confront you within your "comfort zone." You then fall into the heart of that ancient proverb: "The simple minded will believe anything..." Further, you would not like to consider that you will let yourself be manipulated, controlled and made to believe in something which is plainly not true. Ignorance *is* comfortable.

History *is* written by the winner. This simply means that the facts are manipulated in order to show the winner in the best, most benevolent light possible. No person or group would like to consider that she, he or they could do anything which is not constructive. Even the most hardened criminal or most inhuman regime believed that what was being done was the "correct" thing to do and in the "best interests of humanity"—no matter how heinous the action.

This also goes for religions and religious philosophies. The Catholic Church, and later the Protestant Churches, saw absolutely nothing wrong in the murder of many millions of innocent people during the period of the Inquisition using witchcraft as an excuse.[3] Nor did it see anything wrong with forcing Christianity onto "ignorant savages" by coercion and threats of torture and death.

It is a sad fact that the bloodiest wars in all history have been religious wars. These wars have occurred only since the coming of Christianity. They were perpetuated and fought by self-righteous fanatics who were blinded by their own excessive guilt, self-hate, and (especially) greed. The interesting thing about these bloody wars is that both sides invoked the *same* God to help them *destroy* the *unbeliever and heretic*.

The self-righteous fanatics' own self-hatred drives him on in the pursuit of his "holy cause." He has no concept of who he is for his identification is in the religion and he sees himself as "chosen." He believes himself to be God incarnate. As such he will commit all sorts of atrocities in the name of his God believing in his own personal perfection. His rationalization is that what he is doing is

---

3 The Inquisition was promoted by a Pope with the ironic name of *Innocent III*. This was done even *after* The Church had, a few centuries earlier, declared witchcraft to be *non-existent*.

what God wants. In this way he does not have to feel any guilt for his actions. To gain followers he sees nothing wrong with putting words in God's mouth and interpreting the Scriptures whichever he sees fit. He will proselytize in order to gain followers only because he is convincing himself that what he is preaching is true. The more followers he gets, the more he believes his own propaganda and falsehoods. Also, since he hates to give up his ignorance and the comfort that his ignorance provides, with every rejection he becomes more determined to force his limited thinking on to others. Through rejection and his own self-righteous, egocentric ideals as well as his refusal to admit that he is wrong, he feels more strongly toward his irrational thinking, viewing himself as being persecuted. That persecution, he ignorantly reasons, is only part of "doing God's work." With that he becomes more entrenched in his limited position.[4] His fear, ignorance of fact and superstitious beliefs accompanied by a weak self-image and self-concept perpetuate a neurotic state of mind. It is that neurosis that becomes the means of manipulation by unscrupulous, self-righteous, dogmatists.

What you are about to read are historical facts. All are documented and the majority of resources are shown in the bibliography so that your own research will be able to verify it. There are some things which were found before this work was put together and the reference has been lost, but by engaging in your own research surely you will find them.

To begin your own research, the bibliography in the back is a good starting point. Once the truth sets you free you then must accept personal responsibility for your life, your thinking, and your actions. You cannot blame anything on anthropomorphized concepts designed to manipulate and control your mind. Remember, true freedom means that you are not bound by any philosophy, any institution, or any dogma.

---

4 See *The True Believer* by Eric Hoffer, *The Psychology of Self-Esteem* by Nathaniel Brandon, and *Faith and Violence* by Thomas Merton.

This research was initially begun with the hope of proving that the Judeo/Christian religious teachings of the latter half of the 20th and the beginning of the 21st century are correct and unique. Face it, life would be so much easier if all you had to do was to give yourself over to the God of the current religious tenets. You would not have to accept any responsibility for what you are doing and you could blame whatever went wrong . . . or right . . . in your life on something else. What was found, though, was not what was expected. The facts far outweigh the fiction, and, by the way, are much more interesting.

These same facts are available to you. History, with which you are familiar, may have been written by the winner and propagandized in order to perpetuate a mind-set attached to the current mythology, but it does not mean that you have to accept or believe it. You can start now to remove that mind-set and allow yourself the freedom to think, to reason, and to be alive. By allowing yourself the freedom to think, to reason, and to search you will be more of the thinking animal as the title **homo sapiens** (thinking man) implies. You will not be an identification only associated with the membership in a particular group. Remember, it is man who makes up the rules by which gods live and judge. It is also man who creates the scriptures and philosophies that gods were supposed to have handed down.

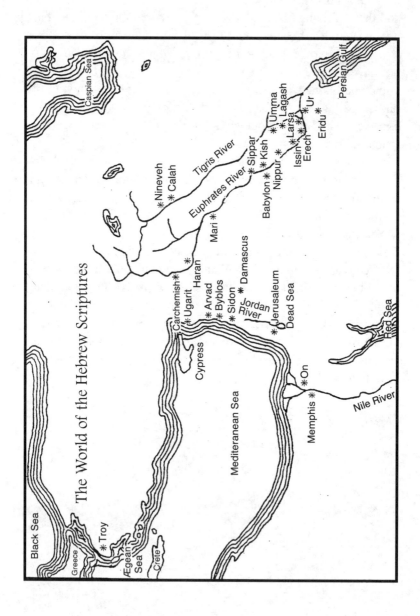

DATING THE HEBREW SCRIPTURES

Group	Date (BCE)	Book
Yahwists (Mushite Priests)	850	1 & 2 Samuel (I)
850-650 in Northern Israel	750	Genesis (I), Leviticus
Elohists (Mushite Priests)		
800-700 in Israel	700	Deuteronomy (I), Judges (I)
Priests (Aaronic Priests) 700		
	650	
Deuteronomists (Shiloah/Levite		
Priests) 650-600 in Judah		
Deuteronomy 1 & 2	600	Exodus, Lamentations
(Jeremiah) 609-587	580	Deuteronomy (II), 1 & 2 Samuel (II)
	530	Judges (I), Joshua, 1 & 2 Kings, Jeremiah, Ezekiel
	500	Genesis (II)
Deuteronomist Redactors		
(Aaronic Priests) 500-450	450	Hosea, Joel, Amos, Obadiah, Nahum, Micah, Zephaniah, Haggai, Habbakuk, Malachi
Ezra's rewriting of the Scriptures	400	Judges (II), Isaiah (I), Ruth
	350	
	300	1 & 2 Chronicles, Zechariah (I)
	250	Ecclesiastes, Isaiah (II), Zechariah (II)
	200	
	165	Daniel
	150	Canticles, Psalms, & Proverbs are non-specific in dating being collections of sayings, etc.

The Roman numeral I indicates the beginning of the writing of the particular book. Roman numeral II indicates the final compilation. Hosea, Joel, Amos, and so on were written during the period from 450 to 350 BCE. Consequently, no specific date can be applied to these books.

Alexánder S. Holub, Ph.D.

PART I

Ye shall not add unto the word which I command you, neither shall ye diminish (ought) from it, that ye may keep the commandments of the Lord your God (Yahweh Elohim) which I command you.

Deuteronomy 4:2

The Hebrew Scriptures*

Many today would like to believe that The Bible is *the* divinely inspired "Word of God" and is a truly unique series of books; that the writers of the Bible were especially "blessed" and had *direct* contact and connection with *The* Universal Deity. What is found upon investigation is that this is *not* the case. The Bible either plagiarized, word-for-word, or directly paraphrased much older *Pagan* mythological and legendary sources. In fact, God's "inspiration" never reached The Bible until after 480 BCE. Also, very little in the Biblical texts are actually unique to the people who wrote them. Further, the God spoken of in The Bible, Yahweh[1] by name, who eventually became *THE* Universal Deity, began as one of a number of Eastern Mediterranean tribal deities.[2] It was only due to

---

1 The *New American Standard Bible* states that the pronunciation of Yahweh for the YHWH (יהוה) is, essentially, incorrect. The fact is that the pronunciation of Yahweh is seen in both Greek and Latin as well as in the Gnostic texts. The most incorrect pronunciation is Jehovah.

2 As you shall see, the name of the god of the Hebrews, later the Israelites/Judeans, and finally the Jews also came from *pre-Hebrew* times and is pagan in origin.

*NOTE: It is important to remember that the writings known to Christians as "The Old Testament" were not Jewish but Hebrew. The term "Jew" was first introduced in 1775 and did not exist prior to that time. The religion we call Judiasm had no name until after that period. In this book, it will be referred to as the Judean religion unless the reference is modern.

the stubborn persistence of the priests[3] of one particular faction of believers that eventually their god was raised in stature. It is also important to remember that several thousand years ago cultural gods were like the national flags that exist today. These gods represented different localities, cities, and countries. Yahweh, for example, as is stated throughout the Hebrew Scriptures, is *the god of Israel* who resides in Jerusalem and *not* the Universal Deity. Whenever one nation would conquer another the conqueror would overthrow the temple gods of their foe and erect their own gods in their place. In this way, correspondences between the gods of different nations and areas could be made. Much the same is done today when the flags of the conquered are displaced by the flags of the conqueror. The fact is, the only real thing that the different priests of the later Judeans and Israelites had in common was the desire to pass on a common history. The common history, though, was interpreted by the diverse priests differently. The fact is that the priests in Israel and Judea did not get along with each other and in many instances their scriptures *and* their concepts of God disagreed. They wrote and preached according to whatever would profit their cause. In essence, it was all self-serving. This is why when you read the Christian Scriptures and other early writings you will read of the Pharisees, the Sadducees, the Scribes, and Essenes. Each group was related to a different tradition. Each of the traditions had different ideas that they were interested in imparting to the people. The one thing that they were all interested in was to get and keep their followers. The Pharisees, for example, were held in high regard throughout the Roman and Parthian Empires. They were a dedicated group who upheld the best of religious ideals in the face of oppression. They supported leniency and mercy in the application of laws and they championed the rights of the poor against the oppression of the rich. The Pharisees wrote volumes of books including prayer books, hymns, books of wisdom, law books, Biblical commentaries, mystical treatises, and

---

3 The priests, of course, obviously would have been disenfranchised if the people looked toward other gods. Anyone who has read the Hebrew Scriptures has seen that these people constantly looked toward other gods.

history. Hence, they were more liberal in their interpretation of The Torah and the Mosaic Laws. They believed in a Written *and* an Oral Law and were more interested in adhering to the Oral Laws and traditions (known as Kabbalah). They professed a belief in the afterlife and that the Messianic prophecies were fulfilled in the person of Hezekiah. The Pharisees regarded themselves as the upholders of the authentic Judean religion. It was the Pharisees who instituted communal education with the synagogue in each community as the place of education. The Pharisees were respected by the common people not only for their upholding of The Torah but also for their piety and wisdom. They were *not* the hypocrites as they have been portrayed in the Christian Scriptures. The title given to a Pharisee was rabbi. The Pharisees became a distinct group around 160 BCE during the rebellion which opposed foreign rule in Palestine. They opposed the Sadducees on both religious and political grounds. When the Roman Empire annexed Palestine, the majority of the Sadducees became Roman sympathesizers and were not very popular with the masses. The Sadducees who were not Roman sympathesizers became the Pharisees and opposed the whole idea of a High Priest. Hence, there was a huge rivalry going on between these two groups and their followers.[4]

The Sadducees were the fundamentalists of the time. They were the priests and took care of the Temple in Jerusalem. They believed in a literal interpretation of Torah and the Mosaic Laws. They rejected any Oral Laws and traditions. They believed that only in priestly blood sacrifice and ritual was atonement for sin. They had no use for interpreters, sages, or rabbis. They believed in a priestly class with the High Priest at its head and defended the status quo. They also believed in the afterlife and the coming of the Messiah. The Sadducees came into existence from the period of

---

4   Many of the other groups that you hear about (i.e. the Nazoreans, Sicarrii, and Zealots) were different insurgent groups who were out to attempt to run the Roman Empire out of Israel. Rome had control of this area since around 150 BCE not because they particularly wanted to be there. They just sort of inherited it. The main advantage of controlling the Middle East at that time was the control of trade routes. Palestine was not directly on the trade routes but trade did pass through Palestine.

around 300 BCE when they were first appointed by the Ptolemaic Greeks who ruled Egypt and Judea. They were *not* descended from the Mosaic period.

Before getting involved in the groups, times, and the authors of the different texts of the Hebrew Scriptures, a little explanation of the construction of the Hebrew Scriptures is necessary.

The first book of The Hebrew Scriptures in English is called **Genesis**. The word "genesis" is a Greek word which means *origin* or *source*. Each book of The Scriptures is named for the first word with which it had initially begun. The term Genesis came into use due to the **Greek** translation of the Biblical texts (the Septuagint). The actual Hebrew **term** which begins the Bible is **b'rashith**. This term literally means *at first*, *beginning*, or *from* the first. It is a term which is used **exclusively** in **epic poetry**. This indicates that **everything** which follows is essentially a **poem**, a **story**, and, prior to it being committed to writing, was **recited**. In modern terminology, the term b'rashith would best be translated as; "Once upon a time . . ."

Transmitting material orally and from memory has some obviously inherent problems. It is a well-known fact that this type of information transmission is **always** at the mercy of memory and has additions, deletions, and whatever is necessary to make a point for the people living at the time and place. This can be seen in the recorded mythologies of many places around the world. In the ancient Greek myths, for example, there were changes made in the myths depending on the era and the message needed to convey. The same goes for the texts of the Hebrew Scriptures.

When you look at the term b'rashith, you will find that it is actually a **combination** of words and not a singular word. It combines the words **b'ra** (bara) which means **to create**, **rash** which means **a head**, and **shith** which has several meanings. Among these meanings are **to put, place, set, make**, and **a garment, a veil**, and **foundation**. Consequently, the strict translation of "In the beginning" for the term **b'rashith** does not take into account its full meaning. It is only through tradition that the term **b'rashith** comes to mean **"In the beginning."** Further, like the mythological material of the time, there is a deeper meaning attached to the term thus making a literal translation untenable.

The first verse of the Bible says: "*In the beginning, God created the heavens and the earth*." One major error here is the use of
the term *God*. In the Hebrew, there are many different words used
to denote God. Unfortunately, the terms are not retained in the
translations. This is a mistake. Each of the terms used to represent
God have a different meaning and represent God in (some of his)
various forms or aspects.

The first term used to represent God as the creator in the Hebrew
scripture is *Elohim* (אלהים) . It is *not* Yahweh (or Jehovah)[5] as
many think. The term *Elohim* is especially important because it is
a *plural* term. Literally it means *gods and goddesses*. It is also
translated as *messenger*, ruler, prince, or *angel*.[6] It, too, is made up
of two words: The first word is the term *El* (אל). *El* literally means
god. It is the word used most often in the Hebrew Scriptures for a
god and it is the name of the major Canaanite deity. The second
part of the name is *-him* (ה.ים-) and it is a *masculine plural* ending. In this way the term literally means gods *and* goddesses. In the
modern *traditional* Jewish interpretation of the term Elohim, in
order to try to reconcile the fact that it is a plural term, and combines male and female, it is said that Elohim represents the *unity*
of God. How does it represent this unity? Since it is a plural term
it is a singular word created from two and hence a unity. Even so,
how can there be a unity of anything unless there is more than one
thing that makes it up? In other words, other gods (usually referred
to as aspects) must exist in order for a unity to occur.

History, as well as the Scriptures, records that the *first* god worshiped by the Hebrews was *not* Yahweh at all but *El Shaddai*.[7] El

---

5 Shortly, it will be explained that the term Jehovah is a very poor translation of
   the particular Hebrew name of God.

6 This is seen in the different interpretations of Jacob's wrestling with "elohim."
   Some interpret it as Jacob wrestled with an *angel* others say that it was *God.*

7 Exodus 6:2-3 states: "And God (Elohim) spake unto Moses, and said unto
   him, 'I (am) Yahweh: And (I) appeared unto Abraham, unto Isaac, and unto
   Jacob, by the name of God Almighty (El Shaddai), but by my name Yahweh
   was I not known to them.'" There are people today who claim the worship of
   El Shaddai. What they don't realize is that El Shaddai required blood (including human) sacrifice.

Shaddai was referred to as "the Great Thunderer." He may have been a storm god who lived on the top of Mt. Sinai for he is described as "thundering from heaven" and "sending out lightning." It is known that Mt. Sinai is an extinct volcano so there may have been a connection with some rumblings from the mountain.

The name Yahweh appears to *not* even be a Hebrew name at all. Some very early records place the euphemism, Jah, (pronounced Ē-Ă) into *pre-Hebrew pagan* Syria. Even before that the major deity of the Sumerians (4th millennium BCE) was Ea (pronounced Ē-Ă). Further, the name Iah (pronouncedĒ-Ă) was the name of a minor Egyptian deity. The earliest references to Yahweh are seen in fourteenth to thirteenth century BCE Egyptian writings. It is also seen in pre-Phoenician writings[8] in Nebo, Samaria and northern Sinai and Syria. Yahweh has been identified with the gods Ba'al and Hadad of west Semitic peoples. What is deduced from this is that Yahweh is a *pagan* deity. It is an interesting note that the name Israel is the Phoenician name for the planet *Saturn*. It is not being too speculative to consider the possibility that the name Yahweh could also represent a specific celestial constellation for it appears to have the literal meaning of "little dove" as well.[9]

What is important about, not only the first verse of Genesis, but also the whole story of creation, is that it is seen *word-for-word* in ancient Babylonian texts which date from somewhere around 2100 BCE.[10] In these ancient texts it is not a *singular* deity which created the world but a *union* of gods. As it is stated in these ancient texts: "When the gods in their assembly had created the heavens and the earth . . ." This beginning is important because the Aramaic texts, which are older than the Masoretic texts that are used today for the Biblical translations, begin in much the same way. The Aramaic language was the language spoken by the *Babylonians* and was the popular language in Judea and Israel at the beginning

---

8   There is also the Sanskrit word from which the name most likely was derived, yahveh, which means everflowing and refers to flowing lava from a volcano. Recall that Mt. Sinai is an extinct volcano.

9   Hence, the sacrificing of *doves* at the temple in Jerusalem as noted by the Christian Scriptures.

of this current era and is still spoken in some areas of the Middle East.

There is also another problem here: The Hebrew Scriptures, up until several hundred years after the beginning of this era, had no separation between words, no punctuation, no vowel marks, and no paragraphing. Consequently, each book of the Scriptures was essentially **one long word or verse**. Part of the Judaic ritual of worship consists of recitations of sections of the Torah. These recitations can go on for quite a long time causing changes in awareness and consciousness. Recitation done in this manner is used to induce altered states of consciousness and deep trance states, not to impart information. The recitations will have a tendency to open doorways to the mind. This same process is used in Buddhist ceremonies during the recitation of the Sutras and Vedas. The choice of what the words mean is essentially arbitrary and based mainly upon tradition.

If you look at the history of the writing of what *eventually* became the Jewish Scriptures of today you will find that there is a fairly reliable pattern that you can follow. Much of the earliest texts were written down in Babylonian, Syrian, and Mesopotamian *cuneiform* script.[11] This dated from prior to 2500 BCE. When the

Sample *cuneiform* script

---

10 As a point to be mentioned, the name Eden comes from an ancient Sumerian word meaning "wild grasslands." Most of the Middle Eastern region 5000 years ago were grasslands, not desert as it is today.

11 Cuneiform was a syllabary and not an alphabet, except for the Ugaritic cuneiform (c. 14th century BCE). The Ugaritic language was a Semitic language and it was extremely similar to later Hebrew in its structure. The first alphabet was an Egyptian alphabet (c. 2000 BCE) followed by the first Semitic alphabet (c. 1700 BCE). The alphabet became most developed with the Phoenicians beginning about the 15th century BCE.

Assyrians captured Babylon about 1300 BCE the Assyrians took the Babylonian laws, their culture, *and* their religion and translated their religious texts into the Assyrian cuneiform. Then later, about 900 BCE the Assyrians took on a modified version of the Semitic alphabet and translated these texts into the Assyrian alphabet.[12] Around 600 BCE Babylon was taken back from the Assyrians and the texts were rewritten in the Chaldean, the early Aramaic, of that period. At about 400 BCE, they were again recopied, this time, into middle Hebrew. It's at this time when "Divine Inspiration" came into the texts. The Scribe (prophet) Ezra was credited with doing this. The fact is, many scholars believe that Ezra was the *actual* author of the Pentateuch (Torah), for its known that Moses, assuming his existence, had *nothing* to do with its writing.[13] Then, about 200 BCE these texts were recopied again with many allusions to the Maccabeans and John Hyracanus. It is important to know that each area of Judea/Israel had their own version of the texts. Hence, there was no coherency between any of them. Finally, at about the beginning of the current era (between the 1st and 4th centuries CE) these texts were again copied into the Masoretic Hebrew which included the addition of the vowel marks and separation of the words.

In all of this copying and recopying, no one knows what the original texts (c. 700 BCE) looked like or even said. There are indications that they were very similar to the Pagan literature of the time and the area and may have included the names of Pagan gods throughout. Further, no one knows what overzealous Scribe or Priest changed, added to or detracted from the originals. The fact is that additions, deletions, and alterations were freely made even after 100 CE. (This was noted by Eusebius [c. 325 CE] in his writings.) It is quite possible that one of the reasons that the Essenes considered themselves the "Elect of God," the "New Covenant"

---

12 Called "Ashuritic" text.

13 History records that after Ezra had recopied the texts from the Aramaic into the Hebrew he read them to the people. Then history states quite unequivocally: "The people heard things that they never had heard before."

and the "New Israel" was because they kept their texts relatively free of alterations from the group's inception (c.200 BCE to 70 CE). An interesting thing has been noted by scholars concerning the Dead Sea Scrolls, which are seen as documents of the Essenes, some of the later books (e.g. Isaiah and Samuel) appear to be pretty much the same today as 2 millennia ago. But with the recent release of some of the previously unpublished material some of the earlier books (e.g. Numbers) are vastly different. Consequently, it is quite obvious that there were huge alterations in spite of Biblical verses forbidding it.

The fartherest back that any actual Hebrew Scriptures can be dated is to about 100 BCE. These are only some fragments in the Dead Sea Scrolls, as was noted. As far as **complete** texts of the Hebrew Scriptures, there is **nothing** earlier than around the 6th century of this era.

From around 400 BCE there were at least **three** different versions of the Hebrew Scriptures. The Masoretic, Aramaic, and Ashuritic are versions of the same materials. As far as the groups of writers, it is known that there were the Elohists (known by the use of the term **Elohim** and a specific writing style), the Yahwists (known by the use of the term **Yahweh** and the anthropomorphic quality of their god), the Priests (who used a combination of the Elohist and Yahwist texts as well as their body of laws), the Deuteronomists (who represented a middle, or a spiritual/ethical religious stage of development), and the Deuteronomist Redactors (the editors who combined and organized the separate documents into one narrative).[14] With a little research you can see that each had a version of their own particular texts. This is one reason that there are two, sometimes three, conflicting versions of the same story. Later, all of the versions were combined into what are known as the Hebrew Scriptures. It was not until the beginning of this current era that the Masoretic Texts were decided upon as being the *correct* "Word of God" by a group of rabbis in Jerusalem. It was

---

14 Do not forget that there were texts not only written in Hebrew but also Aramaic, Samaritan, and, later, Greek.

they who chose which texts were to be included in the canon and which were not, and it was they who did what they could to suppress the other texts as well as they could. The inclusion of a text in the canon meant that the text had been "authenticated" as far as authorship. The only problem is that authorship was authenticated by *tradition only*!

The Bible is a restatement of more ancient myths. With a little research you can easily find that much of the Genesis myth comes from the Babylonians. The flood myth is seen in at least 400 different cultures world-wide and many of those possessing this myth are much older than the Judean/Israelites.[15] The stories of Noah's sons, Jacob's wrestling match (from the wrestling match of Gilgamesh and Enkidu, c. 2100 BCE), Isaac's "sacrifice," Solomon's judgement, the Cain and Abel myth (which is taken directly from the Persians without even changing the names), and the Samson myth including his destruction of the temple via the pillars all came from legends and myths which predated the existence of the Judeans/Israelites by many centuries.

By looking into older texts you can see that Samson's story is actually a conglomeration of several solar myths with the Babylonian War-god/Sun-god, Shamash,[16] being the prototype of the Judge and Savior (messiah) of all men and the destroyer of the wicked. Many researchers have noted the extremely strong parallels between the Greek myths of Heracles and Prometheus in the Samson tales as well.

You can find also that the story of Moses is modeled after a Syrian hero. The Mosaic laws are modeled after the Code of Hammurabi (c. 1750 BCE) and many of these laws were earlier stated in the Mari tablets (c. 2000 BCE). All of these laws are traditional Semitic laws even though they were *all* supposed to be

---

15   It is an interesting thing to note that one of the most ancient of cultures, Egypt, has no universal flood myth. This is interesting due to its position in regard to Israel.

16   Consider also that in the Hebrew Samson's name is pronounced **Shamash**on. The word shamash means "sun."

handed down by their respective cultural gods. Some of these laws even predate the Code of Hammurabi and the Mari tablets for they were seen in the Sumerian codes of Ur-Nammu and Lipit-Ishtar as well as the Akkadian laws of Eshnunna (c. 3000 BCE).

The Solomon legend most likely came from an older Persian legend because when the Israelites were freed from the Babylonian "captivity" by the Emperor Cyrus (c. 500 BCE) and the Persian army, they took on *many* aspects of the Persian religion (Mazdaism or Zoroastrianism). In the Persian legends was the story of a wise ruler named Suliman ibn Doud (*Solomon, the son of David*) who was credited with great wisdom. Actually, history has *no* record of Solomon's existence *anywhere*. More on this shortly. Also, consider that from the Assyrian records comes the great king Shalmenasar I[17] (c. 1300 BCE) who was, likewise, credited with being a wiser ruler. Shalmenasar I ruled at about the same time that Solomon was supposed to have lived.

If you take a look at Solomon's illustrious father, David,[18] you also run into a problem. First of all, if the son did not exist, then most likely the father may not have existed. Again, take a look at the Mari tablets. On these tablets was seen a term, davidum. At first, archeologists assumed that it was a title such as the Roman *Caesar*. Consequently, it was felt that David was a general term. Upon later research and translation it was found that the term davidum actually means *a disastrous defeat*. Hence, you will find that David can be placed in the same category as his famous "son" Solomon. In 1993 there was part of a stele discovered which appeared to be dating from around 800 BCE with the term) translated as ". . . *House of David*" inscribed on them. Immediately the Biblical archeologists claimed proof of David's existence asserting it meant "king of the house (dynasty) of David." Problems

---

17   If you will look at Shalmenasar's name you will notice that the last portion of the name is -asar. This means "king." The first portion, then, is his name **Shalmen**. His name actually means king **Solomon** for the Hebrew letters in Solomon's name are the same as those in Shalmenasar's name.

18   The name David (Doud) is a variation of the name of the Egyptian god Thuti, better known as Thoth.

occurred as soon as this discovery was made—least of which was the strong possibility of mistranslation. In context, the term appears to refer to the country of Israel, not to a specific person. It is important to remember in other tablets and writings when the term "house of . . ." appeared it referred to a *reigning* king, not to a kingly line. The term *"house of..."* also refers to a local ruler of a town but when attached to a name refers to a god or goddess and can be translated as a "temple." Further the Egyptian term "pharaoh" meant "house:" the title Pharaoh Thutmosis literally meant the "House of Thutmosis." Consequently, the use of the term "house" was that of a title, not a lineage.

The term *doud* presents another problem. Even though it is used for the name of a particular hero in the Hebrew Scriptures it occurs as an epithet for a god (and possibly others) in the Mesha Stele dating from the eighth century BCE. Remember, the name David means "beloved" and is used as a metaphor and reference to a god, not the name of a person.

The stories of Job, Ruth, Esther,[19] and Daniel are totally or in part taken from Babylonian myths or legends. It is quite apparent that the years spent under Babylonian and Assyrian influence definitely affected the Israelites thinking. They borrowed the legends and mythology freely from their neighbors. They would have most assuredly found some myths that appealed to them and others that did not and brought whatever they liked with them when they were eventually "released." Finally, the Biblical messiah concept is derived from the Egyptian (Arabic) Mahadi (savior) idea. In fact, many verses dealing with the messiah are copied verbatim from the Egyptian and modified so that they mesh quite nicely with the Persian and Babylonian savior concepts thus creating the idea of the Messiah with which many are familiar.

Are the Hebrew Scriptures unique? The answer obviously is in the negative. In fact, the idea of monotheism is not even a unique concept. All you need do is to check Egyptian history for the 13

---

19   The Hebrew for Esther, Asther (אסתר), is the Hebraized name of the goddess Ishtar.

years of the "heresy" of Akhenaten (c. 1350 BCE), who embraced the monotheism of Syria. This was due to the influence of his mother queen Ti. Needless to say, this angered the temple priests to the point of plotting the overthrow of the pharaoh. According to the records, one of the leaders to get back the old religion was a temple priest named Moses!

The Egyptian religion actually was strongly monotheistic. It was believed by the Egyptians that there was only one creator god. That was Ptah. The Egyptians believed, as they put it; "From the one came the three. From the three, the many." To the ancient Egyptians all of the gods were aspects of the one god and that creator god created the gods which then took on the process of creating everything else.

Monotheism was not unique to the Syrians or the Egyptians either. Nabonidus of Babylon (c. 550 BCE) and Darius I of Persia[20] (c. 525 BCE) both strongly embraced monotheism as well, but this was much later. The Persians all down through their religious history (which is much older than the Judean/Israelite religious history) were staunch monotheists. Their singular deity was Ahura Mazda and he was their "all-consuming fire" as well as "all-knowing," "all-present," "righteous," and so on, possessing about all of the titles attributed to Yahweh now. The fact of the matter is that virtually every Pagan religion was monotheistic at its core.

For many years in the Middle East, archaeologists have been unearthing libraries of cuneiform tablets. They have in their possession several hundred tablets which date prior to 2700 BCE and are Syrian in origin. They link Israel and Syria as a common people with a common language and a common mythology. The Israeli government is adamant about not having these tablets translated and published. In fact, they had gone as far as having placed a bill in front of their parliament which would require an orthodox rabbi be present at every archeological dig to instruct what can and cannot be removed. This supposedly is to prevent the desecration of "religious

---

20   The Persians were extremely strong monotheists. There was only *one* god, that was Ahura Mazda and above him there were no others.

artifacts." The only problem here is that many of these digs predate the founding of Israel/Judea and the religion we now call Judaism, so how can what is being unearthed be an artifact of the religion of Judaism when it didn't exist 3000 or more years ago?

Another historical question that needs to be considered is this: Were the Israelites God's "chosen people?" If you go back to the writings of the Babylonians, you will find that they considered themselves the "chosen" of God. Prior to them, the Sumerians considered themselves the "chosen." As far as the Sumerians are concerned, they were the "chosen" simply because they lived in the fertile Tigres-Euphrates region. It is interesting that half a world away and at about the same time the Toltec, the Mayan and later the Aztec Indians of Mexico considered themselves the "chosen" people of God. The story of the Mayan/Aztec culture closely parallels the march of the Israelites through the desert. The difference is that the Mayan/Aztec march is through the jungles. Also, when the Aztecs took on the Mayan religious structure they took over the Mayan empire the same way as the Babylonians took over the Sumerians. They also took on the title of the "chosen" as well. A point of note here: To the Mystical branch of Judaism *all humanity* is the *chosen* people.

Committing the Scriptures to Writing

***And it shall be, when thou has made an end of reading this
book, (that) thou shalt bind a stone to it, and cast it into the
midst of Euphrates.***

Jeremiah 51:63

As you have seen, keeping material as an oral tradition has some
obvious drawbacks. The least of which is the memory of the individ-
ual(s) who would be reciting the material. It is necessary to remember that oral materials would be changed to fit the times, the group
doing the recitation, and the lessons to be passed on. So, writing
everything down is the solution. But, that has drawbacks as well.

The committing of the Hebrew Scriptures into writing was done
by at least five different groups. You have already seen some of
them. Now you need to look at when they existed and you can see
the approximate period when they wrote down their tradition. The
only problem is that *no one* has any idea what the texts originally
said for each succeeding group would change and modify the
material to suit themselves.

It appears that the earliest group to commit their oral tradition
down to writing were the **Yahwists**. These were *Mushite priests*
who wrote in Judea, in northern Israel,[21] from about 850 to 650
BCE. The Yahwists are seen in the texts by the use of the term
Yahweh as the name of the deity. The group called the **Elohists**,
another faction of the *Mushite priesthood*, existed in Israel from
about 800 to 700 BCE. The Elohists used the term Elohim instead
of Yahweh as the name of the deity. The third faction were the
Deuteronomists. These were *Shiloah/Levite* priests. They existed
from about 650 to 500 BCE. They wrote combining texts and
adding their own statements, observations, and history. Within the

---

21 What we know as Israel was divided into two for many centuries. The northern portion was Judea and the southern portion was Israel. They did not
always get along in politics and religion. We can see this because Israel and
Judea both had kings.

31

Deuteronomist period there were two writings. They are termed Deuteronomist 1 and 2. The books that they produced were from Deuteronomy through I and II Kings. Tentatively, both Deuteronomists (609 587 BCE) have been identified as the prophet Jeremiah (c. 586 BCE) writing and editing in Judea. Next there are those referred to as the **Priests**. These were the *Aaronic priests* who existed from about 700 BCE. They wrote the cosmic version of the flood,[22] the stories of Abraham, Jacob, the Exodus, and the Laws.[23] They wrote an alternate account of the Yahwist's and Elohist's version of the traditions from their position in Judea. Finally, there were the **Deuteronomist Redactors**. These were also *Aaronic priests* existing from about 500 BCE to about 450 BCE. They got all of the material after everyone else had written it and compiled it into a somewhat unified form. They also had their particular point of view and their own interests they were promoting and this influenced their writings.

The Yahwists and Elohists reflected a very early stage of the Israelite religion. This is when it was still essentially a nature/fertility religion much the same as the other pagan religions of the time and region. It contained things like angels (in the text called elohim), talking animals, dreams, and the idea of an anthropomorphic deity. This deity brought both good and evil as any anthropomorphic deity does. There was no Satan to bring the natural disasters which were described. It was God. It was God also who when (he was) displeased with someone simply "removed" him by taking his life. So it was necessary to propitiate and worship this deity in order not to anger him in any way. It was later, after the Babylonian "captivity," that this God became patient, just, and merciful, just like Ahura Mazda.

The Deuteronomists reflected a middle stage of the religion. This was the spiritual/ethical stage. They quoted the Yahwists and Elohists profusely, and were an advanced level of their religious systems.

---

22   The cosmic version of the flood is the "windows of heaven and the fountains of the deep opening up, etc."

23   The laws includes about 30 chapters of Exodus, Numbers, and all of Leviticus.

The Deuteronomist Redactors combined the Yahwist, Elohist, and the Deuteronomist texts into one plus they added things of their own. It is in the Redactor's combination of texts that God became the God with which you are most familiar: just and merciful, angry and compassionate, strict and forgiving—all of the things that people expect from their earthly rulers. You must remember also that at the time these texts were being combined the Mystery Religions were gaining in stature and strength and that the chief god of every one of these religions was referred to as "father" and was just and merciful, angry and compassionate, strict and forgiving. And all of the Mystery Religions were monotheistic.

The Priests reflected the latest stage of the Judean/Israelite religion. This was that of a priest-based religion with sacrifices, ritual and strict laws. The Priests saw God as strict with a set of rules and the only way to expiate sin was through priestly sacrifice. In their version, the Priests rejected all of the stories of angels, talking animals, dreams, and anthropomorphism.

When it comes to gaining a greater insight into what was being said, it is important to look at when it was being said. Without an historical perspective all that is going to happen is a constant assuming of what is meant and these assumptions are virtually unreliable. Another thing to consider is that people are concerned for their own present needs, not for something several hundred years down the road. Simply put, human beings tend to be "short-term hedonists." They are interested in themselves and their own comfort. This means that prophecies cannot give a people anything upon which to rely if they do not **directly** apply to them. That is, prophecies are made to keep the people relying upon the **present** regime in power. They are not to apply to some nebulous time in the somewhat distant future or for some future generation hundreds of years away. This is something that has kept both Judaism and Christianity going for 2000 years: Judaism is still awaiting the imminent coming of their Messiah and Christianity is still awaiting the impending **second** coming of their Messiah and the end of the world. Both of them are, and have been for centuries, interpreting "signs" as to the coming as well. It is essentially the "carrot-on-the-stick" which keeps the followers begging for more.[24]

The dating of the writing of the Hebrew Scriptures can be approximated with a degree of accuracy. There are indicators as to the possible time periods for their committing the books to writing. Again, you must realize that the first books written were not Genesis and Exodus. These came later. Let us go through the Hebrew Scriptures and begin to affix a time period to their writing.

Genesis was done by a combination of writers. It begins with the Elohist version of the creation myth and then goes into the Yahwists version of creation. In all, there are 2 versions of the creation.[25] There are, though, three creations of humankind.[26] This places part of the text around 700 BCE. Other parts of Genesis (i.e. the story of Cain and Abel) came in around 500 BCE because it *is* a **Persian** tale brought in *after* the Babylonian "captivity" (586-538 BCE). There are also many references to older myths and legends in Genesis. These include those from Egypt (e.g. the story of Joseph), Babylon (e.g. the Tower of Babel and the Flood myths),

---

24   In the Scientific American of July 1941 it was stated:

"Mental distress and uncertainty of all peoples has been enhanced by the world's war-like attitude, by international economic and social unrest, with the result that man's age-old query of what lies ahead next week, next year, brings about a dangerous public trend toward futility, and a tendency to turn to so-called mystic rites or cults or individuals in a desperate attempt to find the answer to the future." It is religion which perpetuates this attitude claiming that they have the answers and the truth. It is important to note that fundamentalist Christianity, which is the American version of Christianity with which we are familiar, came about during the latter part of the 19th century and earlier part of the 20th century in the United States and gained momentum in response to the First World War and continued gaining momentum throughout the Second World War.

25   These versions of creation are: Genesis 1:1-31 and 2:1-4 is the Elohist version; and Genesis 2:5-9 is the Yahwist version.

26   These are: Genesis 1:26-27; Genesis 2:7; and Genesis 5:1-2. They are the Elohist, Jahwist, and Priest versions. The third creation uses the term Elohim as the creator.

Ebla, Sumer and Mittianni (e.g. the Abraham story[27]), Greece (e.g. the destruction of Sodom and Gomorrah), and Phoenicia (e.g. the "sacrifice" of Isaac).[28]

Exodus was written down sometime around 600 BCE. You can also see here references to other sources. The title of Moses as "The Good" or "Faithful Shepherd" was given to earlier sun-gods; Dumuzi of Sumer, Tammuz of Babylon, and Yima of Persia. Moses' title of "lawgiver" was given to Bacchus of Greece and Zoroaster of Persia. The story of Moses' river trip as a child also has counterparts in Egyptian, Greek, and Babylonian, as well as other myths and legends. In the **Zend Avesta** of Persia, considered by some the oldest written religious scriptures, Zoroaster is seen talking to God on a mountain top. The laws that Moses were given and he gave, were traditional Semitic laws. In the ceremonies of the Mystery Religions two stone tablets (called **petroma**) were an important part of their "articles of faith." The writing on these stone tablets was also very close to the Shurpu Tablets from Babylon which contained laws similar to those of the Ten Commandments. The Ark of the Covenant comes directly from the Egyptian legends for it is pictured on the walls of the Temple of Philae in Egypt with Egyptian priests carrying the Ark.

The books of Leviticus and Deuteronomy were supposedly given to Moses by God. If you will look at the Babylonian legends you will see the god Marduk giving the laws to Hammurabi in the same manner centuries earlier. Again, these laws were traditional Semitic laws.

---

27 The name of Abraham's wife, Sarah, is nothing more than a Hebraized version of the name of the Syrian goddess Asherah.

28 In the Jewish interpretation of this story, this is called the **Raising** of Isaac. For in the early laws, when it was stated that; "The firstborn that openeth the womb of woman or animal shall be **raised** up..." meant that it was to be placed on an altar to be **sacrificed**. The idea of the ram being substituted was a later addition after the disintegration of the early Judean priesthood.

Leviticus was written sometime around 700 BCE as well. There are references to many different cultures in this text. You can see that the Babylonians play a prominent role in all of the Hebrew Scriptures for much of the Scriptures have Babylonian influence. You can further see later additions through the material that was lifted directly from the *Zend Avesta* (e.g. Leviticus 11: 32-34; 15:19-25; 18:22). One thing that you see toward the end of Leviticus are two verses which state that the covenant with God and the Israelites will *not* be superseded. Hence, there is no "new covenant" as the Christians have claimed (Leviticus 26:44-45). The term "new covenant" as seen throughout the Dead Sea Scrolls indicated an Essene influence in early Christianity. It actually meant a *reiteration* of the former covenant with the Essenes as the carriers of the agreement, not a change.

The last of the "Books of Moses" is Deuteronomy. This, it is known, was pretty much written around 650 BCE and edited after 550 BCE. The books of Deuteronomy, Judges, I and II Samuel and I and II Kings are called the "Early Prophets." It is here where you begin to see references to other books which were mentioned. There are also references to the *Zend Avesta* here as well. Considering that Deuteronomy was edited around the end of the Babylonian "captivity" it is obvious that there would be references to Persian books in here—and there are.

The Book of Joshua represents not the exploits of a singular individual but many centuries worth of legends. Joshua *did not* exist. This book was finally compiled sometime around 550 BCE. The name Joshua (translated as *Jesus* in the Greek) literally means redemption, salvation, victory, and welfare. It is a combination word which means "Yah (or Yahweh) is salvation" or "Yah is our hue and cry."[29] There are also a few references to other cultures in the book of Joshua as well.[30] Mentioned in this book are cities that

---

29 The combination is Yah (a euphemism for Yahweh) and Sh'voh.

30 The archeological evidence shows that the walls of Jericho were destroyed by an earthquake sometime around 1400 BCE. This is around *the same time* that the evidence shows the walls of Troy to have collapsed. Could it have been an immense earthquake or another version of the same tale?

were supposedly destroyed by Joshua and were in ruins at least 1000 years **before** the time of Joshua's supposed existence (e.g. Ai and Arad). It is important to remember that by the time the first century of this era began there were many "Joshua" groups throughout Palestine with their own messianic beliefs and expectations. They all expected another "Joshua" that would lead them to military victory over their oppressors.

The Book of Judges was composed sometime between 700 to 600 BCE. Some evidence indicates that it may have been even as late as 400 BCE thus placing it possibly in the hands of Ezra. In here you have the story of Samson. This has been previously discussed as taken from different earlier legends.

The Book of Ruth was composed about 400 BCE. In Ruth you will find a strong connection between the Moabites and the Israelites. Ruth was a Moabite so this book was kept because of the affinity that the Israelites had with the Moabites. According to the tradition, both Israel and Moab were to be ruled by the House of David.

Parts of both I and II Samuel were composed around 700 BCE. It was finally compiled about 550 BCE. This is the book where the prophets begin to become a force in the Israelite religion and politics. Here is found the story of Saul, David, and Solomon. In I Samuel there are also more connections between the Moabites and the Israelites (i.e. I Samuel 23:4; 12; 24:8-22).

The original texts of I and II Kings were begun about 625 BCE and finally completed about 550 BCE. There are quite a few references to Persian practices thus indicating the influences after the Babylonian "captivity." In I Samuel is where you have the myth of Solomon.

I and II Chronicles have many parallels in both I and II Kings and in I and II Maccabees.[31] Since there are these parallels to Maccabees it indicates a later writing. Most scholars place the writing of these books at about 300 BCE. Other books written about the same time are Ezra, Nehemiah, Esther (which is copied

---

31   Both I and II Maccabees are historical books. Much of Kings and Chronicles are not.

from the Persian), Ecclesiastes[32] (c. 250 BCE), some later chapters of Isaiah, the latter chapters of Zechariah, and all of Daniel (c. 165 BCE).

It is well known that the Book of Job was a paraphrasing of an older Babylonian tale (most likely a play) with some changes thrown in. The date of its final form was about 538 BCE. The reason for this is because of the incorporation of Satan (one of God's *angels*) in the story. You will recall that in the earliest books of the Hebrew Scriptures both good and evil were brought about by God and it was not until after the Israelites were freed from the Babylonian "captivity" that they took on the concept of Satan. Hence, Job did not get its final form until sometime after 538 BCE.

The Psalms and Proverbs are a collection of songs, poems, and sayings that were extant throughout the Middle East at the time and had nothing to do with Solomon. Some are Egyptian, others are Canaanite, and still others have direct correlations to old Indian aphorisms. Consequently, these two books do not have a specific period of time when they were actually written and cannot be attributed to any specific person.

The same goes for The Song of Solomon (Canticles). They are a collection of Egyptian, Mesopotamian, and Hebrew love songs. Hence, no author or period can be fixed for their authorship. These also did not have anything to do with Solomon.

The Book of Isaiah is known to have been written by at least five different people at different times. Chapters 1 through 23 have many references to the Assyro-Babylonian period. Chapter 24 through 27 are known to have been later additions. Chapters 40 through 55 have a totally different style and refer to different times and, consequently, are ascribed to a period about one hundred-fifty or more years after the previous chapters (c. 400 BCE). In all, there are many different styles of writing in Isaiah so it cannot be ascribed to a single individual or period.

---

32   The author of this book is known to be Joshua (Jesus) ben Sirach.

Both the books of Jeremiah[33] (c. 646-587 BCE) and Ezekiel (c. 627-571 BCE) were written close to the same period as the earlier Isaiah and most likely by rival priests or priesthoods. This can be seen in the fact that Jeremiah wrote in Judea and Ezekiel in southern Babylon. There had been a rivalry between the interpreters of Torah, Talmud, and other books in Palestine and Babylon in the ancient Judean religion. This began during the "captivity." Consequently, it is not out of order to see that Ezekiel and Jeremiah were most likely from competing priesthoods and each one wrote about prophecies to prove that their priesthood, and their god, was the best. As you can see, both Jeremiah and Ezekiel lived during the latter part of the Assyrian period. Ezekiel lived closer to the end of the period as his prophetic utterances and descriptions bear out. More on these two "prophets" of God later.

Lamentations was ascribed to around 600 BCE but most assuredly it was written sometime after 586 BCE. Even though they seemed to reflect a life in captivity, they cannot be ascribed to Jeremiah. One reason is that the Babylonian "captivity" began in 586 BCE and Jeremiah died in 587 BCE. Another reason being that if Jeremiah was making prophecies to Nebuchadnezzar (II) of Assyria (604-562 BCE), he was quite obviously in the emperor's court. Life could not have been that rough for him as the Lamentations tell. The same goes for Ezekiel who, you shall see, also supposedly prophesied to the same Assyrian king.

The Book of Ezekiel begins with a very famous description: The Wheel. Did Ezekiel actually see something or was this just a story that he invented for some reason? Many have interpreted the vision of Ezekiel as everything from a flying machine to an actual view of heaven. If you look into different cultures you can find similar descriptions. In Egyptian mythology you find a very strong correl-

---

33 Apparently, the Book of Jeremiah wasn't even written by Jeremiah but by a scribe named Baruch ben Neriyah. His name is mentioned many times throughout. Also, many phrases and ideas of the Deuteronomistic school are common in Jeremiah as well. Hence, it may be that Baruch was in collaboration with the Deuteronomists both editing and writing for both Jeremiah and the Deuteronomists.

ative description. In Egypt it was the description of Horus and his four sons. You can also see that the description of Ezekiel's Wheel has a very similar appearance to that of the depiction of the image of the Persian Ahura Mazda (figure). If the latter is the case, then

we can place the final compilation of this book during the end of the Babylonian "captivity" (538 BCE) and by one of Ezekiel's followers.

Ezekiel has been called "the father of Judaism." It was Ezekiel who dictated the structure of the Temple and the nature of Judean ritual so precisely that it aided the reestablishment of the Judean community after the "captivity." Since the "captivity" ended in 538 BCE and Ezekiel died about 571 BCE it was most probably dictated while still in the "captivity" . . . or it may have been written *after* the "captivity" by one of Ezekiel's followers.

The last of the books to be mentioned; Hosea, Joel, Amos, Obadiah,[34] Jonah,[35] Micah, Nahum, Habakkuk, Zephaniah, Haggai, and Malachi[36] are rather non-descript as far as timing is concerned. They can tentatively be placed between 450 to 350 BCE.

---

34 Known to have been written by 2 different authors.

35 Written as a satire on the prophets and prophecy thus placing it after the era of the prophets.

36 It is known that no such person as Malachi existed. The name means *messenger.*

In the aftermath of the diaspora and the destruction of the first temple, the idea of wisdom attributed to the Scribes was dissolved. The notion of Scribal wisdom assumed the existence of a temple-state, and intellectuals who were Scribes imagined the temple-state as the perfect society. After the destruction of Jerusalem and the whole society as well, more questions were posed than answered. In order to keep the wisdom alive it was said that wisdom no longer resided in the world but only with God. This is when the Jewish Wisdom literature came into being and a mythology of Wisdom emerged. In this literature there was the desire to see the world as a Divine creation and that the epic of Israel was a series of Divine rescues. The books of Moses (the Torah) were considered Divine instruction and Divine inspiration. Eventually the whole Bible received the pronouncement of Divine instruction and Divinely inspired. The popular narratives saw Wisdom (referred to as she) in the act of creating, generating, building, making the rounds of heaven, seeking people with whom to dwell, sending messengers, rescuing, teaching, working, as the consort of Yahweh, nurturing families, and even the Logos (see the writings of Philo). It was after this time when the concept of Satan was introduced into Biblical writings. Remember, prior to this time it was God who brought both good and evil. With the introduction of the good god (Ahura Mazda) and the evil god (Angra Mainyu) from the Persian mythology an explanation of why the destruction of Jerusalem and the temple and the diaspora was given credence. Obviously, Yahweh would never have done this to his "chosen people," so some other force had to have done the deed.

The Prophets

I will raise them up a Prophet from among their brethren, like unto thee, and will put my words in his mouth; and he shall speak unto them all that I shall command him... When a prophet speaketh in the name of the Lord (Yahweh), if the thing follow not nor come to pass, that (is) the thing which the Lord (Yahweh) hath not spoken, (but) the prophet hath spoken it presumptuously: thou shalt not be afraid of him.

Deuteronomy 18: 18, 22

A lot has been said of the prophets of old. A prophet was referred to as *the son of man* (ben-Adam). He was supposedly divinely inspired and in direct communication with God. The era of the prophets had ended sometime between 400 to 450 BCE.[37] Consequently, in the Judean/Israelite religion prophets were not raised up after that period.

The prophets were priests. They followed a specific point of view and directed their prophecies to specific outcomes. As stated in the Hebrew Scriptures, the prophets were called *seers* (1 Sam. 9:9) so there is no difference between a seer and a prophet. The major difference is between that of a prophet and a sorcerer. According to the Scriptures, the prophet of God is 100-percent accurate *all of the time* and apparently foretells *good* things. The sorcerer, at that time, was one who augured ill-fortune through signs and omens. So, if someone told of bad things to occur (e.g. the destruction of the whole world), he or she was considered a *sorcerer*, *not* a prophet of God. There is an interesting point to be made about the concept of a prophet of God being 100-percent right. Prophets were also an extremely important part of the Persian religion as well. According to their writings the prophet of God (Ahura Mazda) is 100-percent accurate as well. Could it be that the era of the prophets actually came *after* the Babylonian

---

37 Don't tell the Jehovah's Witnesses that. If we are to believe the Jehovah's Witnesses, they are the "true" prophets of God even though not one prophecy they ever came up with ever panned out.

"captivity," or was it that the Judean/Israelite religion had to show that they too had prophets and that their prophets were as good as any of the other prophets, or could it be that those who are now referred to as prophets were not considered prophets at all but simply *seers* or the *high priests* of a specific faction of an Israelite religion? It is known that the high priests of literally all of the pagan religions were trained in the art of prophecy and divination. So, it stands to reason that those priests of the Judean/Israelite religion had a similar type of training. This, in fact, is seen in Scripture. A basic meditation procedure to assist in going into the state of prophecy is described in 1 Kings 18:42.

It is interesting to note that there are *false prophecies* in the Bible. Take a look and compare the prophetic utterances of the prophets and actual history. You will find more than you bargained for. Since there are false prophecies in the Scriptures, then it must be concluded that the Bible as a prophecy of God is *invalid*.

It is a fact of human nature that prophecies or predictions must apply to the times and the current group if they are to have any meaning and if it is necessary to continue to generate a following. People will not stick with a group that says 500 or 600 years down the road someone will be born who will save them. The fact of the matter is that in five or six centuries the group could easily not exist at all or have changed enough to not be the same. So, immediacy is the important thing in prophecy. This is what actually kept the Judean/Israelite groups together and focused in a common direction. They always seemed to be conquered by their larger and more powerful neighbors so it was necessary that someone would quickly come to deliver them. Hence, there was an immediate need for a "messiah" and so prophets would be constantly making predictions of rescue. When the Babylonians came and destroyed the Assyrian Empire, the Judean/Israelites thought that the Babylonians were the saviors. That, though, was a short-lived feeling. The Babylonians in a common practice of the time and in order to not have any trouble from this group of people who had a reputation for causing trouble, dispersed them throughout the empire (the diaspora or "captivity"). The main idea was to scatter a people around an empire, have them intermingle and set them up economically so that they would not become trouble later. Then the Persians came and destroyed the Babylonian Empire and brought the Israelites out of the Babylonian "captivity." It is said that the Judean/Israelites had become so prosperous that many of them refused to be relocated back to their original homes after the diaspora. With the rescue, the Persian Emperor Cyrus was called the "messiah." Later, the term Messiah was applied most often to the High Priest of the Temple and often with the King.

Here is a small list of false prophecies. You will notice that they apply *directly* to the times in which they were made and not to hundreds of years into the future.

1. Syria will be delivered to Ahab (I Kings 20:13). This never happened.

2. The Israelites will be in Babylon for 70 years (Jeremiah 29:10). They were there for 48 years.

3. The birth of Immanuel (Isaiah 7:14). This verse is *not* a prophecy of the coming of Jesus for if you will read the accompanying verses you will find that it pertains to events that recently occurred and one that was immediately expected. It actually refers to the installation of a king. It seems that this is part of a hymn that was sung during that installation. The "son" referred to here is the king who is the *adopted* son of the *national god* (Yahweh). For references see Samuel 7:13-14 and Psalms 2:7, the latter of which refers specifically to David.

4. All of the nations shall flow into Yahweh's house in Israel (Isaiah 2:2) and there will be total peace (Isaiah 2:4). This never happened.

5. Jonah's prediction of the destruction of Ninevah (Jonah 3:4). Jonah even brought his picnic lunch up onto the hillside to watch the destruction. When this did not happen he was so irate with God that he even argued with him to destroy Ninevah so that he would not be proven wrong and, hence, be

44

a false prophet. The story says that God "had a change of heart" and could not destroy even one single cow.

6. Micah's prophecy of the destruction of Jerusalem (Micah 3:12). This never happened.

7. Israel's distress will be relieved by Michael, the archangel, rising up (Daniel 12:1-3). This never happened. This verse, by the way, is the verse which the Jehovah's Witnesses use to claim that Jesus was actually Michael, the archangel.

8. Ahijah's prophecy that Solomon's kingdom would be rended from his hand and given to Jeroboam (I Kings 11:30-32). Solomon died and the kingdom passed on to his successor, Rehoboam.

9. The rebuilding of the Temple after the Babylonian captivity (Ezekiel 40-42). As prophesied, it never happened. There are also those that doubt that the first Temple even existed. If Solomon did not exist, what is the possibility of the temple *he* built existing?

10. Isaiah's prophecy to Hezekiah that all Hezikiah's treasures would be carried away to Babylon and his sons would be Babylonian eunuchs (II Kings 20:12-19). Since this did not happen, II Chronicles 32:31 uses the cop-out that it was only "Yahweh's testing" and not a false prophecy. If it was spoken by a prophet of Yahweh then it is a prophecy. Since it was spoken and since it did not happen that makes Isaiah a false prophet. Besides, if God cared about his prophets He would not test them so that they would make false prophecies. I guess that Yahweh is a practical joker.

11. Ezekiel's prophecy of the siege of Tyre (Ezekiel 26). This siege continued for 13 years and ended in a stalemate.

12. Jeremiah's prophecy of Nebuchadnezzar's "successful" attack

on Egypt (Jeremiah 46:13-25). This prophecy was made about 586 or 587 BCE. Historically, Nebuchadnezzar fought Egyptian troops but *not* in Egypt. He *never* invaded Egypt as Jeremiah had predicted.

13. Ezekiel's prophecy of Nebuchadnezzar's "successful" attack on Egypt (Ezekiel 29-39). This looks rather familiar, does it not? Who made the prophecy anyway? They both could not have done it at the same time for historically they did not even live in the same area when the prophecy was made. You will recall that Jeremiah was in Judea and Ezekiel was in Babylon at the court of Nebuchadnezzar. It really does not matter who made the prophecy anyway. They were both wrong. Historically one of Nebuchadnezzar's successors finally invaded Egypt and was soundly driven off.

It is interesting to note that God had *deceived* the prophets so that they would make false prophecies. It is also interesting that an all-knowing, all-wise, all-loving God would *purposely* deceive someone that He chose to deliver His words. You can see this deception in Jeremiah 20:7 when he states:

> *O Lord (Yahweh), thou hast deceived me, and I was deceived: Thou hast overcome me, and hast prevailed; I am become a laughing-stock all the day, everyone mocketh me.*

Later in Ezekiel (14:9) it further states:

> *And if the prophet be deceived when he hath spoken a thing, I the Lord (Yahweh) have deceived that prophet, and I will stretch out my hand upon him, and will destroy him from the midst of my people Israel.*

What this looks like is a convenient cop-out for predictions that did not come true.

As you have seen, neither Jeremiah nor Ezekiel nor any of the other "prophets of God" were destroyed by God for His deceptions. They did, in fact, profit and become well respected and their names are still remembered.

The Hebrew Scriptures makes a very strong point that **all** prophecy that comes from God and every prophet that God "raises up" is 100-percent accurate otherwise it is *false* prophecy and the prophet is a *false* prophet. As you can see, there were "men of God" who were supposedly "Divinely inspired" and were *false prophets.* If any prophet has as few as one prediction incorrect then that prophet is **not** of God and any other prophecies cannot be believed.

The Bible as a History Book

The simple minded will believe anything: but the wise looketh well into everything he does.

Proverbs 14:15

There are many who will argue that the Bible is a *reputable* historical text. This is not true as well. The mention of a few historical names and places and some descriptions of apparatuses and ceremonies does not make a book historically accurate. As a matter of fact, the first Biblical and historical record that does agree does not come until about 702 BCE. This was at the siege of Jerusalem under Hezekiah. The siege appeared to be nothing more than a stand-off and this was only due to Jerusalem's position. It appears also that Hezekiah paid off the Assyrian king Sennacherib for both the Bible and Assyrian records agree on the amount given, but not the reason.

It is important at this point to remember that about 400 BCE the prophet Ezra had taken *all* of the texts available at the time, which were written in the more difficult Aramaic, and *retranslated* them into Hebrew. As you have seen, there were changes made by him and the story of the siege of Jerusalem was one of them. Consequently, he had changed everything to *his* satisfaction bringing mythology and a smattering of history together to have Yahweh *directly* interfering in the lives of the people and affecting their history. This, as anyone who has ever read the classical myths will notice, is not much different than any other mythological tale. Thus, history and mythology were correlated and the mythos becomes confused with facts. Consequently, if something happened historically it was due to Yahweh's intervention. Since the people of the times believed that the gods had control over their lives, if problems befell them it was because the "gods were not smiling" on them. It had nothing to do with the forces of nature or that the army was horribly outnumbered or incompetent. It was the gods' doing. This is one reason why the Judeans/Israelites were constantly seeking after the gods of their neighbors. The

Judean/Israelite god was obviously a weak god for these people were **always** being conquered by other more powerful nations.

One of the most popular writing techniques for centuries[38] was that of using an historical setting and placing fictitious characters in it. The reverse was also done: placing historical characters into mythological settings. This makes it more appealing to a specific peoples.[39] It would also tend to make the material seem to be historically accurate. This was done in much of the epic poetry of the time and it was done in the Bible. If the Bible was meant to be an actual historical book I and II Maccabees and Esdras would not have been removed and Joshua would have followed Exodus.[40]

There are some other facts that show the Bible to not be as historically accurate as some would like to believe. It was mentioned already that Solomon did not exist. You know this because absolutely **none** of Solomon's contemporaries, those with whom he was supposed to have trade agreements with and the daughters of whom he was to have for his 700 wives and 300 concubines, ever mentioned him in **any** of their correspondence. Further, many of the supposedly historical characters mentioned in the Bible are out of time and sequence. According to the Bible, there are kings who supposedly reigned for at least eighty years. There are **no** records of any king **anywhere** in those times ruling near that long.[41] Consider, though, that the Bible is restated mythology and written and rewritten by so many different groups with their own point to make, it would be easier to write these stories with known characters and cultural heroes and giving them long lives and imposing records. This would promote a particular heritage to a

---

38   It's still in use today as a matter of fact.

39   Take for example the epic of Gilgamesh. It is known that Gilgamesh was an early warrior-king so he was placed in the mythology of the time as both a factual and mythical character.

40   Although we know that the Book of Joshua is not an historical book.

41   Unless the reign begins with the birth of the king and ends with his death. Usually this is not so. Many a king's installation was around puberty.

group that needed one. With this, the myths would become believed as reality and a past would exist. It is also easier to remember the heroes within the context of a mythological tale than in the essential facts.

Historically, the first mention of anyone *referred to* as "Hebrew"[42] was around 1400 BCE. This came from several letters to Amenhotep III of Egypt. The "Hapiru" from the "north" were invading Syria and Syria sent to Egypt for aid. These invaders did *not* live at the same time as the Biblical Hebrews and could not be assigned the designation of "passers-over," "passers-by"[43] or Hebrews. Next are two letters concerning a male and female, both called Hapiru or Habiru who indentured themselves as servants to Egyptian families. This was about 1200 BCE. These letters indicate that the two people were from Syria. The Hapiru apparently settled in Syria and obviously had intermingled and intermarried with the peoples of that area, including those who later became the Judeans.

The first mention of Judea is on the stele to Shishonk of Bubastis[44] dated about 925 BCE. Shishonk is called the "king of Judea" on the stele. The first king of Judea actually recorded was Jehu in the reign of Shalmenasar II of Assyria (c. 880 BCE). The first historical Israelite mentioned was "Ahab, the Israelite" who commanded 2,000 chariots and 10,000 soldiers in the battle of Qarar on the Orontes River in 825 BCE. Prior to that time there was neither a mention nor even an allusion to a Hebrew "nation" or to Israelites.

Several decades ago, there had been some material published concerning the Exodus being around the reign of the Pharaoh Tutmosis III (c. 1477 BCE). This is based on the translations of

---

42 This is assumed from the term Hapiru, Habiru, or Apiru, which is Egyptian and was originally translated as "passers-over" or "passers-by." It actually means "outlaws." These were people who were not accepted within the current political and social structures. Today, the term is "gentile." The term is also seen in Sumerian and Assyro-Babylonian texts.

43 This is the root of the word "Hebrew."

44 This is the Biblical Shishak.

Hans Goedicke of John's Hopkins University. He states that this coincides with the eruption of the volcano Santorini. The problem is that Goedicke's translations have been contested by other Egyptologists as being incorrect. They say that he too hastily translated the material in order to be the first to be published. Since that time, though, these translations seemed to fit into just what people want to believe. So, they were accepted as being factual.[45]

Another problem with the Exodus is that, *according to tradition,* the Exodus occurred during the reign of Ramses II (c. 1290 BCE). In the Bible it is stated that there is around 480 years between the Exodus and the period of Solomon. If you are to follow tradition, the 480 years places Solomon in direct conflict with historical Judean and Israelite kings. Further conflict is seen with tradition in that Solomon was supposed to exist around 1200 BCE.

There are some researchers who claim that the Exodus was not a single group movement out of Egypt. It was actually a series of groups moving out at different times with the first group leaving about 1500 BCE and the last group leaving in the time of Ramses II. This surely does rectify some of the tremendous errors in the time lines. But there still is the problem with Solomon.

If you look at the text of the Exodus you find that the Hebrew phrase ***orab rab*** is used to designate the "mixed multitude" that came out of Egypt. This term is used to indicate the stars and constellations. In other words, it has ***astrological*** significance and does not refer to a group of people. It also does not mean that the "mixed multitude" that came out of Egypt numbered like the stars. Orab rab refers specifically to the stars and constellations in the night sky.[46]

---

45   There is absolutely no historical evidence of the army of any Pharaoh who, in pursuit of a contingency of nomads, was destroyed by being drowned in the Red Sea. We know more about the Egyptian civilization than any other ancient civilization because the Egyptians wrote about *everything* in their experience.

46   It is then quite possible that the whole story of the Exodus is from an ancient *stellar myth* with Moses being a specific constellation which leads the procession of the stars. Which one could it be? There is one main suspect: it is the constellation of Perseus for this was an important constellation in ancient times and Perseus led a procession of the stars when he rose and traversed the heavens.

The Development of Yahweh's Divinity

Thou shalt not revile the gods, nor curse the ruler of thy people.

Exodus 22:28

There are many ideas of the Judeo-Christian concept of God which are accepted to be true and unique but which are neither. You have already seen that the concept of Satan came into the Judean/Israelite religion *after* the release from the Babylonian captivity. You have seen that in the early parts of the Bible God was the one who brought both good *and* evil to His "chosen." If you look hard enough at the concept of God throughout the Hebrew Scriptures you can easily see that it changes. In the text itself God tells Moses that he was known by a different name to Abraham, and to Isaac, and to Jacob.[47] As you have seen, this god, the earliest god worshiped by the Hebrews, was El Shaddai. So, God had a different name and a differing function. Also, the divers names of God denote separate concepts, a different period, and divergent groups following that form of the deity. All of the concepts of God were different because they were essentially *different gods* who acted differently (i.e. creator, destroyer, and redeemer). They all became united under the name *Elohim* and followed as Yahweh.

Some of the other concepts of God and life that were taken on by Yahweh as the times and the priesthood changed were:

1. There is one Supreme God that made the world and the world is governed by His providence. Most of the Pagan religions saw this to be true, especially the Egyptians and the Persians. The Stoic philosophers, founded by Zeno (335-236 BCE), also firmly believed in a single Supreme God.

2. One must have a pious fear (respect), love and adoration of God. This is an extremely strong belief in the Persian religion.

---

47 The indication here is that the god of Abraham was different than the god of Isaac and different than the god of Jacob. This idea is mentioned exactly the same way several times in Torah.

3. God is "an all-consuming fire." This is taken word-for-word from the **Zend Avesta** of the Persians. Ahura Mazda was a "fire-god", and hence, an all-consuming fire."

4. God is omnipresent, omniscient, all-wise, all-powerful, independent, just, and exists outside of space and time. He has no beginning and no end. God is the universal creator. This was an extremely strong belief in virtually *every* mystery religion. The Persians, especially, saw Ahura Mazda in this way.

5. There were levels of angels and demons, the heavens and hell. This whole system is directly out of the Persian religion and their Holy Books although some have tried to relate this to Babylon, this is unsubstantiated.

6. If one does not meet retribution for evil deeds in this life, he will meet it in the next. In modern psychology this is called the "just-world phenomenon." This was a very deeply held belief in virtually *all* of the Pagan religions. The Pagans believed firmly in a law of Universal Retribution (karma). Their main concern was how one acted while alive, *not* what they did or said on their deathbed.

7. Covet neither another's wife or be adulterous. Monogamy was a very strong conviction in the Persian society. This can be seen in the very ancient laws and religions of all of the Pagans. In ancient Rome, for example, it was very difficult to get married so one had to really want to get married.

8. "An eye for an eye." This was directly out of the code of Hammurabi.

9. As the Jewish religion of today sees hell, it is a place of temporary punishment or purging of the soul[48] similar to the

---

48   This purging was necessary because according to the messianic tradition, *all* of the souls of the world had to be properly purged or cleansed *prior to* the messiah appearing.

Catholic Church's Purgatory. Initially, hell was seen as a place of "nothingness" or land of the dead by the early Judeans. Later on, it assumed the proportions of a place of temporary punishment as seen by the Persians and this related to the concept of reincarnation. Toward the beginning of this era it became a place of eternal punishment like the one with which you are familiar today. In the Greek mythology Hades had two parts: the Elysian Fields where the righteous lived in peace and love for all eternity and Tartarus where the evil would spend eternity burning in fires and atoning for their sins. In the Talmud, hell is described as a *state of mind* and the majority of Christian churches are agreeing with this idea.

10. Evil does not proceed from good. This was a belief in all of the Pagan religions. The early Hebrews saw both good and evil proceeding from the same source: **Yahweh**. Later this was modified to bring a personified evil deity into play. If Yahweh was good, how could evil proceed from him? Hence, someone or something had to be brought in. That something was Satan. Satan had several models: the Egyptian Set; Angra Mainyu of Persia; and many of the underworld gods such as Ba'al ZeBub. All of these contributed to the *concept* of an evil deity that is called Satan or the Devil.

11. If a man repents, God is merciful. All of the Mystery Religions believed this. All sacrificing religions prior to the Mystery Religions saw the sacrifice as a sin-offering for repentance and that is why blood sacrifice was so important.

12. God's kingdom is eternal. The Persians believed firmly that the kingdom of Ahura Mazda was eternal.

13. *God* (Yahweh) is the Lord of Lords, King of Kings, the Most High. The idea of God being a king reflected the state of mind of the people. Obviously, God had to be a king greater than any of those on the Earth. It was also believed by many Pagans that one's kingship was derived from God (Ex. 22:28). This latter

idea became reflected in the writings of Paul in the Christian Scriptures.

14. There is none like God; He is One. All of the Pagan religions believed that there was only *one* God. All of the others were only *aspects* of that One. Again, Ahura Mazda was the One according to the Persians, Ptah was the One according to the Egyptians, and so on. Virtually *every* Pagan religion saw their main God, the creator God, as *the* One.

As you have seen, much of what many believe—or purport to believe—has little, if any, basis in historical fact. The god of the Judeo-Christian philosophy began as an apparently popular tribal deity in the Eastern Mediterranean area for archeologists have found small temples dedicated to Yahweh all around the Middle East. He was a nature god who was promoted into a national god of a particular Semitic group. Eventually he became *the* universal God. This was mainly due to the stubbornness of the priesthood of the people. The Bible, which has been touted as the "Word of God" is nothing more than a contrivance written by dissenting priests of different groups for that group, at different times, for particular reasons borrowing liberally from their neighbors and, adding to what they borrowed by inserting their own national and personal heroes.

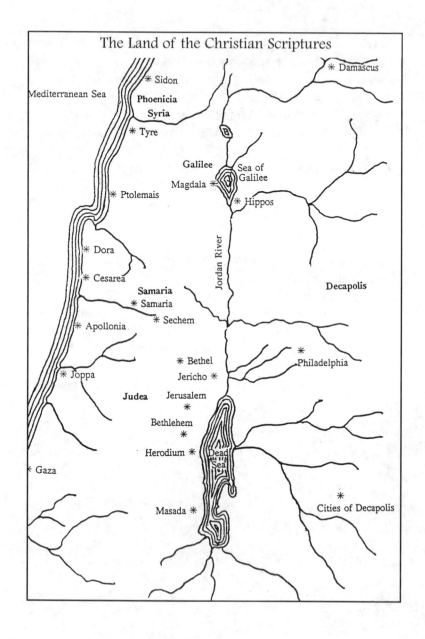

The Land of the Christian Scriptures

Dating the Gospels and Epistles

Date (CE)	Gospels	Epistles
20	"Q"	
30		
40		
50		
60	(Thomas)	
70		Thessalonians
Destruction of the Temple	Mark	Romans
80		
90		James
	Matthew	1 & 2 Corinthians, 1 Peter,
100	Luke & Acts	Hebrews, Ephesians, Phillipians Philemon, Galatians, Colossians
110		Jude, 2 John
	John 2 Peter	Revelations, 1 John,
120		
130		Timothy Titus
140		
150		

Some researchers and historians date the writing of the Pauline Epistles to the period between 40 and 70 CE. This is because they feel that any references to places and events after 90 to 100 CE were added by Church copyists in order to make the Epistles have more meaning for the period. Even with this being true, it is still not known what the originals said, consequently, no one knows what the copyists changed, deleted, or added.

Late 4th century, early 5th century image from a catacomb in Rome. The individual with the wand is Jesus. Notice the short hair and lack of beard. This is an indication that every Christian group pictures Jesus differently.

PART II

Early First Century Palestine

Without an understanding of the times it is difficult to get any idea as to the whys and the hows of the appearance of Christianity. All that you are left with is an *extremely biased* "history" that has little to no basis in fact. With a one-sided viewpoint it becomes impossible for you to get the whole picture.

Traditionally, Palestine was seen as made up of the main Judean religion's areas of Israel and Galilee in the north, Judea in the south, and to a lesser extent Samaria to the west. According to the standard Christian belief, Palestine was to a very large extent saturated with the Judean religion. This is not true. In Palestine there were a mixture of religions and the Judean religion was only one of them.

One of the most important areas to Christianity was Galilee. Galilee was *not* made up of people of Judean beliefs because it was *not* bordering Judea. Galilee, from the time of Alexander, had a strong Hellenistic or Greek influence. Its cities were modeled after the Greek cities with theaters, schools, gymnasiums, stadiums, porticoed markets, and so on. Even the major language in Galilee was not Hebrew or Aramaic but Greek.

Galilee was not culturally the same nor did they ever feel part of "Israel" as the Christians of today understand it. It was a mixture of peoples with many different ideas, philosophies, religions, and beliefs. It had no capital city, no temple, no hierarchy of priests, and no standing army. Galileans had no loyalty to any kings nor particular gods. They refused to join the tribal confederations when they were annexed by Judea because they did not feel that they belonged to Israel/Judean history. To the traditional Judeans Galilee was known as "the land of the gentiles."

Tensions had consistently existed between the traditional Judeans and the Samaritan Judeans from the time of the diaspora (539 BCE). The Samaritan Judeans had intermarried with locals thus "corrupting" their pure Judean lineage. Later, about 135 BCE, the traditional Judeans conquered Samaria and destroyed their temple. About 100 BCE Galilee was annexed. The Galileans were not too happy with this and continued to resist.

Galilee had consistently been a major trade center which supported a thriving, productive economy and an eclectic society. In Galilee was farming, access to Mediterranean sea ports, and trade with Damascus, Tyre, Ptolemais, Caesarea, Samaria, Jerusalem, the Transjordan, and Decapolis. It was a crossroads linking Levant with Egypt, Syria, and the Tigris-Euphrates valley. Most of the people living in Galilee were peasants, small farmers, artisans, and day laborers who lived in small villages and medium-sized towns. The people living in Galilee formed networks of exchange for goods, foods, and craftwork.

Due to the major Greek influence, Galilee being a major trade center, and the eclectic nature of the Galileans they were open to different ideas, philosophies, and religions. The fact is, one of the most important schools of the Greek Cynic philosophy came out of Galilee. Several important Cynic philosophers came from this school: Meleager (100 BCE), Philodemus (110-40 BCE), and Oenomaius (120 CE). The Hellenistic influence was very important to the Galileans; more important than any Judean influence. It was not until *after* the Roman-Judean war (66-73 CE) that a large Judean population came into Galilee and there began to develop more of a Judean influence. This does not mean that Galilee was suddenly converted to the Judean religion.

By the time of Jesus' supposed appearance, the whole area was in turmoil. A century or so earlier the Romans begrudgingly annexed Judea/Israel only after the locals could not resolve their own internal conflicts. The Galileans had refused to get involved mainly because they were irritated with the constant warring. Further, they had no loyalties to either the Romans or the Herodians in Jerusalem.

The Greco-Roman world at this time was ripe for new philosophies to develop. The age itself showed an undermining of older traditions. Old philosophical and religious structures were being questioned and people were left to their own devices. Many new philosophies, cults, and religions began to develop to fill the void. As people were displaced and moved around they were exposed to many different religions and religious practices with the most popular being the mystery religions who claimed to represent the ancient religions and cultures.

The development of new philosophies at this time were made possible by three important phenomena: 1) There was a major preoccupation with ideas, philosophies, and writings in literature. Quite a bit of the interest was in the social area because of the number of social problems of that time. National epics and local histories were revised in order to compete with other histories. Ancient laws were searched in an attempt to find guidance for the present age. Writings on the ideal ruler, humanistic ethics, kingship, tyranny, authority, power, virtue, justice, law and well-being flourished. At this time the writings of the Qumran community were developed and the ideas of the ideal teacher and savior, the teacher of righteousness, came about; 2) There was the formation of small social units or fellowships of people with common interests. These ranged from clubs, lodges, and craft guilds to monastic communities; and 3) There developed a large number of itinerant teachers (philosophical entrepreneurship). For a fee you could have your dreams interpreted, have your stars charted, have sacrificed animal's entrails read and so predict your future. The followers of the particular teachers referred to them as *divine* and claimed miracle workings for them. The others were referred to as *sophists*, a derogatory term referring to what can be termed today as a "con-man."

Onto this stage stepped a new philosophy. The earliest writings were nothing like the Gospels and Epistles of today. Slowly it began to attract listeners. What was it that seemed to attract people? Researchers have been able to piece together the first writings. Originally there was nothing more than a series of sayings and aphorisms. There was no life story around these sayings. They were simply a series of instructions laid out mainly as maxims. What these writings did was to challenge each person to become a unique individual and seek individual freedom as well as to seek a simpler lifestyle. Even though there was nothing really new about this concept, its presentation appeared during a period of searching.

Alexander S. Holub, Ph.D.

The Christian* Scriptures

For it is written, that Abraham had two sons, the one by a bondmaid, the other by a freewoman. But he (who was) of the bondwoman was born after the flesh; but he of the freewoman (was) by promise. These things are in allegory representing the two testaments; the one from the Mount Sinai giving birth to bondage, which is (H)Agar.

Galatians 4:22-24

As we have seen, the idea of the Hebrew Scriptures being the "Word of God" or even of the Universal Deity does not stand up to proof. We have seen that the god of the "Old Testament"[1] had undergone considerable changes to reach the status of a universal "father." From his beginnings as a simple tribal deity to El Shaddai who resided on Mt. Sinai, through the creator of the world named Elohim, to the creator of the universe, to the punisher of the unrighteous named Yahweh, to the father, the Judeo-Christian god has made some incredible transformations.

When it comes to considering the Bible as the *inspired* "Word of God" it is necessary to consider one extremely important fact: The Bible is the product of a rather arbitrary and dubious process of compilation performed by **men** and designed to put forth the particular point of view of these **men**. Many quite beautiful and spiritually uplifting books were excluded simply because someone in the council that was deciding upon the canon did not particularly like the approach of it or of a particular group that happened to be making use of the books. Consequently, it was felt that these expurgated books could be wrongly interpreted and could be dangerous.[2] Other books were excluded due to fierce political and

---

1   I use the term "Old Testament" in quotes because throughout the Hebrew Scriptures Yahweh states that the bargain he made with "his people" is *forever* and shall *not* be superseded.

2   Dangerous to their point of view and teachings, that is.

*NOTE: The term "Christian" will be used throughout even as a reference to the early 1st century CE followers of the philosophy. In the early 1st century, the first "Christians" were members of the Judean religion. It wasn't until later when the philosophy began to penetrate the Roman Empire that the followers got a name.

religious rivalries between sects, factions, Judean, Christian, Gnostic, and Pagan. The **assumed** antiquity and authorship of a book was the primary factor which influenced its inclusion in the canon. For this reason, many competing texts were attributed to great Biblical figures (i.e. Enoch, Isaiah, Matthew, Luke, Thomas, Paul, Peter, etc.) in order to give them both age and authority. The fact of the matter is that it is only **speculation** as to who wrote many of the books and the time when each was written. Historically, the earliest fragments available of the Christian Scriptures date from around 120 CE and much of it was quite different from what has been accepted in the canon.

The period from about the 2nd century BCE to around the 4th century CE was a period of extensive scriptural writing in the Middle East. The problem was that most of the writing *never* made it into the canon. With the absence of texts from this period, with the acceptance of only a small number of repetitive texts, with the total exclusion of **all** later Christian Apocrypha, and **total** rejection and destruction of many Gnostic Scriptures, what you see is a highly censored and distorted picture of ancient religious literature.

Without the scriptures that were written intermediate to the canonical writings, as well as the Pagan sources which influenced them, the general reader is lead to believe that Christianity somehow just popped up on its own with no roots other than what **The Church** has given as its history. Looking at these texts you can see that concepts such as the appearance of the Son of Man,[3] the imminence of the end of the world, salvation through a messiah, the apocalyptic vision in the Book of Revelations, the laying-on-of-hands for healing, the "revealed word" or oracles, and the concept of the **Word** or the **Logos**, all were preoccupations of this intermediate literature and its period. Again, it is important to look at the historical background of the times in order to get an understanding of how the philosophical concepts developed. By doing so you can

---

3   Ben Adam: This is a title that was given to the king of Judea and was a general appellation given to *any prophet.* It meant nothing more than "human being" or "man." In other words, when Jesus spoke it he was referring to himself in the third person: ". . . they will see this man . . ."

get an idea of the thinking of the people who created the concepts in the first place.

What is being practiced as Christianity today, and especially fundamentalist Christianity,[4] has literally *no* relationship, bearing, nor even the slightest resemblance to original Christianity[5] from the beginning or the latter part of the first century. From its onset, Christianity drew from many sources: the Mystery Religions, oriental mythology, astrological doctrines, Iranian (Persian) theology, Judean religious tradition, *the Occult*, and Platonic and Hellenistic philosophies and concepts. Hence, there was, and is, nothing unique about Christianity as there is nothing unique about what we call Judaism today. Some researchers delving into the early first century and early Christianity have come to the conclusion that Christianity originally developed from an Hellenistic *Greek* philosophy and from *gentile* sources. It was adopted into the Judean religious structure later.

Probably the earliest actual religious "Christians" were of the *Judean* religious beliefs of about the first quarter of the first century but most likely it developed quite a bit earlier as a philosophy. The fact is, the first ten "bishops" of the "Jerusalem Church" were all circumcised. Early Christians went to the synagogues. They celebrated all of the High Holy Days and festivals including the Day of Atonement. In essence, what this means is that they did not believe, as later Christians, that Jesus' death atoned for sins at all. They observed all of the Mosaic laws, dietary laws, purity laws, and so on. They had several differences in regard to traditional Judean thought. First of all, these early Christians apparently believed that the messiah had already come and gone (Hezekiah?),

---

4   This type of Christianity began in the United States around the beginning of the 20th century with its roots in the Anabaptists, Calvinists, and so on of Europe.

5   To put Christianity into workable perspective: *The last true Christian was a Pharisee, and he died 2000 years ago!* There are actually *no* records of the actual teachings of the earliest Christians. The records, in fact, begin around the end of the 1st century CE with Clement, Ignatius, and Polycarp. The term "Christian" didn't come into existence until after the beginning of the 2nd century C.E.

although there is no proof of this because there is no written documentation as to the beliefs of the early Judean Christians. We must remember that according to the messianic tradition, there were **three messiahs** who were to come: the *king-messiah* from the line of David who is the great conqueror (the ruler); the *warrior-messiah* from the line of Joseph (the knight); and the *suffering messiah*[6] (seen in mythologies as the fisher-king). The suffering messiah was definitely **not** divine nor was he considered Divine nor was he the Son of Yahweh. There was only one divinity and that was God and Yahweh was considered the Savior, as the name Jesus (Joshua) implies. The second point: The early Christians (especially the gentile Christians) believed that the end of the world was imminent. This is seen in many of the early Christian writings such as the Epistles and there are even mentions of this in several of the Gospels. Further, the writings of Ignatius of Antioch (c. 100 CE) and the Epistle of Barnabas (c. 130 CE) stated bluntly that the end of the world was due. Even down into the 4th century it was believed that the end of the world was coming at any moment. We will consider this concept later. Third, the early Christians after 73 CE believed in community, very much as the Essenes did. They were communists in the general sense of the word. They were more concerned with caring for each other, the poor, the widows, the orphans, the disenfranchised, and so on, than in material gains.[7] Fourth, very early on and especially in gentile Christianity, they believed ignorance and blind obedience to the bishops and the organization to be virtuous. We can see this in the writings of Ignatius of Antioch in both his Epistle to the Philadelphians[8] and in the Epistle of Polycarp[9] as well as the Epistles of Paul.[10] Finally, the early Christians believed that as a

---

6   The symbol of Israel and its tribulations.

7   That's a very far cry from today.

8   See the 2nd paragraph: "...and where your bishop is; there follow him like sheep."

9   See paragraph 7: "So let us have no more of this nonsense from the gutter, and these lying doctrines, and turn back to the Word originally delivered to us."

10   See I Corinthians 1:18, 19, 21, 28.

member of the community, whether a bishop, deacon, or layman, one *must* work. One of the main vices that the early Christians preached against within the Church was that of taking money from the group or the Church for preaching the Gospel: that is, living off of the donations of the group. Rather early on many saw fit to live off of others and for material gain simply on the strength of them being a Christian and the head of a specific Church. We can see statements against this in the Pauline Epistles as well as those of Polycarp and Ignatius.[11] All money collected was to go into the common welfare of the community. One who lives off of the community is *exploiting* Christ. In other words, it is against *all* of the teachings of Christianity to take any money for preaching the Gospel.[12] The most important thing was the community. For it was the community that provided everything that anyone needed: food, shelter, clothing, indoctrination, etc. essentially *everything* that a *cult community* provides.

---

11   See above.

12   Policarp stated in paragraph 6 of his Epistle to the Philippians: "As for the clergy, they should be men of generous sympathies, with a wide compassion for humanity...eagerness for money should be a thing utterly alien to them." See also I Timothy 3:2-4: "A bishop then must be blameless, the husband of one wife, vigilant, sober, of good behavior, given to hospitality, apt to teach Not given to wine, no striker, not greedy of filthy lucre..." Compare this with the description of Jesus in Matthew 11:19 and Luke 7:34.

The Early Church

> *Even so every good tree bringeth forth good fruit: but a corrupt tree bringeth forth evil fruit. A good tree cannot bring forth evil fruit, neither (can) a corrupt tree bring forth good fruit...Wherefore by their fruits ye shall know them.*
>
> Matthew 7:17-20

Some scholars believe that Christianity and early Church organization came from the Essenes. The main reason for this idea is that the Church's organization was very similar to the Essene organization in that: 1) Its organizational system was similar with its hierarchy; 2) It practiced frugality; 3) It promoted celibacy; 4) It had tests and vows to enter and remain in the community. To the Essenes, and the Mystery Religions for that matter, the idea of being ***born again***[13] meant nothing more than to take the ***second set of vows*** of the community. This occurred after a year and a day of probation; 5) It was a closely knit group which practiced communism; 6) It practiced ritual washing (baptism). This was the most common way for a gentile to become a member of the Judean religion in the Diaspora; 7) It rejected the use of oaths; and 8) It had sacred common meals. Since this has been seen historically, some researchers think that the Essenes (or a splinter group of the Essenes), who were considered "gnostic" by some Judeans, may have been the actual first "Christians." Consider also that after the Judean revolt (c. 70 CE) the Essenes completely disappeared and Christianity began to make quite a lot of headway. Until that time, Christianity was essentially considered pretty much a Judean religious sect.

There are problems with this idea though. The Essenes were a breakaway branch of the Sadducees. The Sadducees, though, were Roman sympathizers. The High Priest, also a Sadducee, was appointed by the Roman government. Consequently, neither the Sadducees nor the High Priest were held in much regard by the

---

13   The Hebrew word for being "born again" is *digon* and it referred to taking the second vows of the nazirite. The Greek term is *digonos*.

people. It is, as has been noted that from this break the Pharisees evolved and many of the statements attributed to Jesus were known teachings of the Pharisees.

According to the Christian tradition, the Christian "Church" at Jerusalem, after Jesus' supposed death was headed by his "brother" James. James was executed by the High Priest, Ananas, a Sadducee. After that, it was headed by Jesus' "cousin" Simeon, the son of Cleophas (also called Peter), who was executed by the Romans. Consequently, early Christianity's heads were *not* elected or appointed. The pattern was that of a *monarchical* succession. In Matthew 16:15-19, which is a later addition from around the 4th century when Jesus says that Peter is the rock on which he will build his church, he was appointing Peter to be the *minister* of his organization, not the leader of the Church. (See Isaiah 22:19-23)

The Early Christians

But be it so, I did not burden you: nevertheless, being shrewd, I caught you with deceit.

2 Corinthians 12:16

Whenever you read or hear of the early Christians you get this image of a pious, selfless, saintly group of people who would rather die than give up their beliefs. The early Christians were seen as a group of people who just wanted to be left alone to worship their god but were set upon by the Roman Empire and persecuted simply because they were Christians. This is the picture that you have today handed down by the early Christian writers. It is a traditional picture with literally *no* historical basis in fact. What you have been told and what actually occurred are two totally different views. The Christian writers have told one story, and much of that story is obviously highly colored. The historians and philosophers in many diverse areas of the Roman Empire all wrote of a completely different Christianity than that which you are used to hearing and reading about.

The historians and philosophers of the time were a curious group of people. They wanted to find out whatever they could about everything they could. When a new philosophy surfaced they became interested in the philosophy and wanted to find out more about it. So, they would set out to see what this new cult would have to offer. Literally every new cult would open themselves up to scrutiny for they realized that was the only way to get followers to become interested in them and to get accepted by the Roman government. Unfortunately, the more that the Christians were pressed for information regarding their beliefs the more resistant they became. The early Christians were anything but friendly and willing to discuss their philosophy. They were quite closed-mouth in the company of anyone who had any kind of knowledge and intelligence. Not so when it came to those who were easily manipulated, especially the lower classes and slaves. They would do or say anything to convince the listener that the end of the world was at hand and they had to repent or suffer for eternity in Hell.

The early Christians were, in fact, extremely intolerant. They criticized and persecuted others for their religious practices and beliefs. Quite often, writers of the time had stated that the Christians saw fit to believe their own myths while disbelieving and chastising those Pagan myths which were exactly the same. It didn't matter that they themselves continued to practice and believe much the same things as those whom they persecuted and considered it perfectly correct. This intolerance, as well as the fact that the Christians thought that their religion was above the law, is what caused the Pagan resentment of them. It is the contrived history by the Church that tells you that there were other reasons for the Pagan indignation toward the Christians. Further, historically, any persecutions were few and far between. The most notable of the persecutions was under the Emperor Nero (54-68 CE).[14] Under Nero Christians were not the only group persecuted. You must remember that Christianity was considered a Judean sect at this time so there were Judean believers persecuted as well as Pagan sects that fell out of favor with the Emperor. It is a fact of history that there was no evidence of a persecution under Domitian (81-96 CE). This supposed persecution has been a mainstay "proof" for early Christian oppression for more than 2000 years. There were also *no* martyrs in Carthage prior to Cyprian (248-258 CE). Of the martyrs that there were, it is well known that the Christians were noted for their theatricality in martyrdom, *not* for their bravery or piety. Further, it is known that Christians were *not* the only ones who were martyrs for their religious beliefs. They also were not the only persons who were part of the "sporting" events. The Christians who were placed into the contests were among other criminals and fanatics who were actually attempting to overthrow the Empire.

Christianity and the Christians were considered atheistic blasphemers and contemptible, "*...antisocial followers of a fanatical superstition both perverse and extravagant,*" and were accused of

---

14   Nero had a near riot on his hands at one point when he "treated" the citizens
     of Rome to plain-and-simple *murder* instead of the games of skill practiced
     by the Gladiators.

practicing incest and cannibalism at their nightly meetings. The most virtuous persons of the time saw that through Christianity no one would become generous and worthy, nor did Christianity promote wisdom and learning.

> *For it is written, I will destroy the wisdom of the wise, and will bring to nothing the understanding of the prudent...But God hath chosen the foolish things of the world to confound the wise; and God hath chosen the weak things of the world to confound the things which are mighty. And base things of the world, and things which are despised, hath God chosen, (yea), and things which are not, to bring to nought things that are.*

1 Corinthians 1:19; 27-28

It was a fact well-known at the time that the Pagan writings promoted abstinence, wisdom and justice. The Christians, though, ascribed these writings to Satan and Satan worshippers. Many Pagan writers saw nothing in the early Christian philosophy that was truly beautiful or worthy. It was filled with seriousness, fear and impiety. Many of the ancient writers saw the Christians leading a warped and dishonorable life of lethargy and confusion.

> *For God is not (the author) of confusion, but for peace...*

1 Corinthians 14:33

The early Christians were seen as not gathering the best of the Judean and Pagan religions and philosophies. Historians found only the worst. Early Christianity wove these things together into a "web of evils," as it was described.[15]

What was the original message, if any, of Jesus, assuming his existence? Is it, or any part of it, actually found in the Gospels and/or the Epistles? Who were those people who continued to propagate the Christian philosophy?

---

15   See the writings of the historian Celsus and the Emperor Julian.

71

Today, many people are claiming that they know and understand what the message of Jesus was and that the Christian philosophy of today is the same as was that preached at its inception 2000 years ago. The fact of the matter is that the original message of Jesus, whatever it may have been, is lost in antiquity. There is no record of what he may have said or alluded to in parable although there are ideas of what a parable meant when looking at it *in the context* of history and tradition. By the mid-first century, the actual message had begun to assume a form which became the basis for the theological formation of orthodox Christianity. Hence, the distinct possibility exists that Jesus' (assuming his existence) original message had nothing to do with theology nor did it have a spiritual meaning. It is also a fact that it definitely had nothing to do with messianic prophecies. He may have been, as was suggested by some researchers, someone from a kingly clan only trying to regain his disenfranchised throne. Consequently, he may have related himself to the king-messiah and was attempting to put together an army in the style of Judas the Maccabee. His intent may have been to overthrow the Romans and become the true king and ruler of Judea and Israel.[16] This too is speculation drawn from some implications in the Gospels.

When Christianity went out to the Gentiles, because it was making no gains in the ranks of the Judeans, it had to be changed to fit the audience. It must be remembered that the Mediterranean area was ruled by Rome. Consequently it was important that the appeal was to a Romanized audience. Additionally, at this time the Mystery Religions were extremely popular and it must also have that appeal. So, in order to make Jesus and Christianity palatable to the audience it had to be made to fit the group who was being proselytized.

---

16 There are indications of this idea in the Gospels for some of the statements of Jesus are quite literally seditious. For example, the people that he gathered around him (i.e. Simon Peter, a Zealot and Judas, a Siccarri) were members of seditionist groups, and there were things that he did which were designed to incite rioting (i.e. the temple episode). With the new Dead Sea Scroll translations it is easily seen where these seditionist ideas came from.

> *For though I be free from all (men), yet have I made myself*
> *servant unto all, that I might gain the more. And unto the*
> *(Judeans) I became as a (Judean), that I might gain the*
> *(Judeans); to them that are under the law, as under the law;*
> *To them that are without law, as without law, (being not*
> *without law to God, but under the law of Christ), that I*
> *might gain them that are without law. To the weak became*
> *I as weak, that I might gain the weak: I am made all things*
> *to all (men), that I might by all means save some.*
>
> 1 Corinthians 9:19-22

In order to have a god that appealed to the Pagans it was necessary to make the Christian god comparable to the Pagan gods. In
this way Jesus would be acceptable to the Pagans of the time
whether they be Greek, Roman, Egyptian or any other. In fact, the
idea that the Messiah was divine was **Pagan**, not Judean. The concept of divinity comes from the use of the Greek term "christ"
(christos) and "lord" (adonis), both of which have divine associa-
tions. Each region had to see Jesus as the natural extension of their
sun-god in order to attract the people of that region.[17] So, Jesus
was given: 1) a miraculous (virgin) birth replete with angels and
his own star announcing his birth; 2) miracles; 3) a death and resurrection; and 4) a second coming. All of the trappings of a traditional sun-god. None of these things were mentioned in any of the
writings of the early Church Fathers, nor in the Epistles. As a matter of fact, Paul does not even mention the Book of Acts or any of
the sayings of Jesus, Bethlehem, Nazareth, Jesus' parents, the virgin birth, John the Baptist, Judas' actions, the Sermon on the
Mount, the miracles, the parables, the trial before Pilate,[18] the
Lord's Prayer, or any other "significant" event in Jesus' life or
death. Paul agrees with Peter when he does state several times that
the resurrection was "...in spirit..." because it is only the spiritual
body that can be raised, **not** the physical.

---

17 The first people to listen to Paul were the merchants of Corinth. Merchants then
as now dealt with debt and repayment. Hence, we have the introduction of the
birth and death cycle equated to the debt and repayment process. Jesus is the
offering to repay the debt supposedly incurred by Adam and Eve.

18 Paul does not mention a trial before Pilate, only that Jesus lived during the
reign of Pilate.

All scripture is given by inspiration of God, and (is)
profitable for doctrine, for reproof, for correction,
for instruction in righteousness:

2 Timothy 3:16

After the mid-first century, Christianity had no mission and made no organized or official approach to unbelievers. Everything was left up to the individual. What sold the story of Jesus was the improbabilities and fantastic tales rather than the strength of credible texts. This is so because there were *no* canonical texts nor historical writings available. To the early Christians, all of the "good news" was given by inspiration only, not in written form. The main text that the early Christians used was the Septuagint, the Greek translations of the Hebrew Scriptures.

The term "Christian" did not come into use until early in the 2nd century and by the first half of the 2nd century Christianity was called The Catholic Church. Originally, the Christians were called "Nazarenes." Nazarene, Nasorean, Nozrim are all titles that the Essenes gave to themselves. Consequently, any references to The Church in any of the Gospels or Epistles indicate that the writing— or rewriting—was after the beginning of the 2nd century.[19] Prior to the 2nd century, the term chrestian or *chrestos*[20] meaning "*a* righteous person," was generally used to describe Christians. Before that time, the Christians were considered either a part of the Judean religious structure, as an itinerant Judean sect, or a new cult that had sprung up. The title "Christian" developed out of Antioch, not Jerusalem.

Unlike the Christians, the Pagans of the time were extremely tolerant. They were interested in any new religions and philosophies that came up. They realized that they could gain knowledge from everywhere and anywhere. Consequently, the Pagans had a

---

19   There are those who would argue this point due to the Greek term *ekklesia* (ecclesia) which means literally a *calling out* (the word evocation has the same meaning). It refers to a meeting, especially a religious congregation or assembly but translated as "church." It was Marcion, the Gnostic, who first established Christian churches. That was around the middle of the 2nd century.

20   The title "chrestos" was a common name given to the gods of the mystery religions.

major preoccupation with finding ways to develop spiritually. They had a great interest in anything new and this new philosophy interested them. Remember, this was a period when the Mystery Religions were very popular and the majority of people who could afford it belonged to at least *two* of them. Unfortunately, whenever the Pagans tried to learn about this new sect they were met with closed-mouth intolerance, hatred, and hostility and it was impossible for them to find much out about it.[21]

Due to this attitude by the Christians, the information that was gleaned from apostate Christians, observations, and what was known about them, the Pagans saw the Christians as: "*... a contemptible, anti-social group hated for their vices...and practicing incest and cannibalism at nightly meetings,*"—Tacitus; "*...possessing a squalid superstition,*"—Pliny; "*...a tribe obscure, shunning the light, <u>dumb in public</u>* (emphasis, mine) *though talkative in corners,*"—Origen (a Christian himself); "*...impious and atheistic, for throwing up their ancestral gods,*"—Porphyry; "*It is generosity toward non-members, care for the graves of the dead, and <u>pretended</u>* (emphasis, mine) *holiness of life that have specially fostered the growth of (this) atheism,*"—Julian (4th century); Lucian of Samosata (c.119-200), a Greek satirist, said the early Christians were an "*ignorant body of people*" who were "*duped by rogues and charlatans;*" and Apollonius Sacceas charged the Christians with impiety for they took out their rage and bitterness by overturning temples and altars, and cutting the throats not only of those who remained firm in their own religion, but also other Christians who did not believe the same way as they did (e.g. the lamenting of a dead body differently, or when to celebrate a holy day such as Easter). Even early Christian writers had some derogatory things to say about some early Christian groups: "*...they met in secret to eat human flesh and once the lamps had been upset, to participate in promiscuous incestuous intercourse*" — Justin Martyr: "*...the names of brother and sister hallow fornication as incest. Their foolish superstition makes a boast of crime; a condemned criminal in the object of veneration. Finally, there is infant murder, cannibalism and the banquet with incestuous intercourse.*" – Minucis Felix

---

21   There goes the idea that the Christians were willing to talk to anyone about their philosophical ideas.

For it hath been declared unto me of you, my brethren, by them (which are of the house) of Chloe, that there are contentions among you. Now this I say, that every one of you saith, I am of Paul; and I of Apollos; and I of Cephas; and I of Christ.

1 Corinthians 1:11-12

From 100 to 300 CE, Christianity was a small, unimportant sect, looked at with disdain due to their intolerance of others. It was centered mainly in the cities and was taught to believers only. Christians refused to allow anyone outside of their group to learn of their philosophy. From its earliest beginnings outside of Galilee, it was charged that the Christian doctrines had gained credence only with a public unable to tell truth from nonsense. The thrust of Christianity was to the ignorant, depraved, the slaves, the children, to women,[22] and the old. It was these people that were actively sought out by the Christians to make them believers. Consequently, the stronghold of Christianity was in the cities and among the lower classes. The main focal point of conversion, as was noted by Celsus, was in private houses, *not* in public, as we have been told. Those who could not be convinced by the witnessing of a "miracle" and were beyond the proselytizer's grasp were called "possessed by the devil," casters of spells, witches,[23] soothsayers, cunning women, crystal gazers, and other names of practitioners of the occult arts. Anything intelligent, just and wise was even ascribed to Satan and Satan worshippers.

"*Jesus,*" as Celsus stated, "*was presented by the Christians as if he was a great god, but is not so much as an ordinary one, nor even a daimon.*[24] *Christians believe in eternal punishments and threaten others with these punishments.*" The god taught by the early Christians was a god of wrath, a monstrous concept that was blasphemous and against all common sense. This was expressed by

---

22 About 500 years earlier Plato had commented on how women were given to belief in silly religious ideas and experiences.

23 The correct term is necromancer for the term *witch* was completely unknown until the Middle Ages.

24 A daimon is a lower level spirit. It is also called a *demon*.

both Cicero and the Emperor Julian. The Christian god was similar to the Pagan in that he was: a monarch on a throne; had angels and other supernatural beings in servitude; and had an evil deity which opposed him. So convinced were the Christians that their philosophy was right that they taught freely from **Pagan** literature interpreting it as they saw fit.[25] The same was done with the Torah, adding to, deleting from, and interpreting it as they needed and desired. This convoluted interpretation of the writings was Scripture given by "inspiration."

You can get a fairly good understanding of the reason that the early Christians were looked upon with such disdain by the intellectuals of the time by looking at their teachers: the Church fathers. The Church fathers taught not only a now defunct form of Christianity but also their own superstitions and incomprehensible beliefs. The three Church fathers given credit for the founding of Christianity were Irenaeus of Lyons (115-202), Clement of Alexandria (160-215), and Tertullian (160-210). All of their arguments and assertions were inconsistent, lacking critical thinking and supporting data, and were weak and intellectually inferior to the Pagans. When they were confronted by Pagan arguments they couldn't counter their consistent retort was that it was of Satan. They were seen to use "tasteless and infected language" and exaggerate in order to "clothe the poverty of their own thoughts," (e.g. Alexander of Abonuteichus [c. 317] was referred to as, "a religious huckster who created a huge puppet of a snake" to deceive people).

The actual beliefs of the founders of Christianity were rather unusual. Clement of Rome (d. 100), Irenaeus, Tertullian, and Origen (185-251) believed that the Phoenix actually existed. Origen went so far as to say that the sun, moon, and stars were living creatures with reason, free will and were able to sin. Clement of Alexandria, Hippolytus of Rome (176-236), Justin Martyr (c. 100 - c. 163), Theophilis of Antioch (c. 170), Athenagoras (c. 180), Minucis Felix (d. c. 211), Cyprian of Carthage (c. 258), Lactantius (245-323), Origin, Tertullian, Irenaeus, Jerome (340-

---

25   For example, the early Christians taught that Virgil's *Fourth Ecologue* was messianic prophecy and Socrates was called a "Christian before Christ."

420) Eusebius (c. 263-340), Tatian, and Augustine of Hippo all believed in the reality of demons. Justin Martyr claimed that demons were the offspring of angels who had sex with human females. Since angels were bodies of light demons were from the darkness. Both had ethereal bodies and this gave them extraordinary powers of perception and movement. They also believed in the existence of nature spirits: sprites, elves, and goblins.

Justin Martyr also believed that insane people were possessed and tortured by the soul of someone wicked who died in their sins. This, he claimed, proved that the soul was immortal. Theophilis of Antioch said that the pains women endure in childbirth and the fact that snakes move on their bellies are proof of the "fall" as described in Genesis.

Tertullian believed that the hyena changed its sex and that the stag renews its youth by eating poisonous snakes. He said that eclipses and comets were signs of God's anger and forerunners of natural disasters. Volcanos, he believed, were openings into hell and that the volcano was a punishment inflicted on a mountain as a warning to the wicked. He further claimed that the chirpings of birds were prayers.

These early Christian fathers were seen with quite a bit of derision in the beginning centuries of this era. They were superstitious and neither intelligent nor versed in philosophical argumentation. Hence, the thrust of their preaching was originally to the lowest classes, the uneducated, children, and elderly. It wasn't until centuries later that Christianity became the religion of choice because of the material and social advantages that were available, not for anything spiritual.

What Were the Early Christian Churches Like?

For God hath not given us the spirit of fear; but of power, and of love, and of a sound mind.

2 Timothy 1:7

One of the early Church writers, John Chrysostom (C.347-407), made note of what went on in the Christian churches. Far from being that with you may be familiar, he stated that: "*...for ours are not of that sort* (e.g. the synagogues), *but, rather, truly fearful and filled with shuddering. For within is the God that has the power over life and death—so fearful is the place. And within, 10,000 sermons on eternal punishments, on the rivers of fire, on the poisonous worm, on unbreakable bonds and further darkness,*" Pelagius (c. 380) said the texts read by the priests contained "*a series of strange hallucinations which only a few weak women believe and perhaps a few womanly men.*" Galen of Perganius (d.c. 199) saw the early church gatherings as a "*place of resort to the curious, the speculative and the idle.* So, as you can see from this description, apparently the important aspect of the early Christian teachings was fear, ignorance and superstition. It seems that this was one of the main teachings that brought the poor, downtrodden, and ignorant to accept the Christian point of view and this is what kept them in bondage to that point of view. It is not much different than that of today especially in the fundamentalist Christian churches. As was stated by St. Augustine in the late 4th and early 5th century: "*There is no conversion from hope, only from fear.*" It is fear which continues to keep people's mind bound to this philosophy two millennia later.

Alexander S. Holub, Ph.D.

What Constituted Conversion to Christianity?

But in vain they do worship me, teaching (for) doctrines the commandments of men.

Matthew 15:9; Mark 7:7

From the very earliest times of gentile Christianity the fear motive was necessary. In virtually every case in early Christianity the stimulus which would underlie the giving up of a Pagan religion for Christianity was the avoidance of Divine and eternal punishment. Later on, especially from the 4th century onward, it became advantageous to be a Christian. Being a Christian meant that you would gain the benefits of this world, not the next, as these benefits were promised by the local adherents.

In the first few centuries of this era, conversion from one philosophy to another was the rule rather than the exception. Hence, people converted to Christianity mainly through the desire for "blessings," fear of physical and spiritual pain, and belief in "miracles."

All cults need to have a "hook" that will attract the attention of prospective followers. Today there is the idea of "chanting for world peace," or being able to "think clearly," or "the world is coming to an end," or any number of other devices. The "hook" that the early Christians had which grabbed the people first off was a "miracle" or sign as it was called. It must be remembered that it was a time of immense superstition. There was a great belief in magical spells that can change people into something else, and in gods and demons all of which can directly affect human existence. As has been noted by many writers of the time, the Christians seemed to be quite adept at prestidigitation and other forms of illusion and manipulation.[26] The people of the time believed in and came to expect miracles to occur so that they were looking for them to happen. In the vernacular Greek of the time, of which the Christian Scriptures were written, the word *pistis* is commonly mistranslated as *faith*. It actually means belief or

---

26 This is not unlike the fundamentalist ministers of today. James Randi (The Amazing Randi), the stage magician, has caught quite a few pulling a lot of old carnival tricks. These old tricks are referred to as "articles of faith" by the evangelists. To any honest, reputable individual they are just plain deceptions.

trust.[27] In non Christian inscriptions it is translated as salvation and represents the results of merely witnessing or being a spectator at a "miracle." The Greek word used for spectators of miracles was also used to denote conversion. Consequently, anyone who did nothing more than be present at a magic show or "miracle" was considered converted! This technique, though, was not the exclusive right of the Christians. Many of the cults of the time followed the same procedure. If you saw it and believed that it happened, you were automatically considered a convert. Then you could begin the indoctrination.

Pagans, who were members of the Mystery Schools, were well-versed in the manipulations and tricks that were used. So they were extremely skeptical regarding "miracles." This obviously caused the performing Christians to be outraged and the Pagan would be accused of all sorts of things and be condemned to hell. The Christian approach was summed up quite aptly by Celsus when he said: *"Their* (Christians) *injunctions are like this: 'Let no one educated, no one wise, no one sensible draw near. For these abilities are thought by us to be evils. But, as for anyone ignorant, anyone stupid, anyone uneducated, anyone who is a child, let him come boldly...' Moreover, we see that those who display their trickery in the market places and go about begging would never enter a gathering of intelligent men, nor their presence; but whenever they see adolescent boys and a crowd of slaves and a company of fools they push themselves in and show off...But they alone, they say, know the right way to live..."* To this, the Christian Father Origen said——NOTHING!

To the early Christians, as it is with many Christian sects today, ignorance was considered a virtue. It was important to have blind obedience to the bishop.[28] As it was stated by the Emperor Julian, *"No one will become generous and worthy from Christianity for it does not promote wisdom and learning and the Pagan writings that promote fortitude, prudence, and justice are ascribed to Satan and those who worship Satan."* Further, he stated, *"Christians collected from the Greeks and (Judeans) what is pernicious, impious,*

---

27 See Mark 9:23; Matthew 15:28; 17:20.

28 Recall Ignatius' Epistle to the Ephesians and that of Polycarp as well as Paul's first Epistle to the Corinthians.

depraved, indolent, audacious and confusing and put it together in their philosophy." The Emperor Julian was one of the most intelligent emperors that ever ruled Rome. He had written many a volume of work against the Christians to which the Christians wrote many an apology. After they had him killed, the Christians destroyed *all* of his writings and all that exists are portions of the apologies which contain a small number of Julian's statements.

One of the main selling points of early Christianity was that it preached the end of the world as being imminent.[29] This helped to induce fear and anxiety into the unaware and ignorant individual and, hence, gain followers. In fact, after the turn of the 1st century, when the world did not end, it was believed that by 170 this would certainly occur. From then on, it seems, every turn of the century or so the Christians have been awaiting the end of the world. Even Eusebius, the Church historian, (c. 320) had reached the conclusion that the end of the times was about to occur due to circumstances which had taken place. Further, going from the year 999 into 1000 people sat on their rooftops watching and waiting for the end of the world. It promised to be quite a spectacular show. They definitely did not want to miss it!

The problem here is one of interpretation of the Greek writings in the Christian Scriptures. In these writings there are four Greek words translated as world: cosmos (adorning, world: the sky); *æon* (an age or era); oykoumenay (land, globe, or earth); and ghay (soil, region, country, or land). Some of the most quoted verses referring to the end of the world actually state the end of the *era* or *æon*.[30] Further, each of the Greek terms had more than a literal meaning attached to it. Their significance extended into the mystical areas as well. You will recall that the beginning of this era saw the Mystery Religions as being extremely popular. Much of the philosophical writings of the day were done by those who were members of Mystery Religions. Hence, their writings had both a surface meaning and a deeper meaning. The deeper meaning would be seen by those who were initiated into the Mystery Religion. So, a literal translation of the texts renders them quite sterile of meaning.

---

29   See Matthew 24:34; Mark 13:30; Luke 21:32; 1 Peter 4:7; 2 Peter 3:10.

30   See Matthew 12:32; 13;22, 39. 40; 24:3; 28:20; Mark 4:19; 10:30; Luke 1:70; 18:30, 34, 35; John 9:32; Acts 3:21; 15:18; etc.).

What Were the Influences on the Christian Philosophy?

> *...Who also hath made us able ministers of the new testament; not of the letter, but of the spirit: for the letter killeth, but the spirit giveth life.*

2 Corinthians 3:6

Traditionally Christians have been led to believe that Jesus was responsible for the teachings of Christianity. If this were true, the Gospels would have been written *before* the Epistles and the Epistles of Paul would not overshadow the Gospels. Throughout the Epistles Paul states that what he is preaching is *his* version of the Gospel.[31] He also *never* mentions the Gospels which are included in the canon of the Scriptures nor does he mention anything actually said by Jesus.

The individuals most responsible for Christian thought, as it has been handed down, are Irenaeus, the bishop of Lyons (c. 180 CE), Clement of Alexandria, (c. 190 CE) and Tertullian of Carthage (c. 190 CE), all of whom stressed three main things: 1) a fixed dogma (for there was none at the time); 2) a theological system; and 3) a structure that allowed *no* individual interpretation of the scriptures and was chosen by the Church. There had to be a single "Catholic" or universal church resting on an Apostolic foundation and succession with the bishops' and priests' authority as most important. It must be remembered that the Papacy was not set up until the time of Constantine some two centuries later.

It was Irenaeus who set out to create a Christian canon in response to the canon of the Gnostic Marcion of Sinope (c. 170). It was later left up to Athanasius Bishop of Alexandria and the Council of Laodicea (365) to compile the list of the books for the canon which were to be used in the Christian Scriptures. This was eventually ratified at the Council of Hippo in 393 and again in the Council of Carthage in 397. Prior to Irenaeus' response to the canon of Marcion of Sinope the Christians used the Septuagint (Greek) version of the Hebrew Scriptures as their Scriptures.

---

31 See: Romans 2:16; Galatians 1:12; and 2 Timothy 2:8.

Tertullian saw Christian life as a battle with the devil. He bluntly stated that Christians believe in their tenets "...*because they are absurd*"[32] and impossible. Tertullian had a great influence on a lot of Christian thought although he ended his days outside of The Church as a Gnostic.

Some of the most important doctrines that Christians now believe were **not** even part of earliest Christianity. Heaven, hell, the resurrection of the dead, and the Second coming were seen as *symbolic,* not actualities. The idea of the Trinity was a very hotly debated item until well into the 3rd century. The debate first began about 180 when Theophilus of Antioch[33] first coined the term "Trinity." It was not until the 3rd century that the doctrine of the Trinity, an essential *Pagan* belief, was incorporated into Christian thought. The main reason that early Christianity did **not** see the Holy Spirit as part of the god-head was because it was seen as *female*. The fact of the matter is that many influential Church thinkers still did not believe that Jesus was God even into the 5th century. Therefore a belief in a trinity would be baseless.

The problem with discussing Christianity is that today's writers use today's beliefs, attitudes, mores, traditions, and concepts with little or no historical perspective. We are **led** to believe that Christianity began with a certain person at a particular time who taught a specific philosophy. None of this is true. Christianity, as we know it, is the product of a lot of debate, much of which was extremely heated and hostile. Mainly, *it is a product of the Councils of The Catholic Church.* To put it mildly, what was not politically and economically advantageous for the ruling priests was discarded and became anathema and heretical. In contrast to Paganism's freedom of choice and toleration, Christianity presented ideas that demanded belief. You had to believe as a certain individual or group did or you would be accused of all sorts of horren-

---

32 "Prorsus credibile est, quia *ineptum* (stupid or ridiculous) est." Later, St. Augustine writes, "I would not believe the Gospel if the authority of the Catholic Church did not compel (force) me."

33 See the dedications at the beginning of the Gospel of Luke and the Book of Acts.

dous activities. Later on if you chose to question the beliefs you were ostracized and condemned to hell. This is not any different than what happens with many Christian sects today.

In the Pagan Roman Empire there was complete religious tolerance and freedom of religion. All religions were permitted to practice and believe in any god in any way that they saw fit.[34] Unlike the Judeo/Christian monotheism, Pagan polytheism actually promoted religious tolerance. The Pagan priests, whenever they encountered other religious beliefs and myths, would attempt to learn everything that they could about the religion and create lists for comparative religious study (syncretism). In this way, they would learn what the other religions had to offer that could strengthen their own. They never looked down on any other religious belief nor did they criticize another's practices or mythologies. This toleration continued throughout the days of the Pagan control of the Roman Empire...unless the religion became an actual threat to the functioning of the Empire. It was then that the religion and its adherents were denounced. In fact, about a century before Christianity began the Dionysian Mystery religion had caused such a large problem, because of its followers (mainly women) becoming quite inebriated, and going about at night murdering people. The Roman government put an immediate stop to this religion and its practices. Later on it received limited permission to practice until it "straightened out its act." It was not until Christianity had total control of the Roman Empire (i.e. the "Holy" Roman Empire) that real religious intolerance began.

From its earliest inception, gentile Christianity refused to allow any freedom of belief and thought. This is what actually caused the resentment between the Christians and Pagans. The Christians felt that they could do anything they desired because their religion was above the law and that their god could beat any other god and, besides, the end of the world was coming. With the end of the

---

34 The Roman government wanted to keep the people occupied while they did what they wanted and made the gains that they wanted. The two things that they used to keep the people occupied the most were sporting events and religious cults. While they were happy in their pursuits the people would not know or interfere with the operations of the government. Governments have not changed in more than two thousand years.

world they knew Jesus was coming back at any day to destroy the unrighteous. As you have seen, their intolerance not only included murdering those who refused to accept their philosophy, but also those who had accepted their philosophy but did not believe exactly the same way.

After 312 Christianity was in vogue in the Roman Empire and there were social and material rewards for becoming a Christian. Further, Pagan temples were expensive to keep up while Christian churches were not. This along with banquets for the poor, made it seem attractive to the people. We must remember that the Mystery Religions were on a decline by this time and that many temples of the Mystery Religions were abandoned. Then, too, the gods of the Mystery Schools seemed far removed from human emotions and Jesus just seemed easier to reach for the average individual. Consequently, it was easier to relate to the Christian god than to many of the Pagan gods for Jesus was supposed to have been alive only a few centuries earlier. Hence, Christianity prospered not on the basis of it being pure, holy, sincere, honest, and loving but on the basis of politics, economics, fear, and ignorance. *People who are taught to worship a Divine teacher are not taught to think with any form of morality or responsibility.* The worship of that teacher is paramount, not the relationship one has with his/her fellow human beings or the rest of the world.

Who were the Gnostics?

For God, who has said, "Light shall shine out of darkness,"
is the One who has shone in our hearts to give the light of
the knowledge (gnosis) of the glory of God in the face of
Christ.

2 Corinthians 4:6

You cannot possibly discuss early Christianity without discussing the Gnostics. They were an extremely important part of the history of the Christian movement. Their fate was to create a strong influence on the Christian beliefs, be ostracized by those now considered orthodox, to be persecuted by those same orthodox Christians who eventually took on many Gnostic beliefs that they persecuted, and eventually rise from time to time in different forms.

The word Gnostic comes from the Greek word gnosis which means "knowledge." The word itself became sort of a catch-all word for non-orthodox religious movements (Remember the Essenes?). Gnosticism itself existed in the Hellenistic Roman Empire at least a century prior to Christianity. Later on, the early Church fathers (e.g. Iranaeus) had written against those who were "false knowers" and spoke of other than orthodox teachings. The Gnostics were not attempting to find any ideal philosophical intellectual or theoretical knowledge. Their quest was to find a knowledge which was both liberating and redeeming at the same time. The extent of this knowledge is based upon your personal investigation of yourself, others, and Divinity. It is a knowledge given by revelation which has been made available only to the chosen who are capable of receiving it.[35] Anyone who has this "knowledge" or gnosis is a redeemed individual. This person is fulfilling the Divine Will of the Creator. The true Gnostic is like one who was asleep and is now awake and can tell the difference between the two states. Standing in contrast to the Gnostic is the ignorant individ-

---

35   See Romans 16:25; 1 Corinthians 14:6, 16; Galatians 2:2; Ephesians 1:17, 3:3 etc.

ual. The ignorant simply has faith, which is considered the opposite of knowledge. It was this opposition of faith and knowledge which was one of the central themes in the debates of the orthodox Christians and the Gnostic "heresy."

Almost as soon as original Christianity went out to the gentiles Gnosticism spread. In reality, the majority of Christian proselytizing was Gnostic and their philosophy and influences are seen as far away as in India and China.[36] Further, if, according to tradition and several verses in the Gospels, Jesus was an Essene, then he was a Gnostic (in the most general use of the term) Judean.[37] What he would then have preached was *not* traditional Judeanism nor, what later became orthodox Christianity, but actually Gnosticism! With this a possibility, then orthodox Christianity and its dogma is the true heresy and these early Christian "heretics" were closer to the actual Christianity.

The Gnostics were an early part of Christianity and Gnosticism existed before Christianity. They believed that true self-knowledge was the knowledge of God. Their practices ranged from total asceticism to total decadence, although most scholars do not believe that they actually were as decadent as they wrote. No matter what they did or believed, the main characteristic of Gnostic Christianity was the freedom to think and Gnosticism rested firmly on a personal experience and union with Divinity. This, of course, was an effrontery to the orthodox Christians who saw blind obedience to the hierarchy and faith as important.

The early Gnostics saw Jesus as either a full-fledged god or a mortal prophet.[38] The latter view was seen especially by the (Judean) Gnostic Ebonites.[39] They also saw that the term "Christ"

---

36 As much as many followers of the Indian philosophies would not like to admit it, there are quite a few strong Gnostic Christian influences in the *Bhagavad Gita*. The basic idea of this book is seen in *The Mahabarata* but the text itself was not actually put into writing until the 6th century CE.

37 We will soon find that this tradition cannot possibly be relied upon.

38 Recall that the term "Son of Man" is a title of a prophet. Also, we find that Jesus being (a) God was a Gnostic Creation.

39 The Ebonites, even though they were from the ranks of the Judean religion, were treated as deviationists by the orthodox Christians.

was nothing more than a ***title*** as was that of "messiah" and had nothing at all to do with Divinity. All that these terms did was to indicate a position ***near*** God, not that of being God. Consequently, the Gnostics believed there were other "Christs."

The first Christians to compile a teaching canon were the Marcionite Gnostics. This group was considered definitely heretics by the early Church, for they were the first Christian "fundamentalists."[40] Their canon was compiled about 144 CE. The books that they used were the early Book of Luke (which was quite different than the present version) and the ten Pauline Epistles. It was not until around 180 when Irenaeus compiled the books with which you are familiar as the essential canon for the orthodox Christians and it was not until more than two centuries later that these books were finally approved of as the actual "word of God" for Christians. In fact, it was said that Marcion of Sinope (the compiler of the Marcion canon) so angered the followers of the ***new*** religion of Jesus Christ and so provoked the Christian Fathers (Irenaeus specifically) that they then established their own canon of texts for Scriptures.

There is the distinct possibility that the earliest Gospels, and maybe even the Epistles, were written by Gnostic sects.[41] There are literally hundreds of Gnostic ideas expressed and very strongly emphasized in the Gospels and Epistles. These include: being God intoxicated; receiving the "call;" being cast or thrown out or fallen; being ***reborn*** or born again; being saved by the blood; and being ". . . in the world but not of it." There are also too many Gnostic terms used in the same allegorical ways as the Gnostics to consider it mere coincidence.[42] This, along with many other allegorical terms, leads to the strong possibility that the Gospels were

---

40   You will recall that the "word of God" was given by *revelation*, not by text.

41   Or could it be that Paul was a Greek who was very familiar with Gnostic teachings and simply incorporated early pre-Christian Gnosticism and Paganism into what he understood Christianity to be?

42   i.e. the Light or Life of the World; outer darkness; house, dwelling place, or garment; King of this world; living waters; the wind; living fire, etc.

written by the Gnostics, heretics, and later they were modified by the Church fathers for their own purposes. For the Gnostics taught mainly through the use of allegory (parable) and allusion.[43]

---

43   See Matthew 13:34 and Mark 4:34. It is a well-known fact that the Kabbalah, and all of the Mystical and Mystery Religions, taught mainly through metaphor and allegory and never directly. The main reason that there are injunctions against literal interpretations of the Scriptures is that all that is written are *teaching tales*. They were never designed to give true facts. This is why whenever you begin to search for historical documentation for the Scriptures you find very little if any. Each of the tales can be interpreted differently as you learn more from life and grow mentally, emotionally, psychologically, and spiritually.

The History of the Christian Scriptures

Now I beseech you, brethren, mark them which cause divisions and offenses contrary to the doctrine which ye have learned; and avoid them. For they that are such serve not our Lord Jesus Christ, but their own belly; and by good words and fair speeches deceive the hearts of the simple.

Romans 16:17-18

Today, virtually all of Christianity follows the teachings of Paul. Without Paul and his teachings Christianity would not be. The teachings of Jesus, as espoused in the Gospels, are *not* the same as Paul's. We must remember that Paul supposedly encountered Jesus "in spirit" on the road to Damascus. The only problem is that there are three detailed accounts of this story and they all differ.[44]

According to tradition, Paul was born Saul in the city of Tarsus in Asia Minor. Tarsus was an important center for trade and information at that time. One of the most important Mystery Religions of the time, The Mithraic Mysteries began in Tarsus.

Paul, according to this tradition, was a tentmaker by trade and an ex-rabbinical student (a Pharisee) supposedly taught by one of the most respected teachers of the time, Gamaliel. Nowhere in any of Paul's writings is there even anecdotal evidence of this nor is it mentioned. This is only stated in Acts.

Paul was supposedly from Tarsus. Being from Tarsus, a city on the major trade routes between the eastern and western Roman Empire, and a supposed former rabbinical student, Paul had to have been rather familiar with the mythologies of his day and the more non-traditional philosophies such as those of the Essenes and the most popular Mystery Religions and their gods, their mythologies, and their slain and risen saviors, as well as the Essenes' Teacher of Righteousness. He may have heard the stories of a teacher in Judea who had a following and these stories may have inspired his thinking. He may have done nothing more than add to

---

44   See Acts 9:1-19; 22:6-21; 26:12-18.

the teachings the myth of the crucified and risen savior. Because of his familiarity with the Pagan mythologies, Paul naturally assumed that this teacher was a god, for only a god can die and rise again. One thing to remember is that the earliest teachings of Christianity had no virgin birth, nor a death and resurrection story. There was, in fact no life story at all. It is not known exactly when this began. Consequently, none of Paul's writings say anything about any of these concepts.

Another important aspect of the development of Paul's philosophy was the city of Tarsus. Tarsus was one of the most important cities in the Near East. Not only was it a center of trade but it was an exchange point for information from all parts of the Roman Empire and Asia. By this time it was completely Hellenized with a very strong Greek influence. As Tarsus was the city where the Mithraic Mysteries had began, it was obvious that Paul was familiar with them. The Mithraic Mysteries began a bit earlier but rose pretty much concurrently with Christianity and vied for the religion of choice of the Empire. In fact, the Mithraic Mysteries were the religion of choice for the Roman Army. The Mithraic Mysteries continued to remain the religion of choice for the Roman Army up into the 4th century. After that time, Christianity had its material advantages. If it was not for Constantine, Christianity would have eventually died out and the western world would have most likely been Mithraic.

Paul, obviously, had been familiar with the Mithraic Mysteries. In them were described many of the beliefs which eventually made their way into orthodox Christianity including that of "true" salvation and the end of times.

Paul's Epistles are written in Hellenistic Greek and in them Paul makes use of the Hellenistic Stoic style of rhetoric, not that expected of an ex-rabbinical student and especially someone who claimed to have studied to be a Pharisee with one of the most respected teachers of the time. In fact, for Biblical quotes and "proofs" of his version of Christianity, Paul uses the Greek Septuagint, not the Hebrew.

Today, there are scholars who are beginning to doubt that Paul had even existed. One of the reasons is that Paul was never mentioned by Gallio, the proconsul of Achaia (52-64 CE) Paul was supposed to have had an audience with Gallio and was to have preached there for a year-and-a-half. Further, the Epistles which are attributed to him were actually written by at least a half-dozen different people: 1 Corinthians was written by Stephanus, Fortunatus, Achaicus, and Timotheus; 2 Corinthians was written by Titus and Lucas; Hebrews was written by Barnabas; Romans was written by Tertius; and Ephesians was originally called Laodicians and no one knows who wrote it. It is totally unthinkable that Paul, having been a businessman prior to preaching Christianity, did not know how to write or had forgotten how to do it when he converted. Further, if you will look closely at the Epistles it is easy to see differences in the writing style and philosophy being expressed. This is an indicator that different people and time periods were involved. Consequently, no one knows who the actual writers of the Epistles were even though several Epistles are considered "genuine" Pauline.

Historically there was no mention or record of the Epistles until after the middle of the 2nd century. Justin Martyr (c. 140) who wrote many volumes of works concerning early Christianity *never* mentioned Paul or his Epistles. Nor were they mentioned by early Church Fathers (i.e. Clement [c. 96], Ignatius [c. 107], Polycarp [c. 108]).

The Beginnings of the Gospels

For over a century Biblical scholars have suspected and suggested that the Gospels had at least one precursor. Some had reasoned that there was a basic story line the Gospels came from. Others were not sure about the story line idea at all. Many agree that there had to have been an oral tradition of teachings more so than a story line. What these latter scholars reasoned was that the deeds of a movement's founders are secondary. The teachings are most important. These latter scholars, it appears, were probably correct.

It is a fact that the Gospels came into being *after* the Roman-Judean war. That is quite a few decades after the incidents supposedly occurred. If the events were so important to the followers of this teacher they would have been written down almost immediately. They were not, consequently the events are highly suspect. Further, since there are some fairly strong parallels in the teachings in the Gospels there most likely had to have been a common source from which they were drawn. This common source was accidentally discovered by scholars who were wondering which Gospel was written first. As the Gospels were set side by side for comparison they noticed two kinds of correspondences: 1) the story line in Matthew and Luke agreed only when it followed the Gospel of Mark. This indicated that Mark had to have been the earliest and the source for the story line; and 2) Matthew and Luke contained a large quantity of identical sayings not found in Mark. This meant that Matthew and Luke had used a second written document in addition to the Gospel of Mark. This document was given the title of "Q", from the German word *Quelle* which means "source." It is this Q gospel which is now recognized as the source for the Gospels and the text which the earliest followers of the movement, which later became Christianity, had taught and learned from.

The interesting thing about these early followers of Q is that they were ***not*** Christian. Many of them were most likely not even Judean. There is a good possibility that the movement numbered many of its followers as Palestinian born ***Greeks*** and members of different Semitic groups. The teachings of Q indicate that there was no messiah, or even a messiah or Christ concept. There was no reproach of the traditional Judean religion. There was no death and resurrection that would transform the world. None of the later mythological additions existed in the Q gospel. Instead there were teachings of how to live in the troubled times.

The Q gospel developed out of the Galilee area. You will recall that Galilee of 2000 years ago was not a stronghold of the Judean religion. Rather it was one of the most Hellenized areas of the Middle East. Its Greek influence showed throughout. The most popular philosophical school in Galilee was the *Cynic* school. Today's representation of the Cynics is inaccurate. The Cynics were actually the social critics of the time. They would comment, often humorously, about the traditional values, oppressive forms of government, and society in general.

Cynics were known for their begging, voluntary poverty, renunciation of needs, severance of family ties, fearless and carefree attitudes, and troublesome public behavior. Their main areas of criticism were the rich, pretension, and hypocrisy. Their style of speech was clearly proverbial. They were taught how to handle criticism of their movement, nonretaliation, and the authenticity of their vocation. All of these behaviors are dealt with in the earliest portion of the Q gospel.

The Q gospel itself developed in three stages. The first stage (referred to as Q^1) was a series of theses, reasonings, and analogies that come to a conclusion. For example:

Thesis -   I am telling you, love your enemies, bless those who curse you, pray for those who mistreat you. If someone slaps you on the cheek, offer your other cheek as well. If anyone grabs your coat, let him have your shirt as well. Give to anyone who asks, and if someone takes away your belongings, do not ask to have them back.

Reason -   As you want people to treat you, do the same to them.

Analogy -   If you love those who love you, what credit is that to you? Even tax collectors love those who love them, do they not? And if you embrace only your brothers, what more are you doing than others? Does everybody not do that? If you lend to those from whom you expect repayment, what credit is that to you? Even wrongdoers lend to their kind because they expect to be repaid.

Conclusion -   Instead, love your enemies, do good, and lend without expecting anything in return. Your reward will be great, and you will be children of God.

Each part had seven sections. Each of these sections had some terse sayings with a distinct tone. This tone was very Cynic-like in that the precepts showed a strong sense of vocation corresponding to the Cynic life-style. Beliefs were not a major concern. What mattered most was behavior in public. What we see here is that the pre-Christian movement began as a grass-roots version of the Cynic philosophy during a time of social change in Galilee. Unlike the later Christians, these people were not out to overthrow the Roman government or to reform the traditional Judean religion. Nor was social reform that important. They were simply out to show people a better way to live: a change of life-style which involved a personal challenge. In essence, they practiced what they preached.

The Q^1 gospel did not have any apocalyptic view of the world. The mention of the kingdom of God was in keeping with the philosophical discourse of the day. The kingdom of God concept represented more than the ideal kingdom ruled with integrity by a righteous, wise king. It represented the individual who lived by showing and telling others how to live. This was highly compatible with the Cynic way of life.

It was not until after Q^2 where the location of the kingdom of God was found in the social formation of the movement itself. What is seen here is a fully self-conscious movement. It is in Q^2 where a basic story line begins to develop. It is also in Q^2 that the John (it is assumed to be the Baptist because his is the only name that is mentioned)/Jesus relationship begins (they were not relatives here), and where there are judgements on the generation, what is to come, and the final judgement is introduced. In Q^2 the pronouncements against the Pharisees are laid down. Probably the movement began to lose steam because it could not stand up to its critics. So its adherents began to make outlandish claims for its founder (miracle worker, son of God, etc.) and induce fear into it through judgements and pronouncements about the immediate coming of the kingdom of God because "this generation" has rejected the founder.

In Q^2 Jesus was seen as a wisdom teacher; a child of the Wisdom of God. This was not an idea that would have ever occurred to a Cynic because being Divine and the Wisdom of God was not part of the Cynic style of instruction. Remember, all the Cynics and the Q^1 people were doing was showing a better, more natural way of living. This idea of a Wisdom teacher is not that far removed from the Essene idea of a Teacher of Righteousness. This may be where the Cynic ideas and traditional Judean religious beliefs came together.

Q^2 introduces the concept of the Son of Man. Literally it means a "child of humankind," or a *human being.* It was a term in use at the time when a speaker did not want to use the pronoun "I." In the Book of Daniel it was a term to describe a human figure that appeared in an apocalyptic vision (Dan. 7:13-14). Daniel uses it to refer to a mysterious figure that looked human to whom God granted sovereign power. This was later placed in Revelations (1:13). Here in Q^2 the term Son of Man is used to instill a "group think" (a "buzz-word") and loyalty adding links to an earthly and heavenly Son of Man. The real cultishness of later Christianity most likely began forming during the mid or latter part of the Q^2 period.

Finally, there's Q^3. This is nothing more than much later fragmentary additions that have to do with the growth of traditions. These additions have an air of finality and judgement which indicate writing around the time of the Roman-Judean war.

Another important early writing was the Gospel of Thomas. Some scholars place its writing after Mark and between Matthew, Luke, and John. This seems to be a direct descendent of Q^2 because it contains all of the aphorisms of Q^1 with the pronouncements of Q^2. It's easy to see, when reading this Gospel, the development of the other Gospel stories because many of them are there. The indication is that by this time a mythological life had been set up around the Q^1 and Q^2 teachings. There are some differences between the Gospel of Thomas and the synoptic Gospels. In the Gospel of Thomas there is an allusion to Jesus' apostles being referred to as "stones" who will minister and five trees in Paradise referring to the number of his apostles. This indicates Jesus had five apostles, not twelve. This is most likely a reference to the five apostles of Jesus ben-Sedata (c. 100 BCE). The implication here is that the Jesus of the Christian Scriptures was ben-Sedata! (More on him later.) There are also many references taken from Pagan and Wisdom literature. Further, it is filled with parables and allusions. The Gospel of Thomas is considered a Gnostic text because of the many symbolic references in it.

The Gospels

The Gospels that are in the present Christian Scriptures were, according to tradition, written between about 60 and 80 CE. Even using that time period, that makes the Gospels rather suspect for factual information. The first of the Gospels would have been written at least 30 years *after* Jesus had supposedly lived. Consequently, their validity can be called to question. The Epistles, assumed to have been written before the Gospels, never mention the Gospels at all. Therefore, even the earliest dates of the writings of the Gospels are suspect—or it may be that the Gospels were not written by orthodox Christians in the first place. With that being a possibility it is easy to see why they were not originally accepted until they were modified to fit the teachings of the Church in the latter part of the 2nd century. With the modifications being completed they became canon.

As we have seen, Paul, assuming his existence, in several of his Epistles even states that what he is preaching is *his* version of Christianity. Unfortunately, what is his version is taken by many to be the *only* version. The actual first mention of any of the four Gospels, with which you are familiar, was not until Irenaeus. His first mention of the Gospels was the Gospel of Luke.[45] This was in chapter 16 of his Book 2. Prior to this, there was no mention of the Gospels in *any* of the other Christian writings. There was, though, statements made by some earlier Church fathers (c. 90-100) indicating their possible familiarity with a Gospel in its earlier form.

The antiquity of a Gospel is based on several things. Among the most important are: first, the language style being used; second, the repetition of certain statements and ideas; and finally, if there

---

45   You will recall that Marcion of Sinope had chosen the Gospel of Luke to be part of *his canon.*

is a mention of the destruction of the Temple which occurred in 73 CE. With this in mind, the earliest of the Gospels is attributed to Mark. Some claim that this was written sometime around 66 CE. The fact is that it was most likely written closer to 75 CE.—and probably more likely some time afterward (some historians say as late as 90). A couple of indicators that this Gospel was written, or at least compiled, later is the mention of the name of the coasts of Decapolis (7:31). This name was unknown until after the middle part of the 1st century because there were no coasts of Decapolis until into the 2nd century. Also, there is an allusion to a persecution supposedly by the Emperor Domitian (c. 90 CE) in this Gospel as well[46] but as you have already seen, there were no persecutions under Domitian. There was one under Trajan (c. 112 CE) which may be indicating the time of the writing. Finally, there is a further allusion to the destruction of the second Temple. This places its writing directly *after* the destruction of the Temple.

Looking at the Gospel of Mark, there are known deletions and additions. As an example, in Chapter 14:51-52, these two verses seem to be rather strange and out of context. What could this naked young man mentioned in these verses have to do with Jesus?

Well, in 1958, Prof. Morton Smith of Columbia University found a fragment of the Gospel of Mark that was expunged and suppressed at the insistence of Clement of Alexandria (c. 190 CE). Clement, in a letter to an individual named Theodore, acknowledges the authenticity of this fragment and instructs him to **deny** it even under oath. This fragment reads:

> *And they came to Bethany, and a certain woman, whose brother had died, was there. And, coming, she prostrated herself before Jesus and says to him: Son of David, have mercy on me! But the disciples rebuked her. And Jesus, being angered, went off with her into the garden where the tomb was, and straightway a great cry was heard from the tomb. And going near, Jesus rolled away the stone from the door of the tomb. And straightway, going in where the youth*

---

46 See chapter 13.

was, he stretched forth his hand and raised him, seizing his hand. But the youth looking upon him, loved him and began to beseech him that he might be with him. And going out of the tomb they came into the house of the youth, for he was rich. And after six days, Jesus told him what to do and in the evening the youth comes to him, wearing a linen cloth over (his) naked (body). And he remained with him that night, for Jesus taught him the mystery of the Kingdom of God. And thence arising, he returned to the other side of the Jordan.

This is called *"The Secret Gospel of Mark."* The description given here is that of a typical mystery school initiation—it is a ritualized and symbolic death and rebirth sequence. There are, in fact, mentions of secret teachings several times throughout the Gospels and Epistles.[47]

There are also inaccuracies in this Gospel. In chapter 2:26 it relates a story from the Hebrew Scriptures. The high priest mentioned in Mark was Abiathar. The actual high priest was Ahimelech.[48] The reference to Decapolis was already mentioned. There are also several names mentioned in Aramaic (chapter 5:41 and chapter 7:34) which should have been Hebrew names. In chapter 11 verses 9 and 10 is describing the entrance into Jerusalem. The translation of "Blessed (be) the kingdom of our father David, that cometh in the name of the Lord: Hosanna in the highest" is incorrect. It should read: "Blessed is the *coming* kingdom of our father David; Hosanna in the highest." Also, in chapter 14 verse 24: "And he said unto them, This is my blood of the new testament (covenant), which is shed for many" the word "new" was not in the earliest of the texts. Finally, verses 9 through 20 of chapter 16 were non-existent in the earliest texts. Verses 17 and 18 actually came from Gnostic texts of the 2nd and 3rd centuries, hence, they are totally bogus. The problem with these verses is not so much that

---

47   See chapter 4:11-12 and all references to parables.

48   See 1 Samuel 21:1.

they came from that particular period, but that they were not added until the 16th century!

The Book of Matthew is generally considered the next of the written Gospels. Traditionally, this was ascribed to the period around 80 CE. More appropriately the writing of this Gospel was closer to 100 CE. This Gospel begins with a proposed genealogy of Jesus. The only problem is that it is contradicted by the genealogy in the Book of Luke. The usual explanation for this is that the Gospel of Matthew supposedly traces Jesus' ancestry through the Davidic line (his mother) and the one in the Book of Luke supposedly traces it through the line of Joseph (his "father").[49] Remember, Joseph was not Jesus' real father but his step-father so he could not have possibly been of the line of Joseph.

The Book of Matthew was originally called The Gospel of the Hebrews and it originally began with a genealogy of Jesus according to the flesh with *no* virgin birth. It did not reach its familiar form until around 173 and was ascribed to Matthew by Apollinarius, Bishop of Hierapolis (c. 310-390). The Gospel of the Hebrews could not have been written until after 80 and most likely its writing was closer to 100.

There are many who believe that both Mark and Matthew were compiled pretty close to the same time. But the fact is that Mark, Matthew, and Luke contain a lot of similar materials and references. There are, though, some references in Mark that are exclusively in Luke and not in Matthew thus indicating that each compilation had some similar and different sources. When we take a look at the Book of Luke, we will see some other problems in reference to dating the texts.

Why does Matthew begin with a genealogy on the "Davidic" line? As you have seen, different Messiahs were expected: a king-messiah, a warrior-messiah, and the suffering messiah. The king-messiah was to be in the Davidic line and the group at the time which expected the king-messiah was the Pharisees. The warrior-

---

49   You will recall the two messiahs, one from the line of David and one from the line of Joseph.

messiah had come in the person of Hezekiah. This genealogy was supposed to convince the Pharisees that Jesus was *the* messiah. The only problem with the genealogy was that it contained errors. These include the fact that the women in the Davidic ancestry were considered stains on the line and also Jechonias (1:11) actually had no legal right to the Davidic line. Further, it states that there were 14 generations between Abraham and David, 14 generations between David and the Captivity, and 14 generations between the Captivity and Jesus' birth. That makes a grand total of 42 generations. If a generation is 20 years that is only 840 years. This time sequencing is in great error. But then, we must look at the Greek word used to indicate a generation in this instance: genea. The meaning of this word does not mean a span by a particular number of years but the age of the individual at death. Hence, it refers to the life span of the particular person mentioned. So, if one individual lived to 65, those number of years represents *his* lifetime or generation (the number of years he could produce offspring). Then, if we give each "generation" approximately 50 years, the number of years then extends to 2,100 years. This is about the time period that modern researchers have found Pagan clay tablets bearing the name of Abraham. But, this does not make the genealogy valid. Remember, the genealogy starts with Adam and there was no way of keeping track of the years then as we have now. Lest we forget, Paul in the Epistle to Titus admonished:

> **But avoid foolish questions, and genealogies, and contentions, and strivings about the law; for they are unprofitable and vain.** (3:9)

There are also errors in Matthew. In chapter 2 is the story of Herod's learning about the Christ child. In verse 6 is a misquoting of the "prophecy" of Micah (5:2). Then we read of the killing of all male children under two years of age which was supposedly prophesied by Jeremiah (31:15-19). This so-called prophecy does not deal with the killing of children but with The Babylonian

Captivity. Further, there is *no* record of Herod issuing any orders to murder children.[50] If he would have done this he certainly would have gotten into quite a bit of trouble with the Roman Government for Herod was a Roman puppet and had to administer according to the laws of Rome. Besides, which of the writers was there during this episode to write about it? Further, who knew what was happening so that they knew of its importance? In verse 23 there is the statement that the prophets said the messiah would be called a Nazarene. Nowhere is it stated in any of what are considered prophecies that the messiah would be called a Nazarene or from a town named Nazareth.

Another interesting error is in chapter 19 verse 12. The reference here is to a particular Christian Gnostic sect where the males castrated themselves to try to eliminate their carnal desires. How could this have been said by Jesus when that version of Christian Gnosticism did not exist at the time? This sect actually did not come into existence until well into the 2nd century CE.

A problem has long been overlooked in this Gospel. When Jesus went into the desert for 40 days[51] there is a relatively detailed description of the temptations. There is also a rather detailed description of what happened to Jesus when he was praying in the garden before he was arrested. The question is, who saw it in order to report it with such detail? No one was with Jesus in the desert and the apostles that Jesus brought with him in the garden fell asleep. You must remember, the writers of the Gospels claimed to be eye-witnesses to *all* of these events. These two events in particular were witnessed by no one. How could they have been reported?

---

50 In the legend of Buddha, when the local king heard that the Buddha had been born he issued an order that all male children under the age of 12 were to be killed.

51 The number 40 is used rather often in the Bible, from the raining of 40 days and 40 nights, through the 40 years wondering of the Israelites in the desert, Moses' 40 days on the mountain to get the Commandments, to Jesus' 40 days in the wilderness. The number 40 represents a period of purification.

There are quite a few references to mythological tales throughout this and the other Gospels. Here is a list of a few:

1. **The Star in the East**

   A star appeared in the east to herald the birth of literally *every* sun-god[52] as well as a host of other dignitaries. Among these were Confucius, Lao-Tsu, Zoroaster, Moses, and Buddha. According to ancient Judean tradition, a star appears in the east at the birth of every *prophet*.

2. **The Temptation in the Desert**

   According to the Persian legends, Zoroaster was tempted three times by Angra Mainyu while in the wilderness, Buddha was tempted more than 3 times while fasting under the Bo Tree by Mara, and Quetzalcoatl was tempted by an evil spirit while he was fasting during his 40 days in the desert.

3. **John the Baptist**

   According to the Egyptian mythology, the Egyptian god Thoth[53] is heralded by cynocephalic apes[54] who went before him announcing, "Make ready the way of the lord."

4. **The Virgin Birth**

   Literally *every* sun-god was born of a virgin and under miraculous circumstances. In India, Krishna and the Buddha, in Meso-America, Quetzalcoatl, in China the sages Lao-tsu, Yu, and Confucius, in Egypt Horus or Ra, in Persia, Zoroaster and Mithra, in Greece, Prometheus, Bacchus, and Apollo among others.

---

52 It is obvious that the "star" in the east that represents the birth of the sun-god is the sun. The star which heralds the birth of the sun-god is the morning star: Venus.

53 Who had the title of the "Word."

54 The description of John the Baptist is similar to that of these apes. These apes were considered "wild men of the desert." Cynocephalic apes are the baboons.

5. ***The Walking on Water***
    There are many mythological deities and legendary persons who walked on water: Poseidon, Orion, and even the Buddha walked on water. For centuries rumors had circulated out of India about yogis who could not only walk on water but levitate. The walking on water was a way to put Jesus on par with Moses in order to attract the Judeans.

6. ***The Entrance into Jerusalem***
    In the ancient epic of Gilgamesh, after Gilgamesh and Enkidu defeated the mighty bull of heaven, they rode into the city of Ur on the backs of donkeys. According to the ancient Judean tradition, Pagan gods are depicted riding on the backs of donkeys.

7. ***Jesus as a Carpenter***
    In India there was Tvashtar who was a carpenter and in England, the Druidic sun-god, Hesus, was a wood-cutter.

The third Gospel is that of Luke. Its period of compilation was traditionally set at about 75 CE. The fact of the matter is that it could not have been written until at least 100 and probably much later, possibly as late as 160. The Gospel of Luke and Acts are both dedicated to a Theophilus at their very beginning. Who was this Theophilus? He was most likely Theophilus, the Bishop of Antioch (d. 117 CE).[55] In fact, the first 2 verses of Luke indicate that the book is a contrivance, and since both Luke and Acts were most likely written by the same person they were both made up and cannot be relied on for historical accuracy or philosophical content.

The author of Luke and Acts uses some aspects of Matthew and Marcion's Gospel, which later became the Luke with which you are familiar. In the 4th century, when the canon was being compiled John Crysostom stated that few knew of the book or the

---

55 Apparently, this was the first Theophilus, Bishop of Antioch. There was another about 180.

author of Luke and Acts. It was included in the canon only because it contained aspects of the already accepted Mark and Matthew.

There are also many inaccuracies in Luke as well. First of all, there was no decree that went out from Caesar Augustus to tax the whole world. There was no census taken during Augustus' reign at all. There was a small census in a relatively newly acquired region of northern Asia Minor taken by Tiberius Caesar,[56] Augustus' successor. Besides, a census that involved everyone to go to their place of family origin would cause an horrendous mess. The problems that such an idiotic census would leave would be unbelievable especially for an empire that considered paperwork so important. Second, when Jesus and his parents went to Jerusalem and his parents found Jesus in the temple conversing with the teachers,[57] they seemed to forget all about the miraculous birth that they witnessed only twelve years earlier. Third, in chapter 3:2, it was mentioned that the high priests of the Temple were Annas and Caiaphas. This is incorrect because there is only *one* high priest of the Temple. Annas was the high priest at least 15 years earlier than the assumed time in Luke. Fourth, in chapter 5:19 the "miracle" mentions the tiling on the roof of a house in Judea. The roofs of the houses at that time in Judea had straw or thatch covering, not tiles. Fifth, the name in chapter 3:37, Cainan, in Jesus' supposed genealogy is out of place. This would make the other names somewhat askew. Sixth, in chapter 3:23 it quite bluntly states that it was *supposed* that Jesus was baptized by John at the age of 30, hence, no one knew. Finally, verse 34 in chapter 23 was not in the earliest texts, nor was the last section of verse 51 of chapter 24: "...and carried up to heaven."

The last Gospel is that of John. This book has continually had a lot of controversy surrounding it. John claimed to have been an eye-witness to all of the things that he was writing. There is a small problem with this idea: it is known that the book of John was written *after* 115 CE. It was in use by the Valentinian Gnostics for

---

56 The census was about 14 CE.

57 See chapter 2:42-49.

many years prior to its induction into the accepted canon of Irenaeus. Consequently, the Book of John *is* a Gnostic book and it shows to have been greatly influenced by Philo Judea.

This Gospel is the only Gospel of whom direct authorship has been assigned by the Church. The author of the Book of John, according to Epiphanius, Bishop of Salamis (367-403) was Leucius, a supposed disciple of John. But Leucius was definitely *not* the actual author of the Book of John with which you are familiar. If you look at the writings of Irenaeus you find this statement:

> *John, the disciple of the Lord, wrote his Gospel to confute the doctrine lately[58] (emphasis mine) taught by Cerinthus, and a great while before by those called Nicolaitans,[59] a branch of the Gnostics; and to show that there is one God who made all things by his* **WORD***: and not as they say, that there is one the Creator, and another the Father of our Lord: and one the Son of the Creator, and another, even the Christ, who descended from above upon the Son of the Creator, and continued impassible, and at length returned to his pleroma or fullness.*

This book was originally called the Acts of John and was well-known to Clement of Alexandria, hence, it *is* a Gnostic text. The Church attempted to replace the Gnostic text with a more watered-down and "safer" version known as the Acts of Prochorus. This book was still in circulation in the 10th century. The implication here is that the author of the more familiar and safer version of the Gospel of John is none other than Irenaeus himself for Iranaeus admitted to altering the originals of the Gospel of John. He most likely adjusted it to be more in line with the Synoptics. It was edit-

---

58   How could the Gospel refute something that had not been in existence, known of, or even thought of many decades *before* it happened? In essence, the Book of John, that we are familiar with, came into existence around the latter part of the 2nd century of this era.

59   Existed in the early 2nd century CE as a Christian Gnostic sect but actually predated Christianity.

ed in order to refute the Gnostic teachings that were prevalent at the middle to end of the 2nd century as well as those Gnostic groups which would teach from the text.

There has been, as mentioned, quite a lot of controversy surrounding this book. All of this starts right at the beginning of the text. Here we shall begin as well.

In verse 1 chapter 1 the text begins with the *title* of "Word." The Greek term here is "Logos." The translation of this term is quite difficult because there are over 100 different meanings for it. Among the meanings are the ideas of: a study (e.g. bio*logy*, psycho*logy*, etc.); to reason (e.g. *log*ic); to speak, talk, express (e.g. *logo*type), *myth,* to *think, self-expression, message, logic, the thought that gave words their meaning by coming to expression in sentences, speeches, stories,* and *history*. The idea of a "logos" is not one that is unique to Christianity either. One of the earliest religions to have it were the Egyptians. This was in relation to their Trinity. The second person in their trinity was called the Logos or Word.[60] Engraved on the tomb of Apollo in Delphi was the inscription that he was called the Word. The Assyro-Babylonian god Marduk was given the title of Logos or the Word. The Greco-Roman god Mercury was given the title of Logos or the Word. In the Zend Avesta, Sraosha was called the "holy incarnate Word." This term did not come into Christian parlance until after the middle of the 2nd century. The idea of the Logos was an important one to Philo Judea (c. 40 CE) as well. In fact, it is quite possible that the concept of the Logos came into Christianity through Philo. To Philo, the Logos represented the rational and creative aspect of Yahweh. It was the Logos through whom the world was created. The Logos "expressed" the thinking of the creator god. It was Philo who related it to Yahweh and speaks of it metaphorically as the "image of God" or the "son of God;" actually a *second god*. He had then discussed the Logos in reference to a distinct being. It was the "incarnation" of God and the "interces-

---

60   The term "word" is an ancient term that, loosely translated, means "substance" or "thing." It refers to "nothing." This is the same as the "no-thingness" of the Existential Philosophers, the Ain Soph of the Kabbalists, and the Tao of Oriental Philosophy. This does *not* make the "Word" *(the)* God.

ʒor" to God. In essence, it was both *a* god and God. Hence, there are some who translate the first verse of John as: "In the beginning was the Logos, and the Logos was with God, and the Logos was *a* god." The argument here is the "*a*" which appears before the final "god." It deals with the ending of the word "god" in Greek. In order to lure a Roman and Greek audience (i.e. the Gentiles) Jesus would have to be *a* god, not *the* god. [61]

What most translators seem to forget is the concept behind the Logos. Recall that the word Logos is a *title*. This title is given to specific *gods*. Every one of the gods that this title was given to was a god that was involved in the act of creation. In fact, these gods were the gods who took the orders and did the actual job of creation itself. In John 1:3-4 this is expressed, but this statement is directly out of the Essene Book of Hymns. Another Essene concept comes in verse 7, but this verse was not in the original text of the Book of John. The Gnostics used the title Logos. The orthodox Christians did not. Other Gnostic concepts in the book of John are: the "Light" (v. 8); the "only begotten of the father" (v. 14); being "born again"[62] (3:3); being "born of water and the spirit" (v. 5); the bride and the bridegroom; the "lifting up of the Son of Man" (v. 14); the "spirit quickeneth" (6:63); the writing on the ground (8:6); the "prince of this aeon" (12:31); the "father's house has many mansions" (14:2); secret teachings (16:12); and many more.

Probably the major problem with the book of John is the fact that it was originally a Gnostic text that got abbreviated to be made more acceptable. If you look deeper into the text you can see some other areas which are problematic. In 3:2, Jesus is referred to as "...a teacher come from God..." This is an Essene reference to their "teacher of righteousness." This teacher was never named. In 3:16 is the verse that virtually all Christians quote: "For God so loved the world,..."etc. The problem here is that it is contradicted quite strongly by Exodus 4:22 and 13:2, as well as a reference to Genesis

---

61 This statement ought to please the Jehovah's Witnesses. The only thing is that none of them would ever read this material.

62 The actual translation is "to be born from above."

32:28. The idea that Jesus was the "first-born" and the "only begotten son of the Father" is countered by the above Old Testament verses. In 4:5-40 Jesus supposedly taught in Samaria with his disciples. In Acts 8:14 it seems that they had totally forgotten about it and sent Peter and John back there to preach. In 4:47-52 we have a miracle being performed by Jesus. This was a traditional Christian story. The problem here is that verse 48 was inserted and did not exist in the original tale. In 6:15 there is the idea that Jesus perceived that after the feeding of the multitude that the people would take him and forcefully make him their king is totally wrong. This could never have happened. The Roman government would never have permitted it for one thing, and for another, the performance of a "miracle" is not grounds for crowning anyone a king. Simply, the people would not have done such a thing because "miracles" were being done all of the time. In this Gospel, as in Luke, there is the problem of Jesus' relatives forgetting about his "miraculous" birth (7:5). Chapter 8:1-11 describes the story of the "casting of the first stone." First of all, this is a later addition and did not exist in the original text. Second, according to Judean law, only witnesses to the act were to cast the first stones. If there were no witnesses, the accusations were considered false. Finally, in verse 6, there is the addition of half of a sentence: "...as though he heard them not." This whole verse is from the Gnostic idea that only the most perfect would write in sand, for the spoken word was preferred to the written word.[63] In chapter 9:22 we have the idea of excommunication from the synagogue. This was not done in the Judean religion until *after* the 2nd century. The title of "the good shepherd" (10:14) was given to Moses, to Mithra in Persia, to Dionysus in Greece, to Tammuz in Babylon, and Dumuzi in Sumer. In chapter 13:26-27 we have the story of Judas being given the bread dipped in wine and told to do what he had to do. The problem here is that dipping a crust of bread into wine was done to honor a guest in Judean tradition, not for anything else. The reference to Jesus sending the Holy Ghost in chapter 14:26 the transla-

---

63   Recall the Pauline concept that the revealed word takes precedence over the written word.

tion is "...he shall teach you " The correct translation is "...*she* shall teach you ..." Finally, all of chapter 21 is a later addition and did not exist in the original texts of the Book of John.

There are many great discrepancies between the Synoptic Gospels (Matthew, Mark, and Luke) and the Book of John. In Matthew you can see Jesus as a man, but in John he is a mysterious being (the Logos). In the Synoptics Jesus' ministry is three years long, in John, it is about a year. In John he made one journey to Jerusalem. In the Synoptics, he made many. In Matthew, Jesus was a strong traditional Judean. In John he was anti-Judean.

The major difference between the Synoptics and John is the development of the religion. In the Synoptics everything was in the present, including the coming Messianic Kingdom, but in John it was all in the remote past and rather ambiguous. In Matthew there is a constant reference to the nation of Israel. In John there are only scornful references.

In the traditional Judean concept of the era of the Messiah several things are supposed to occur *before* the appearance of the Messiah. First of all, the forerunner of the Messiah is expected to usher in an era of peace and harmony between fathers and sons with the reappearance of Elijah the prophet[64] (Isaiah 53:9; Malachi 4:6). This did not happen. In fact, Jesus stated that there *must* be discord within families in order to follow him (Matthew 10:34-35; Luke 12:49-53; 19:27). Further, in the Gospels, John the Baptist denied that he was Elijah or his spirit. Second, the Messiah is seen as a *servant* of God, not co-equal to God (Ezekiel 34:23-24) and definitely *not* God. Finally, prior to the appearance of the Messiah, all of the souls of the world had to be properly purified and cleansed. None of these things occurred at any time around Jesus' ministry—and we definitely do not have that now as well.

It was also stated by Jesus that he came to fulfill the law, not to change it (Matthew 5:7). But Jesus violated many traditional Judean laws. For example, it was against the law to conduct business on a festival (Exodus 12:16; Leviticus 23:6-7; Numbers

---

64   This is interesting because Elijah never said that he would return to introduce the Messiah to his people.

28:17-18; Nehemiah 10:30, 32). Jesus did conduct business on a festival day (John 13:29). It was also against the Judean law to destroy a fruit-bearing tree (Deuteronomy 20:19). Jesus cursed the fig tree because it would not bear fruit for him out of season (Matthew 21:18-22; Mark 11:12-14, 20-25). Finally, it was against Judean law to work on the Sabbath (Exodus 20:8-11). But Jesus worked on the Sabbath by doing healings (Matthew 12:9-14).

Here, also, is a list of some other of the major discrepancies in the Gospels:

1. Matthew, Mark, and Luke agree that the crucifixion occurred the day *before* the Passover. John, you will remember claimed to be an eyewitness, says it was the day *after*.

2. The original Gospel of Mark ends with the crucifixion, burial, and the empty tomb. The latter section from the resurrection onward is totally bogus and was added much later.

3. The sign above the cross at the crucifixion differs in all four Gospels.

4. The miraculous birth occurs in only two of the Gospels.[65]

5. In the Sermon on the Mount, Jesus goes *up* the mountain in one version and *down* the mountain in another. The sermon itself is a patchwork of Hebrew Scriptural statements. It also follows the standard pattern for a Mystery Religion hymn as well.

6. Only one Gospel speaks of an ascension into heaven.

7. In Matthew Jesus instructs the apostles to, "Go not into the way of the Gentiles..." Later he says to "Go ye therefore, and teach all nations..."[66]

---

65 The whole story of the birth of Jesus comes out of *The Gospel of James*, a Gnostic text.

66 The latter statement actually agrees with the first if the appropriate translation is made. The word for *nations* used here is *ethnos*, the word from which the English word *ethnic* is derived. The reference here is then to a *particular* group or nation. The translation would better read: "Go ye therefore, and teach all (of the) nations (*of Israel*)..."

8.   John's Gospel, more than the others, promotes Jesus as God

There are also historical discrepancies that exist. These include:

1.   There was no such Judean custom as the releasing of a prisoner at Passover or in Springtime. This was a Greek and Roman custom at the Dionysian Festival in Springtime.

2.   Roman law denied burial to a crucified man consequently, Pilate would never have given Joseph of Aramathia permission to take Jesus' body for it would have violated Roman laws. (More on this later.)

3.   The Sanhedrin could pass a sentence of death for heresy and this death was by stoning. After this, the body was denied burial by being hung by the neck on a tree or impaled on a stake.

4.   When Jesus entered Jerusalem prior to the Passover, it was during the Feast of the Booths and that is the reason that the people were waving palm branches and yelling "Hosannah!"

There is a unity of teaching which is conspicuously absent from the Christian Scriptures, especially the Gospels. Much of Jesus' teachings were put in his mouth and were known to exist *prior* to this period either in the Hebrew Scriptures and other Judaic writings or in Pagan sources. The ethical precepts that appear are frequently obscure and contradictory.

After having looked deeper into the writings of the Gospels it is time to turn our attention to the other texts in the Christian Scriptures. This means the Acts of the Apostles, the Epistles, and Revelations.

The Book of Acts

As we have seen, Luke and Acts was most likely written by the same person. The main reasons being that the style of writing is similar and they are both dedicated to Theophilus. You will notice that the book of Acts tends to deal quite a bit with the city of Antioch, consequently the dedication, and most likely it was written in Antioch. We can, then, date the writing of this book to around the same time as Luke: 100 CE.

In Acts you first encounter Paul. You are familiar with the story of how he became a Christian from being a persecutor of Christians. Some scholars have proposed that Paul may not have existed. What many do not know is that the name "Paul" actually means "little one" and it is a term which was given to student initiates of some mystery religions. If we take a look at the story of Paul we can see another version of a mystery religion initiation. In virtually every mystery religion initiation there was a "death and resurrection" portrayal. We have seen this in the expurgated section of the book of Mark, the "raising of Lazarus," and we can see it again in the story of Paul's conversion.

Here we have problems in the Acts of the Apostles just as we have problems in the Gospels. In chapter 2:22 it is stated quite unequivocally that Jesus was a *man* who was approved of by God. There are also many references that there is a difference between God, Jesus, and Christ and, as many of the Gnostics had believed, the Christ aspect of Jesus was different than Jesus and God (2:24, 30, 31, 32, 36; etc.). In verse 32, chapter 2 it is stated: "This Jesus hath God raised up, whereof we are all witnesses..." has a translation problem. The term translated as witnesses has the meaning of *recorded* and does not mean that those who are writing the text actually saw what they were discussing. It simply means that it was written down. Again, *much of* what is discussed in Acts has no way of being verified because the author obviously was *not* there to see and record it.

Major Problems in Acts

1. In chapter 5:1-5 we have Peter murdering a man with the power that Jesus had given him. Recall 1 John 3:15 "Whosoever hateth his brother is a murderer: and ye know that no murderer hath eternal life abiding in him." Lest we forget, there is a commandment against committing murder.

2.   In chapter 5:30 and 10:39 there is a reference to Jesus' death in these terms, "...slew and hanged on a tree." In 2:23 it states that Jesus was crucified and slain. To many this is not much of a problem but if we look into Judean law and history we find that according to the Judean tradition the method of dealing with a heretic is that of stoning (slaying) and hanging the body by the neck from a tree or impaling it on a stake. In Judean history this was done to more than one heretic. About 100 BCE this was done to the heretic Joshua (Jesus) ben-Pantera (ben-Sedata). It was this man whom Judean history refers to as "Jesus the Nazarene." His followers and the early Christians were referred to as "followers of the hanged man."

3.   Some grave (no pun intended) errors exist in chapter 7:14-16. In verse 14 it states that the kin of Joseph were 75 people. In Genesis there is listed only 70 persons. In verse 16 it states that Jacob was buried in Shechem. In the Torah Jacob was not buried in Shechem, only Joseph. Abraham's tomb was in Hebron. It further states that Abraham bought the tomb from Emmor. It was actually bought from Ephram.[67]

4.   A major problem is encountered in chapter 13:42 when it is said that there were Gentiles in the synagogue. This cannot be in any way, shape or form possible. Gentiles were **never** permitted in the synagogues.

5.   In chapter 15:1-11 is the story of the dissension that occurred in the early Christianity. This was the feud between Paul and Peter and dealt with two things: one was the admittance of the Gentiles into Christianity and the other was the circumcision rite for proselytes. This culminated in a council that convened in 48 CE to decide on the circumcision of the Gentiles. It seemed that Peter lost on both counts: the Gentiles were let into the ranks of Christianity and they didn't need to be circumcised.

---

67   See Genesis 23:17, 19; 33:19; 49:29-30; 50:13; Exodus 1:5; Deuteronomy 10:22; Joshua 24:32.

6. In verse 20, by the way, the abstinence from blood refers to blood sacrifice or the shedding of blood.[68]

7. Chapter 16:6 states unequivocally that the Holy Ghost absolutely forbids the Gospel to be preached in Asia. There should not be a single Christian church or mission anywhere in Asia even at this present time if that had been followed for the Holy Spirit does not change her mind.

8. In verse 14 it is said that a certain *woman* named Lydia was baptized by Paul. At the time that Acts was written, Lydia was a *man's* name.

9. In chapter 20:35 it was stated that Jesus said, "It is more blessed to give than to receive." The problem is that this isn't stated in any of the Gospels. Chapter 23:2-3 is contradicted by Luke 6:28 and Romans 12:14.

10. In chapter 26:14-18 we see one of the stories of Paul's conversion. This story is actually an old Greek proverb laden with a series of Hebraic Scriptural phrases. Consequently, its validity as an actual occurrence is in doubt.

11. In chapter 22:25 Paul was bound and was about to be scourged when he said to the centurion, "Is it lawful for you to scourge a man that is a Roman, and uncondemned?" By invoking his Roman citizenship he is bearing allegiance to the Emperor and this is the same as admitting that the Emperor is a god and is an object of personal worship. In early Christianity, this, in essence, is a denial of Jesus and of being a Christian.

---

68 This is misconstrued by the Jehovah's Witnesses to mean that you are not to have a blood transfusion. The whole verse refers to: 1) eating the offerings given to idols; 2) the adoration of idols, not sexual relations; 3) eating any animal that is not kosher (not bled to death); and 4) eating any animal used in blood sacrifice.

The Epistles

After the book of Acts begins the Epistles. The Epistles to the Romans, 1 and 2 Corinthians, Galatians, Ephesians, Philippians, Colossians, 1 and 2 Thessalonians, 1 and 2 Timothy, Titus, Philemon, and Hebrews are all considered Pauline. As we have seen, and shall see, most of these Epistles were not written by Paul due to differences in writing style, ideas and concepts, and specific references which had nothing to do with the period attributed to Paul. We must consider several things before getting into a discussion of the Epistles. The Epistles are considered to have been written *before* the Gospels and the Epistles do not mention things that the Gospels elaborate. In fact, the Epistles do not even mention anything that Jesus was supposed to have said. The authority in all matters of faith is Paul or more appropriately, the writer (whoever he may have been). For example, there is no mention of: any acts, sayings, or parables of Jesus; no Bethlehem or Nazareth; Jesus' parents; no virgin birth; no John the Baptist, no Judas and his "betrayal;" the "sermon on the mount;" any miracles; a trial before Pilate; no "Lord's Prayer;" nor any of the other significant events in Jesus' life or death. Paul most certainly had contact with those who knew Jesus intimately (e.g. Peter) so he surely would have had this information given to him. Paul, though, does not even imply that any of the events written in the Gospels had occurred. Further, throughout the Epistles, Jesus was to destroy Satan and evil with his birth and death. If you will but look around you will see that evil is still with us, hence, the effect that Jesus had on the conquering of evil was negligible. Finally, the Epistles bear a close resemblance in construction and style to the Gathas from the Zend Avesta of Persia, especially beginning with Yasna XXX onward.

Before getting into the writing of the Epistles it is necessary to have an understanding of the person to whom these writings are attributed.

As you have seen, traditionally Paul is seen as an ex-rabbinical student, but he could not have been so. If we look at his writing style, his arguments, and the Biblical quotes we find that they are all Greek. According to the Judean Christian (Ebonite Gnostic) tradition as well as many early Christian historians, Paul was a Greek proselyte to the Judean religion. He came to it because of his admiration of the Pharisees. At that time the Pharisees were held in high regard throughout the Roman and Parthian empires. They were a very dedicated group who upheld religious ideals in the face of tyranny, supported leniency and mercy when applying the laws and championed the rights of the poor against the oppression of the rich. They, in fact, regarded themselves as the upholders of the authentic religion.

Paul apparently attempted to become a Pharisee but was unable to understand their form of argumentation. Many who have noted that the Epistles contain Pharisaic logic are unfamiliar with the complete logical process that the Pharisees had gone into. Paul's attempts at this logic fall very short.

In the beginning of the Book of Acts when we first meet Paul (Saul of Tarsus) he is acting on the authority of the High Priest of the Temple of Jerusalem rounding up Christians. As you have seen, the High Priest was a Sadducee and his authority did not extend any further than Jerusalem and the High Priest had no authority to enter synagogues unless it was to arrest those who were attempting to overthrow the Roman government—and that was only in Jerusalem. The synagogues were the domain of the Pharisees. If Paul was going to Damascus to chase Christians and bring them back to Jerusalem, he could get into quite a bit of trouble if found out. Damascus was not under Roman rule at that time. Aretas IV, the king, would not have permitted an emissary of a Roman ruled area to arrest his citizens or even aliens under his protection. So, his association with the Judean religion had to have been with the High Priest and the Sadducees, not the Pharisees.

Paul was **not** held in much high esteem by the early Church Fathers even through the 2nd century. He was not even considered a faithful "pillar of the Church" either. In fact, a 5th century Judean Christian manuscript describes Paul as a falsifier of Jesus' teachings. He was further identified as a Roman sympathizer (a sadducee) who abandoned the Torah for personal gain and may have been responsible for the destruction of the Temple in Jerusalem.

But then, we have the story of how Saul of Tarsus the persecuting tent maker, who became Paul, a Christian, in the Book of Acts. Can this story be trusted? There is the possibility that it may have had some tradition behind it, but how much is unknown. For if you will look at Acts and the Epistles attributed to Paul, you will see that there are direct contradictions in this story between Acts and the Epistles...as well as the contradictions in the story in Acts itself.

The Epistle to the Romans is considered to be Pauline, but it is not. It was written by Tertius (see 16:22), consequently, attributing its authorship to Paul is incorrect. The period attributed to its writing was about 60 CE but most likely the actual writing was after 75 CE. There are some rather important references to the Essene organization in this Epistle which may be indicators of the Essene membership in early Christianity. For example, chapter 1:28-31 is out of the Essene Manual of Discipline. The reference to the "remnant" in chapter 11:5 is an Essene idea for the Essenes considered themselves to be the remnant of the true Israel. Finally, in chapter 13:13 is another verse out of the Essene Manual of Discipline.

At the beginning of the Epistle to the Romans Paul (Tertius) says that Jesus was made of the seed of David *according to the flesh.* This contradicts the idea of a miraculous birth and that he was declared to be the Son of God by his resurrection from the dead. This goes along with the Gnostic concept that it was at his death where the Christ-consciousness came upon him and he became the Son of God and was resurrected *in spirit.* It was from that time, as some Gnostic groups believed, that certain persons were "called" to be his followers. You need to remember that the terms **God** and **Savior** were terms that were used to deify rulers at that time, and the term *Son of God* was a title for the kings of the period and area as well as a title for the High Priest. Attributing these terms to a teacher was **not** out of the ordinary either.

Another rather important Gnostic reference is in 16:16. It is the "holy kiss." This was a Gnostic custom and did not enter into orthodox Christianity until later. The indication is a later writing, possibly after 90 CE. The reference to a **church** in 16:5 further indicates a later writing.

There are also contradictions and incorrect references to Hebrew Scripture in this Epistle as well. Chapter 4:9 states:

(Cometh) this blessedness then upon the circumcision (only), or upon the uncircumcision also? For we say that faith was reckoned to Abraham for righteousness.

This verse is contradicted by Romans 3:20; 4:2; and James 2:20-21, 24, and 26. If you take a look at Genesis 26:3-5 you will see that God blesses Abraham not for his faith, as this verse claims, but for his keeping the laws, statutes, etc. set up by Yahweh. It is a distortion of Genesis 15:6; 17:10-11; 18:19; 26:35; and 28:13-15. This kind of misconstruing of text is not unusual at all for it was liberally done by all Christian writers. The early Christians consistently distorted the Hebrew Scriptures to suit themselves whenever they deemed it necessary. Some other incorrect references to the Hebrew Scripture in this Epistle are: 8:31-32, 36; 10:12; and 11:26-28.

In 1 Corinthians you find references to problems that occurred in Corinth in the mid to late 90s, but that does not save it from being considered Pauline. These problems were discussed by Clement of Rome in his writings in 96 CE consequently giving a later date to these writings. In 14:33 there is further mention of churches indicating later writings. There is also the mention of Sosthenes (Acts 18:17), Apollos (Acts 19:1),[69] and Timothy (Acts 19:22), and, as you have seen, Acts was written sometime around 100 CE.

In 1 Corinthians you find that the main thrust of the Christian teachings about Jesus was that of Christ crucified. There is no reference to him being any kind of miracle worker. You also find that wisdom is *not* a Christian virtue and is not to be sought by the true believer. What is to be sought is blind faith and the following of the teachings of the writer of the Epistle.

You also find here the first indication that the end of the world is imminent. In 7:29 it states that "...*the time (is) short*..." Here the writer states that it is best that no one marry because it is implied that the world shall pass away quickly. This is why the statement in 7:36: "...*let him do what he will, he sinneth not*..."

---

69   Apollos is also mentioned in Titus 3:13.

There is also an indication that celibacy was more important than marriage in early Christianity (7:32-38). This is interesting because all down through the history of humankind any cult that desired to control the minds and lives of others promotes celibacy over marriage. Even in marriage, abstinence was considered a virtue. If one were to have sexual relations with his wife, only certain acts were permitted.

In chapter 10:4 there is a reference to Jesus being the "spiritual Rock" that Moses and the Israelites "drank of." This is another distortion of the Hebrew Scriptures. Many times throughout the Hebrew Scriptures, Yahweh is referred to as a *rock*: Psalms 18, 19, 28, 31, 42, 62, 71, 89, 92, and 94. There is not even the slightest allusion to anyone other than Yahweh as the "rock and redeemer." The Persian sun-god, Mithra, was also referred to as "the rock."

Chapter 15:14 describes one of the greatest arguments in the early Church. This was with those who said that Jesus was not actually raised from the dead and those who said he was in one way or another. Now, this argument goes into many different versions. There are groups of Christians who did not believe that Jesus was really resurrected. Others believed that he was physically raised from the dead. Still others believed that his resurrection was spiritual and not physical. Finally, there were those who believed that the resurrection was symbolic. You would figure that with something as important as this is to Christians they would know for sure if and when it happened. In verses 44 and 50 are indicators that the writer of this Epistle believed that the resurrection was a spiritual resurrection. This goes along with 1 Peter 3:18 as well.

The first letter to the Corinthians gives the basic organization of the early Church. This organizational system is taken directly out of the Essenes. In it were the apostles, prophets, teachers, miracle workers, healers, helpers, and administrators (12:28). The letter to the Ephesians lists these jobs a bit differently (Ephesians 4:11). More will be discussed on this later.

The second letter to the Corinthians is also considered Pauline. Again, at the beginning of this Epistle is the mention of a Church. This indicates a later writing. Another indicator that this may be a later writing is the mention in 8:9 that Jesus started out rich and became poor. This is contrary to the traditional teachings of Christianity. You will recall that according to the tradition Jesus was the son of a poor carpenter. The fact of the matter is that a carpenter would be anything but poor in those days. That was a vital trade. In this Epistle, this is not the case. One thing that must be remembered is that after the Zoroastrians, who believed in proselytizing, the Buddhists began proselytizing in the first century CE. Buddha was born a prince and became an ascetic in order to gain enlightenment. This verse seems to signify a possible Buddhist and/or Persian influence.

Again, there is a mention of the fact that Paul would do anything to gain a new proselyte. In chapter 9:19-22 Paul makes this a statement of fact and in 12:16 he states that he *lied* in order to get followers. If we look in the Hebrew Scriptures, Deuteronomy 27:18, liars are cursed. In 1 Peter 2:22, 24 the writer states that Jesus *never* lied, deceived or had any guile. Paul, on the other hand, was just the opposite: the ends justify the means. Remember, he was a salesman before he became a Christian.

Finally, in chapter 13:1 the writer mentions that it is the third (time) that Paul journeyed to Corinth. In Acts only 2 journeys were mentioned.

Here there is the first mention of the name of Silvanus. This name will be encountered in both 1 and 2 Thessalonians and in 1 Peter. Consequently, Silvanus must have been a rather important individual at the time. But why is Silvanus seemingly disregarded in the history of Christianity and the Church? One reason for this neglect may be due to the fact that he either was a Gnostic or turned from orthodox Christianity to Gnosticism. If you look in the Gnostic texts you find a text entitled "The Teachings of Silvanus." These writings are an early example of Christian Wisdom texts. They also give an idea of the importance of Silvanus to the early Christians. Those who have studied the Gnostic Gospels have noted that the name of Silvanus in the Gnostic text is part of the common practice of attributing a prominent person's name to the writing of an important text. This is the practice throughout all of the Scriptures both Hebrew and Christian. Consequently, Silvanus must have been important in early Christianity.

Even with this practice, it is obvious that the writing of Corinthians, 1 and 2 Thessalonians, and 1 Peter had to have been later than generally ascribed because of the fact that there was *no* mention of the Gospels or Epistles until *after* the middle of the 2nd century.

The Epistle to the Galatians is also considered Pauline. Here also is a mention of churches as well. Also you have a similar problem as that mentioned in 1 Corinthians: The problem was that of different Gospels being preached (1:6-8). This situation occurred when Gnosticism began to gain followers. You will recall that the Gnostics were the first Christians to proselytize and the orthodox Christians most likely set about proselytizing in order to attempt to thwart the Gnostics. The Gnostic Christians were also more open with their teachings as well as being more tolerant of others.

Here in Galatians (4:4) we also have another verse which contradicts the doctrine of the virgin birth. Jesus was "...*born of a woman, made under the law*." There is not even a suggestion of a miraculous birth; no star in the east, no visitation from ancient magicians, no angelic choir singing, nothing of the sort.

One thing that is *not* recorded in the writings of early Christianity is the concept of *love.* Important to the early Christians was their *faith* and complete allegiance to the bishops and other Church leaders. Any reference to love in Christianity came *after* the middle part of the 2nd century. It was the Gnostic Marcion of Sinope who introduced this concept into Christianity. Hence, any references to love in any of the writings indicates a later writing or a later compilation as well.

The next Epistle is that to the Ephesians. The style of writing is different than those considered Pauline and its attributed period of writing is after 90 CE. One of the clues of this is the mention of Tychicus who was mentioned in Acts 20:4. Another is the mention of the Church as an organized body. Supposedly, this Epistle was written to the congregation at Ephesus but the mention of Ephesus in 1:1 was not in the original. Consequently, there was actually no indication as to which congregation this letter was intended.

In the Middle Ages the doctrine of predestination began to surface. It was believed by certain Protestant groups that no matter how you lived your life the fate of your soul was predetermined and there was nothing that you could do about it. This doctrine came about due to chapter 1:4-5 of the Epistle to the Ephesians. In these two verses it is stated that Jesus had predetermined who was going to be his and who was going to go to heaven and who was not. To go along with this verse was Matthew 7:13, Luke 13:24, Romans 9, and Revelations 17:8. This idea also came into orthodox Christianity through the Gnostics.

There are several other important concepts in Ephesians that are Gnostic. First is the mention of "the prince of the power of the air" (2:2). Second is the Gnostic mystical description of the cross of the crucifixion (3:18). Third is the idea of the ascending and descending (4:9-10). Fourth is the raising of the dead (5:14). Finally, is the idea, "For we wrestle not against flesh and blood, but against principalities, against powers, against the rulers of the darkness of this world, against spiritual wickedness in high places" and taking on "...the whole armor of God..."(6:12-13). All of these ideas are strictly Gnostic and were anathema to the early Church.

The sixth Epistle is that of Philippians. This is a very short letter most likely written in Rome. The writing of this Epistle is placed about 96 CE. One of the main reasons for this is the fact that in 4:22 is a statement that is mentioned by Clement of Rome as well as the mention of Clement himself (4:3).

Next is the Epistle to the Colossians. This one is not considered Pauline. This Epistle was most likely written after 100 CE, and most probably around the middle of the 2nd century. The reason for this is the mention of the worshiping of angels (2:18). There were some Gnostic groups around the middle of the 2nd century who believed in the worship of angels. Consequently, there was an admonishment of this practice. Also, there is a mention of Tychicus in this Epistle indicating its writing as being later than 100 CE. There are other Gnostic references in here as well. These references, though, are an accepted part of the dogma. They include: the firstborn of every creature (1:15, 17); thrones, dominions, principalities, powers (1:16; 2:10, 15); the hidden mystery (1:26, 27; 4:3); and the treasures of wisdom and knowledge (2:3).

The eighth Epistle is that to the Thessalonians. This one is considered Pauline. It was written about 70 CE and some say possibly as early as 50 CE. The chances are that the date of 70 or later is more accurate. One of the reasons for this is the use of the term the "elect of God" in 1:4. This, you will recall, is a term that the Essenes used and it came into use in Christianity after the Essenes dispersed in 73 CE. There is also the mention of love in 3:12 and you will recall this concept did not come into Christianity until the 2nd century. There is also a mention of a persecution going on at the time. This was either during the reign of Nero (which was mainly in Rome, c. 60 CE) or that of Trajan (c. 112 CE). There is also the allusion that Jesus will be descending from heaven to take up the faithful at any time. Hence, the indication is that this was written around or after 90 CE.

The 2nd Epistle to the Thessalonians has been traditionally attributed to the time after 70 CE and is considered Pauline. It has a style similar to the 1st Thessalonians. If this be true then its writing after 70 could be quite accurate. There are suggestions in this Epistle of Gnostic proselytizing. The references to deception, falling away, holding fast to the traditions, and so on all reveal a concern for non-orthodox Christian teachings being propagated. Historically, the Gnostic "heresy" began to make more headway in the Roman Empire later in the 1st century so an admonission against its teachings would be made.

The next Epistle is that to Timothy. By the concepts being expressed it is most likely Judean Christian (Ebonite). In this Epistle Jesus is seen as a *man* and revealer of the "word" and God is the savior. It is definitely *not* Paul's writing style. It is a pastoral Epistle in the same style as the 2nd Epistle to Titus. The writing of this Epistle is attributed to the period between 100 and 140 CE. Other reasons for the lateness of the writing of this Epistle are that there are references to a specific Church body (chapter 5), a reference to a heresy which occurred in the early 2nd century (4:3), and the reference to payment to those who are in charge of a congregation (5:17, 18). All of this began in the early 2nd century.

After the 1st Timothy is 2nd Timothy. This Epistle is also attributed to the period between 100 and 140 CE. It is also a pastoral letter having a different philosophy than that of 1 Timothy but in the same style as 1 Timothy and Titus. Some of the indicators of its later writing are the mention of the name of Tychicus (4:12) and a reference to a heresy that began in the early 2nd century (2:18). We also find here an indication that the early Christians had **no** written texts. All scripture was given by revelation or inspiration only (3:16-17).

The twelfth Epistle is that to Titus. It has the same style as both 1 and 2 Timothy and is a genuine pastoral letter. The dating of its writing is between 100 and 140 CE. Again you find the names of Tychicus as well as Apollos (Acts 19:1) being mentioned. This letter deals mainly with a code of conduct of respected persons in the Church (i.e. bishops, elder men and women, etc.). One of the more interesting parts of this Epistle is the fact that the writer got caught in the paradox of the philosopher Epimenides [c. 600 BCE] (1:12): Epimenides was a Cretian. He had stated that;

> "All Cretians were liars." Now, since he was a Cretian and all Cretians are liars then he is a liar. Then, if he is a liar and he is stating that all Cretians are liars then he must be telling the truth. But since he is a Cretian, he is a liar, but then...

The writer of this Epistle could not figure out that this was a paradox and got hooked into it. So much for early Christian intelligence.

After Titus is the Epistle to Philemon. This is a very short Epistle and it begins by mentioning Timothy. This is a confirmation that it is also of a later writing. Further, the mention of Epaphras, the same person that we find in Colossians 1:1 and 4:12 indicates a writing after 90 CE.

The last Epistle traditionally attributed to Paul is that to the Hebrews. It is definitely not in a writing style attributed to Paul nor is it his theology or arguments. It was originally written in Alexandrian Greek and may have been a sermon. Portions of it were first used about 96 CE by Clement but the version that has been entered into the canon is from a 2nd century compilation. It appears to have been originally written to a Judean Christian or Essene group after the Temple was destroyed (73 CE). The reason for this idea is that the arguments are directed toward a Judean religious audience. The arguments posed in this Epistle are that of attempting to prove that Jesus was the Messiah and that the

Hebrew Scriptures had predicted this: that Christians are saved of God through Jesus.

Throughout this Epistle Jesus is referred to as a high priest under the order of Melchizedek. The name Melchizedek means king of righteousness. He is without mother or father and has neither a beginning nor an end of life. This comes from the Hebrew Scriptures. In Genesis 14:18; Exodus 21:6; 1 Samuel 6:14; 2 Samuel 6:17-18 the story of Abraham's meeting with Melchizedek is recounted. In chapter 7:2 Jesus is alluded to as the King of Salem or the King of Peace. In 7:3 Melchizedek was made "*like* unto the Son of God" to "abideth a priest continually." By equating Jesus with Melchizedek the writer attempts to prove a correlation between the two thus verifying Jesus as a high priest, the Son of God[70], and the Messiah. There is also reference to an "old" covenant with Israel and the "new" covenant with Jesus being the mediator. This, it is hoped, will convince the Judean (probably Essene) group that Jesus was the anointed of God.

As far as the Second Coming is concerned, this Epistle has a totally different idea of when that would occur. In 9:28 you see that the second coming *is not* a physical coming at all. It is a personal one which occurs within an individual. To the author of this letter it becomes more of a *symbolic* coming: "*...And unto them that look for him shall he appear the second time...*"

After the Epistles generally attributed to Paul we come to those attributed to other "apostles." The first is that ascribed to James. In the mid-1st century there was a leader of the congregation at Jerusalem named James. Many feel that this was the "brother" of Jesus but this is not known. The term "brotheren" was used to indicate someone of like mind, not necessarily a blood relative. The time period listed as to the writing of this Epistle is between 60 and 100 CE. It actually came into use around 200 CE. Even though this Epistle is ascribed to James, and even though James is mentioned in 1 Corinthians 15:7, there is nothing said of the concerns of the James of Corinthians. Hence, the true author is not known.

---

70 You will recall that the term *Son of God* was a term attributed to the *High Priest* of the Temple as well as to many of the kings.

The Epistle of James had been a disputed book when the canon was being compiled. It was accepted quite late. The reason for this is that it keeps total silence concerning Jesus' life, death, resurrection, and teachings. All that it does is to show Christianity as an ethical way of life with little reference to Yahweh and very little reference to Jesus. There are rather vague ideas about Jesus' supposed existence and there are conflicting estimates of its importance. A Judean religious group breaking from a traditional synagogue or a group still holding fast to Q could have come up with these ideas.

The 1st Epistle of Peter is known to have not been written by Peter. Traditionally it has been ascribed to the period from 60 or 70 CE. Most likely, it was written after 70 and probably during the persecutions of Trajan in 112 CE for there is a metaphor referring to those persecutions (4:12). Also, there is the mention of Silvanus as well (5:12). Another reason for a later writing is in 1:1 where the author calls the members of the congregations "strangers." This is another title that the Essenes used to denote the "elect."

In 1:2 there is a statement, "...*elect according to the foreknowledge of God the Father*..." This is a reference to the Gnostic practice of casting lots to decide which person will do which part in the service. The Gnostics didn't have a set hierarchy and would cast lots as to who would perform which part of the service. Hence, one week one could be the minister and the next week a helper. It was believed that God selected each individual for their particular part for a reason.

Chapter 5:13 presents a problem. It mentions the (Church) that is in Babylon. The problem is that at that time Babylon was not in existence. The Babylon referred to here was Rome. Here is an implication that the Epistle may be actually of Gnostic production. This idea is presented because of the reference to the "kiss of charity" that you had previously seen as part of a Gnostic rite.

The second Epistle of Peter was written sometime between 100 to 130 CE. It expanded the Epistle of Jude for it is written in a very similar style. It was written to explain the "Second Coming" and the name of Peter was attached to it in order to give it authority.

There are direct indications that this Epistle was written after the beginning of the 2nd century. The beginning of chapter 2:1-3 denotes the many different Christian teachings which were prevalent at the beginning of the 2nd century. In 3:16 there is a mention of Scriptures. This means that it had to have been written by about 140 for no Scriptures were discussed or used until after that time.

The first Epistle of John appears to have been written by the same author as the Gospel of John. Consequently, its date of compilation is around 120 CE. Then, if you attribute the same author as the Gospel of John, you would have to place its date of authorship at the latest around the *end* of the 2nd century. If it has the same author as the Acts of John then it is definitely a Gnostic writing, and there are indications that this is so. The main indicator is the use of the term antichrist. This *is* a Gnostic term that was adopted by the orthodox Christians late in the 2nd century.

The 2nd and 3rd Epistles of John are very short Epistles. They are so short that no author can be attributed to either one. As far as possible dates of their writings, the 2nd Epistle mentions the term antichrist and the idea that there are many who are deceiving. Hence, the most likely time of its writing is the beginning of the 2nd century. The 3rd Epistle mentions the names of Demetrius and Gaius. The name of Demetrius was mentioned in the Book of Acts. Gaius was mentioned in Acts, Romans, and in 1 Corinthians. This may be used to date its writing around the end of the 1st century.

The Epistle of Jude came into use about 200 CE. It was most likely written some time after 100 CE. This is a rather interesting Epistle because it mentions the Book of Enoch (v. 14), a known Kabbalistic text which was expunged from the Hebrew Scriptures. It further mentions one of the important concepts from this book (v. 9); Michael the archangel contending with Satan over Moses' body.

This Epistle also states that the end of the world is coming (v. 18). Hence, there are two possible periods for its writing. One is the latter part of the 1st century. The other is the middle to latter part of the 2nd century.

The Book of Revelations

The last book of the Christian Scriptures is The Revelation of St. John the Divine, which is also called Apocalypse. Supposedly this was written by the same author as that of the Gospel of John. The problem is that this *is* a known Gnostic text and is replete with Gnostic symbolism. It was compiled in the early part of the 2nd century and has been attributed to the Gnostic Cerinthus (c. 100 CE) by some researchers. The fact is, no one knows for sure who wrote it but there are too many Gnostic references for it to be orthodox Christian. Even so, there are several facts that emerge concerning this book:

1. The book was ***totally*** plagiarized from earlier mystical writings of Phyregian, Egyptian, and Hebrew origins. It is filled with mystical symbols from both the Phyregians and the Egyptians which the Gnostics used. It also contains writings directly taken from the Hebrew Scriptures, especially the Book of Daniel and portions of Isaiah.

2. Its watered-down version was written by Irenaeus. The main purpose may have been to do nothing more than use Gnostic ideas and concepts to turn Gnostic "heretics" to the Church. The book also tried to bring together both Christian and Pagan philosophies. One reason for attempting to do this was that when Christians tried to convert any intelligent Pagan, the Pagans retorted and ended up converting the Christians. This book fuses Gnostic Christian and Pagan symbolism.

3. There is also some indicator that this book may have been intended to satirize orthodox Christianity. As an example, the star which fell from heaven (called Wormwood)[71] is the Bethlehem star that preceded a false teaching (Christianity) which poisoned mankind.

---

71 Wormwood is a poison.

4.   Another well-known writing technique that existed prior to the 1st century BCE was that of stating something in allusion as if it was being written long before the fact or that it was a "prophecy." The actual writing occurred sometime *after* the occurrence. By placing no historical names or events to it and making only allusion, the events could be applied to any time and any era—and this has been done with this book all down through the centuries.

5.   The most famous number from this book is that of *666.* This number is used to denote the "antichrist." As you have seen, the term antichrist is a purely Gnostic term. The problem here is that in some of the oldest available texts of this book, the number given is *616.* How is that?

The number 666 has been associated most often with Nero Caesar. The reason being that *parts* of the book were apparently compiled before, during, and after Nero's reign. It was not completed until around 110.

The numerology of 666 is done in this manner: The written Hebrew name of Nero is written as KSR NRVN in one instance and according to the Hebrew numbering system this equals 666. The other spelling of Nero's name is KSR NRV. Spelled this way the number equals 616. It is through this method that the number was chosen. Irenaeus also listed several other names with the number 666. They were: Teitan, Lampetis, Antemos, and Lateinos. Since the earliest number of 616 and 666 both can be found with Nero's name, it comes to reason that the individual spoken of was Nero and no one else. In fact, Martin Luther, using a Latin letter/number system, claimed that the antichrist was the Pope. This claim has persisted down through the centuries by many Protestant sects, especially today many fundamentalist Christian sects and cults claim this.

The Hebrew and Greek Numbering system

Hebrew:		Greek:			Hebrew:		Greek:		
Aleph	א	Alpha	α	1	Samech	ס	Xi	ξ	60
Beth	ב	Beta	β	2	Oin	ע	Omicron	ο	70
Gimel	ג	Gamma	γ	3	Peh	פ	Pi	π	80
Daleth	ד	Delta	δ	4	Tzaddi	צ	Episemon Bau	z	90
Heh	ה	Epsilon	ε	5	Qoph	ק	Rho	ϱ	100
Vau	ו	Digamma	f	6	Resh	ר	Sigma	σ	200
Zain	ז	Zeta	ζ	7	Shin	ש	Tau	τ	300
Cheth	ח	Eta	η	8	Tav	ת	Upislon	υ	400
Teth	ט	Theta	θ	9	Hebrew Ending Letters:				
Yud	י	Iota	ι	10	Kaph	ך	Phi	φ	500
Kaph	כ	Kappa	κ	20	Mem	ם	Chi	χ	600
Lammed	ל	Lambda	λ	30	Nun	ן	Psi	ψ	700
Mem	מ	Mu	μ	40	Peh	ף	Omega	ω	800
Nun	נ	Nu	ν	50	Tzaddi	ץ	Sanpi	⅍	900

Take a look at what some prominent Church fathers had to say about the period of the antichrist, the end of times: ". . . *and reason teaches us that the number of the Beast's name is shown according to Greek numerical usage by the letters in it . . . I, for one, dare not risk making any positive assertion regarding the name of the antichrist. Had there been any need for his name to be openly announced at the present time* (c. 180 CE), *it would have been stated by the one who saw the revelation. For it was not seen a long time back, but almost in my own lifetime, at the end of Domitian's reign*" (Iranaeus). This was noted by Eusebius (c. 325 CE): "*Everything indeed has been fulfilled <u>in my time</u>.* (emphasis, mine) *I saw with my own eyes the places of worship thrown down from top to bottom,. . . the <u>inspired</u>* (emphasis, mine) *holy Scriptures committed to flames . . ., and the pastors of the churches hiding disgracefully in one place or another, while others suffered the indignity of being held up to ridicule by their enemies— a reminder of another prophetic saying: for contempt was poured on rulers, and He made them wander in a trackless land where there was no road.*" Here we have two different writers at two different times saying much the same thing as "predicted" by the Book of Revelations. Obviously both of them were wrong for neither saw "the end of times" nor did the antichrist appear. This is evidence of the astounding and "reliable predictability" of this book.

Regarding the "predictions" in the Book of Revelations, the Emperor Julian noted that the Pagan oracles foretold not only events but how, when, where, after what, and by whom. This book is vague and inconcise and, consequently, up for interpretation. Since prior to its inclusion in the canon in the 4th century, people have attributed all sorts of things to its writings and *all* of the predictions have failed. The rationalization constantly used is that, "Only God knows when things are to come." According to the Hebrew Scriptures, all predictions which are inspired by God are 100-percent correct all of the time. Due to this quite shabby record, it's obvious that the Book of Revelations is *not* inspired by God.

6.   The Book of Revelations bears a striking resemblance to the Book of Daniel in the Hebrew Scriptures. You will recall that Daniel was compiled about 165 BCE and it was taken from an older Babylonian book. There are also statements lifted directly from Ezekiel and Isaiah.

The Book of Revelations and the Gospel of John are the two most mystical books of the Christian Scriptures. Both are filled with mystic symbolism and numbers and both have a similar writing style. For example, the number 7 is the most mentioned number in Revelations (as well as the whole Bible itself).[72] In Revelations it is seen in the context of the 7 candlesticks representing the 7 known planets and the 7 seals representing the 7 ganglionic centers up the spine (the 7 stations of Mithra).[73] Remember

---

72   The number 7 in Revelations is borrowed mainly from the Book of Daniel.

73   These 7 ganglionic centers are the *chakras*. These were *not* unknown to the Mediterranean mystical cultures. This was, for example, the "ladder of Mithra" and the seven vowels between Alpha and Omega in the Greek alphabet and the intertwining serpents on the Cadeuces actually had seven spaces.

that the Christian Scriptures were written in Greek after they were copied from earlier versions. You can also find the number 7 being very prominent in the Mithraic Mysteries. On the floor of one of the Mithraeums of Felicissimus at Ostia, Italy is a mosaic with 7 stations decorated with the symbols of the 7 stages of initiation. At another in Ostia are the 7 stations marked with 7 arcs which are associated with the 7 planets. At a third are the 7 gates of heaven that the soul ascends and these are associated with the 7 planets and the 7 metals. (Revelations 1:20)

One of the most interesting descriptions in Revelations is found in 1:13:

> *And in the midst of the seven candlesticks (one) like unto the Son of man, clothed with a garment down to the foot, and girt about the paps with a golden girdle.*

This description is claimed to be the mystical description of Jesus. There's a small problem here. This comes with the last part of the verse: ". . . girt about the paps with a golden girdle." The term "paps" here is a medieval term for female breasts. The Greek term which is being translated is *mastos* which also means female breasts. Also, the girdle or cord was worn by the women under the breasts. Men wore the girdle around the waist. Does this indicate that Jesus was female or hermaphrodite? If this is not the mystical description of Jesus, what is it?

In order to find out who this is you *must* go to the Gnostics. The image presented here is an androgynous image: part male and part female. This androgynous being went by different names. It was called Anthropos (Primal Man) and sometimes Eleleth and it was the archetypal progenitor of humankind. It was bright and shining in form and resplendent in beauty. This figure most certainly is not Jesus. After all, Jesus did not have female breasts, did he? The idea of an androgynous being came out of Paganism and was reinforced by the Hebrew Scriptures. In Genesis 1:27 it states: *"So God created man in his image, in the image of God created he him: male and female (emphasis mine) created he them."* To the Gnostics and in the mystical Judean tradition the original creation of humankind of the male and female created by God was androgynous and not separate. It was later when God brought a "great sleep" upon Adam and created Eve from Adam's rib was there a separation of the sexes.

In Revelations it is stated, as in many of the Gospels and Epistles that ". . . *things which must shortly come to pass*", ". . . *the time (is) at hand*", ". . . *the things which must shortly be done*" and ". . . *Surely I come quickly*." Again, we have the idea that the world is coming to an end very soon, so be prepared.

As you have seen, many of the concepts that Christianity has acquired are not even Christian. In this book there is the concept of the millennium, the 1000 years of peace. This idea came directly from the Persians. Another is the title of "Alpha and Omega." This was a title of the Greek god Dionysus. Yahweh was referred to as the aleph and tau (the first and the last). Again, taken directly from Persian mythology is the statement in chapter 12:9 and 20:2, ". . . *that old serpent, called the Devil and Satan, which deceiveth the whole world*." The idea of the binding of Satan is from the Persian Zend Avesta. In the Persian myth Thraetaona conquered Azi, the foe, and bound him up in Mt. Damavand where he stays to the end of the world when he will be loosed and killed by Keresaspa. Also in Norse mythology is Thor killing the Midgard serpent and the gods' enemies falling in battle. In this battle the whole universe burns, the sun dims, the stars fall from heaven and a new heaven and earth are made where men and the gods live happily. Finally, the description in chapter 19:11-16 of Revelations is found as an image engraved on a Bactrian coin from the 1st century BCE.

As you have seen, there are also ideas lifted directly out of Daniel, Isaiah, and Ezekiel and others. This does not prove that these earlier books were prophecies of things to come. It just means that the material was known to the author. Here are some other examples. Chapter 1:7-8 comes from Daniel 7:13, Isaiah

44:6, and Zechariah 12:10. Chapter 3:5 comes from Exodus 32:32, Psalm 69:28, and Daniel 12:1. Verse 7 of chapter 3 is from Isaiah 22:22. In chapter 4:7 and 5:6 is a description of four beasts. This is directly out of Ezekiel 1:10 and Isaiah 6:2-3. Chapter 5:6 is from Isaiah 6:2-3. Verse 10 of chapter 10 is from Ezekiel 2:8-10 and 3:1-3. Chapter 11:8 (which was added later) comes from Ezekiel 6:5. Chapter 12:3 is taken from Daniel 7:8. The name of Armageddon in chapter 16:16 is from 2 Kings 13:29. Chapter 19:20 has the statement: "These both were cast into a lake of fire burning with brimstone." This is lifted directly from Daniel 7:10. Chapter 20:8 has the names of Gog and Magog which are taken from Ezekiel 38:2. The largest copied text comes in chapter 21:12-27. This is taken directly out of Ezekiel chapter 48. Finally, the description in chapter 22:16 can be found in Isaiah 14:12.

Finally, the Book of Revelations claims to be a book of prophecy. As you have seen, it has not predicted anything in 2000 years and isn't predicting anything now. Since its inception in the canon the "believers" have tried to attribute all sorts of things and people to the vague descriptions in this book and none of what they have said has even the slightest semblance to prophecy and predictions. The consistent excuse of God being the only one to know when these things will come about just does not hold water. So, was this book inspired by God? Quite obviously, it was not.

As you have seen, any Christian Scriptures were unknown to the early 1st century Christians. The text that they used was the Septuagint or Greek translation of the Hebrew Scriptures...and they used this translation in order to "prove" their "correctness."[74] Also, as you have seen, there are a *lot* of discrepancies in the Christian Scriptures. With this being factual, and knowing that the early Christian fathers forged, removed, and otherwise obliterated the original texts, how can any of what exists today be considered the "inspired Word of God?"

---

74   Actually, it was to prove their *self-righteousness.*

The Miracles of Jesus

But we preach Christ crucified,...

1 Corinthians 1:23

Prior to the 4th century there were about 5000 manuscripts which could have been used in the Christian Scriptures. The ones chosen to become the canon were used because they proposed Jesus to be a "miracle worker;" a magician. As the part of the verse above shows, the main teaching of the early Church was "Christ crucified,"[75] not "Christ, the magician" or miracle worker.

As you have seen, the thing that caused the conversion to Christianity was the witnessing of a "miracle," not Christian arguments or teachings. Jesus was referred to by many Pagans as a *"swami,"* a swindler holy man who practiced trickery and successfully fooled the people.

The attribution of magical powers to religious healing was and always has been a feature of almost any new messianic cult. This does not matter whether the cult arises among a people subject to foreign rule or among people who feel "spiritually oppressed."[76] Communities similar to the early Christians were found to offer certain psychological rewards and these were attractive to converts and those who felt something was missing from their lives.

The Gospel stories have direct parallels in older Pagan mythologies and legends. As was noted earlier, the Roman emperor Julian stated that Christians believed their own myths while disbelieving others which were exactly the same. Further, Julian stated, *"Jesus and Paul have surpassed all magicians and impostors that have ever lived. Neither Paul, nor Matthew, nor Luke, nor Mark dared to say that Jesus was God; but John began the concept."*

---

75   The term here in Greek is *staroo* that literally means *to impale on a cross. It actually refers to the subduing or extinguishing of passion or selfishness.*

76   Even the Church of Scientology claims that its techniques can perform "miracle cures" which modern medicine cannot explain. Like a good 99% of all "miracles," they are based upon the placebo effect or the manipulation of trance states (i.e. hysterical healings).

Virtually all of the leaders of all religious movements have had the reputation for performing miracles. This has always been a major selling point for religious movements. Examples are still quite extant:

1. Krishna cured a leper as one of his first miracles. He made the lame to walk, raised the dead,[77] and restored limbs.

2. Buddha's history is replete with miracles, healing both soul and body, curing whole villages of plagues, and easing the pain of childbirth. It is said that Buddha's presence could be felt more than 200 miles away.

3. Zoroaster (Persian) performed miracles in order to confirm his Divine mission.

4. Horus (the Egyptian sun-god) performed miracles, including the raising of the dead.

5. Osiris, as well as Isis (both Egyptian deities) performed miracles. Isis raised Osiris from the dead.

6. Serapis (Greco-Egyptian god who became the physical model for Jesus) was called "The Healer of the World" and had healed the sick.

7. Marduk (Assyrian) was called Logos, "He who made heaven and earth," the "Merciful One," the "Giver of Life," etc. He performed miracles as well as raising the dead.

8. The prophet Elisha raised a girl from the dead and fed a multitude.

---

77 Today there were witnesses who saw Sai Baba in India raise a man from the dead. This man stayed alive for five more years. Then of course, there are those involved in fundamentalist Christianity who have made claims that their pastor has raised someone from the dead. But if it wasn't in the *National Enquirer or the Weekly World News*, who can believe it?

9. Dionysus/Bacchus (Greek) performed miracles, among which was the changing of water into wine, in the same manner as recorded in the Gospels.[78] He was called the "Giver of Joy," the "Healer of the Sick," the "Law-Giver," the "Promoter of Peace," the "Giver of Wisdom," and the "Revealer of Hidden Secrets of the Future."

10. Aesculapius (a Greek physician) was reputed to perform miracles. He cured the sick and raised the dead. Even after his death, miracles were performed in his name and he was called "The Savior."

11. Apollonius of Tyana, who lived in the early first century, cured the sick, stopped plagues, exorcised demons, and raised the dead in the same manner as Jesus: he took the hand of a maiden who had recently died, uttered a few words and the girl stood up and talked. He also vanished before a tribunal in Rome who put him on trial for his life. In fact, Justin Martyr said of Apollonius:

    > "*How is it that the talismans of Apollonius have power in certain members of creation? For they prevent, <u>as we see,</u>* (emphasis, mine) *the fury of the waves, and violence of the winds, and attacks of wild beasts, and whilst our Lord's miracles <u>are preserved by tradition alone, those of Apollonius are most numerous, and actually manifested in present facts,</u>* (emphasis, mine) *so as to lead astray all beholders.*"

    This is one of the reasons that all of the books of Apollonius were destroyed by the Church...and Apollonius wrote more than 60 volumes!

---

78 In one of the works of Praxiteles is the story of Dionysian Priests who were able to make wine appear in empty vessels in front of witnesses with the building and jars sealed off.

12. Simon Magus (Simon the Samaritan) was called, "The Wisdom of God," "The Word of God," "The Paraclete," "Comforter," "The Image of the Eternal Father Manifested in the Flesh," "The First-Born of the Supreme." It was told that he could appear and disappear at will, levitate, animate inanimate objects, produce trees from the earth, cause a stick to reap without hands, do shape-shifting, fling himself from high places without being hurt, etc. All of these "miracles" were attested to by the early Church. Simon Magus was a Gnostic Christian and it is thought it is he who is spoken of in the Book of Acts.

13. Poseidon walked on water. There are also very ancient tales of Egyptian Temple Priests who could walk on water. Indian Yogis have been reported to have been able to walk on water as well as levitate.

14. Meander (Roman) was called "Wonder Worker."

15. Many rabbis of the time could perform miracles including the casting out of "devils."

16. The Emperor Vespasian (emperor from 70-79 CE) cured a blind man in *exactly* the same manner as Jesus (i.e. spittle on the eyeballs) and cured a lame hand just by his touch. He was reputed to cure by his shadow merely passing over a person or by a touch of his garment. It was also reported that he raised a girl from the dead.

17. The raising of Lazarus from the dead is taken directly from an ancient Egyptian legend. The raising was done in exactly the same way and the name of the person being raised: *Lazar-is.*

There is an ancient Greek adage: "*Miracles are for fools.*" The Romans had their counterpart which states: "*The common people* (literally, vulgar) *love to be deceived—deceived let them be.*" The

Book of Proverbs puts it this way: *"The simple minded will believe anything; the wise looks well into all his doings."* In the 4th century John Crystostom stated: *"Miracles are proper only to excite sluggish and vulgar minds, men of sense have no occasion for them,"* and, *"They frequently carry some untoward suspicion along with them,"* In other words, miracles are performed for some sort of nefarious purpose. They are not performed to show "the Power of God" but to hook the unaware. Eusebius was the one who coined the term "miracle." The correct translation is "sign."

The historian Celsus had this to say about Jesus' miracles: *"His miracles, <u>granted to be true</u>,*(emphasis, mine) *were nothing more than the common works of the enchanters, who, for a few obli, will perform greater deeds in the midst of the Forum, calling up souls of heroes, exhibiting sumptuous banquets, and tables covered with food, which have no reality. Such things do not prove these jugglers to be sons of God: nor do Christ's miracles."*

Even as late as the 4th and 5th century, Jesus' miracles were called to question by many of the bishops of the Church. In fact, St. Augustine had stated that Jesus had been initiated into the Egyptian Mysteries while in Egypt. This makes these miracles less than Divinely instigated. There were some who had charged that Jesus did not perform his miracles as a Judean prophet, but as a magician, an initiate of the Heathen temples. In fact, on several ancient Christian manuscripts depicting Jesus' miracles he is seen with a wand in hand exactly the same guise as a necromancer (the term **witch** is used in the King James version of the Bible).

Many ancient historians of the time and area have recorded the miracles performed by other persons, but not one word is mentioned of those supposedly performed by Jesus. The Christian writers are known to have freely suspended natural laws in order to get their point across to make followers. All of Jesus' miracles can easily be seen in their entirety by searching the mythologies of Egypt, Phoenicia, Greece, and Rome for the gods and persons who performed them. The use of sleight-of-hand was a common way to gain followers in the opening centuries of this era. Even the ancient Mystery Religions made use of this same scheme. He who could perform the best miracles would gain the most followers.

Can Jesus' miracles also be explained in any other way?

The answer to this question is in the affirmative. Today evangelists make quite a bit of use of "ringers"[79] and old carnival tricks (i.e. the "growing leg" trick). These same practices were used by the early Christians. But what about Jesus' miracles? Since they were not of Divine origin what other natural explanations could there be for them?

There are several things that you need to look at from that time period. First of all, it was a period of immense superstition. Gods and demons interfered with people's lives and if someone became ill it was either (a) God that had failed to have been propitiated or a demon of some sort causing the problem. If someone had a mental illness, in the Middle East especially, it was caused by "possession" by a demon. So, if someone saw something which appeared to be against natural law, as it was understood, it was miraculous and obviously of Divine origin. Also consider that the medical and psychological care was exceptionally poor. The recommended treatment for most physical and psychological ailments was to make a sacrifice (propitiate the gods) and the use of strange elixirs, concoctions, poultices, magical spells, and etc. Having a priest or priestess perform some sort of magical incantation over the ailing person (not unlike praying for the sick today) was a common practice. Further, there was no knowledge of hysterical or psychosomatic illnesses. These are illnesses which are caused by the mind and are cured by the mind being activated via hypnosis or some other trance or belief state. Then, there was also no knowledge of the placebo effect. The placebo effect is just now beginning to be studied seriously by medical researchers.

Secondly, there is absolutely *no* way of knowing the actual condition of the people who were supposed to have been healed or out

---

79 A relative of the author was paid to be a ringer for Oral Roberts back in the mid-1950s. She was out hanging clothes when one of Roberts' cohorts asked her if she wanted to make $100. Being from a rather economically deprived area, she said "yes."

142

of which "demons" had been cast,[80] Everyone is to just accept everything at face value as being factual with no other source than what, essentially, the Church has stated. If, as Augustine had stated, Jesus was initiated into the Egyptian Mysteries it would be quite obvious that he would have had a good knowledge of hypnotic effects and trance states. Hence, he could have easily worked with hysterical healings and posthypnotic suggestion. Further, since it was a time of immense superstition and ignorance, people would tend to believe what they see without question.[81]

Third, you need to consider that the Gospels were altered from their original form. Iranaeus (c. 180 C.E.) admitted to altering the Gospel of John and implied he did it to others. There is no way of knowing the changes that he made. Why would the Gospel of John need altering? Simply, it was written by the Gnostics and the original most likely contained a lot of symbology that was very Pagan. He adjusted the symbolism *and*, probably added "miracles" for Jesus to perform for five of the seven miracles in John are the same as in the Synoptics.

---

80 One of the more interesting exorcisms occurs in Matthew 8:28-32 and Mark 5:11-14. One reason being that this is from an old Babylonian spell. Second, there was no such place called Gergesenes. The third reason comes in the form of a question: What are pigs doing in Israel?? Swine were anathema to the Middle East at that time. Finally, here was this "son of God" who just ruined a man's livelihood.

81 The same thing goes on today and it does not matter whether it is with evangelical "healings" or "psychic surgery." Any layman who has been to either will come back telling of how this was "the real thing."

Christianity and the Mystery Religions

He answered and said unto them, Because it is given unto you to know the mysteries of the kingdom of heaven, but to them it is not given.

Matthew 13:11

Early Christianity could easily be termed "the poor man's mystery religion." It began when the mystery religions were in vogue, it borrowed profusely from the mystery religions, it appealed to those who could not afford to belong to the more expensive mystery religions, and it most likely was a spin-off of a Greco-Judean Mystery Religion (i.e. the "gnostic" Essenes?). In fact, one of the main Church Fathers, Clement of Alexandria (c. 180 CE), presented Christianity as a mystery religion.

In the 1st century BCE through the 1st century CE there were some Judean religious practices that showed strong similarities to the mystery religions. When Christianity began, it too showed similar resemblances to the mystery religions. In the eastern portion of the Roman Empire the Judean religion and Christianity were pretty much the religions of choice. Initiates into these religious systems, like their parallels in the other mysteries, went through baptisms, purifications, fasts, ceremonial rites (e.g. circumcision), vows, and so on in order to be admitted to the community. From the middle to the latter part of the 1st century CE Christian baptism represented a death and rebirth experience where the emergence from the water meant the beginning of a new life. Once one became a member he or she was required to relinquish all identifications with their past and assume the title given them by the religion. They were then a member of the "brotherhood."[82] The numerous ceremonies and holy days that were celebrated by the communities were meant primarily for the initiated and many of them had a sacred feast involved (e.g. the Jewish Seder and the Christian Eucharist). Like the mystery religions, these Judean and Christian brotherhoods had vows and these vows would be taken

---

82   This is not unlike what the pseudo-religious cults do today.

again after a period of probation. It was taking this second set of vows that was regarded as being "born again."

Different theories have been expounded regarding the strong similarities between the mystery religions and Christianity. Most probably what occurred is that when Christianity began to become organized it adopted the practices, philosophies, and teachings of its neighboring religions. Consequently, since the mystery religions were so prevalent it was from the mystery religions organization where much of Christianity came. Later, when Christianity became all the vogue (late 3rd and 4th centuries CE), what mystery religions still existed had to borrow from Christianity.

Out of the mystery religions came many important Christian concepts: concepts that became dogma after the mystery schools had died out and were forgotten. They become dogma by Church councils who debated, argued, and created Christianity as it is known. It is a definite fact that not one of the members of all of the Church councils was inspired by God.

Christianity absorbed many details of the Pagan cults. As examples: Jesus had a virgin birth like literally all of the sun-gods; Dionysus, Mithra, and Horus were born in a manger, a stable or stone cave and wrapped in swaddling clothes; Dionysus/Bacchus turned water into wine; Aesculapius raised men from the dead and gave sight to the blind; Attis, Osiris, Adonis, and Tammuz were mourned at their crucifixions and rejoiced over at their resurrections by women; Mithra and Osiris were scourged at a pillar and resurrected from a rock tomb; Mithra was seen as humane, a beneficent god, a savior, and redeemer, eternally young, Son of the Most High, preserver of mankind from the Evil One and had *no* loves; from the Osirian and Mazdean Mysteries came the seamless robe; Dumuzi (Sumerian god), Tammuz (Babylonian god), Moses, and Apollo were all called "The Good Shepherd"; Mithra and Hermes carried the lamb on their shoulders; and Peter's denial is the same as that in the myth of Proteus and Janus.

As you have seen, the term "logos" was most likely brought into the Judean religion from Babylon where it first emerged from the vast accumulation of fancies and speculations in their lore. It was used, along with other terms such as Monogenes (the Only

Begotten), Prototokos (the First-Born), and Hyiostou Theou (the Son of God) that applied to Greek gods.

From the Mithraic Mysteries Jesus received the titles of: Mediator, Savior, Incarnate Word, the Holy Word, and the Rock.[83] Mithra stated of himself, "I am Alpha and Omega, the first and the last, which is, which was, and which is to come, the Almighty." It is through the Mithraic Mysteries where the Father and the Son are coequal. Jesus was considered the controller of the cosmic forces, but Mithra had that job before him.[84] The idea of a cosmic, astral, or heavenly immortality is a Mithraic doctrine. This was stated by Celsus and attested to by Origen. Finally, interestingly enough, the Mithraic Mysteries began in Tarsus—the same city in which Paul was born and grew up.

From Proteus and Janus Jesus borrowed, "I am the door," "I stand at the door and knock," "I am in the Father and the Father in me," "I have the keys to death and hell," and "I come not to bring peace but a sword."

Listed below are a series of other concepts taken from the teachings of the Mystery Religions and used exclusively by Christianity as *their* teachings:

1. Monotheism

2. The religion of the spirit and love

3. The religion of God manifest

4. God-fearing

5. The Divine Trinity. This concept flourished in India, Egypt, Mesopotamia, and in Platonic philosophy centuries before Christianity. There were heated arguments in the early Church concerning this doctrine and many still did not believe it into the 6th century.

6. "Many are called but few are chosen"

7. The slain and risen god/savior

---

83 As we have already seen, Yahweh was the rock according to the Judean religion.

84 See Philippians 3:20-21 and Galatians 4:3-5.

8. The things of the earth are in sympathy with the things of heaven. This is stated quite appropriately in the Hermetic mysteries where Hermes Trismegistus states: "As above so below; as below so above. As without, so within; as within so without."

9. Teachings are in allegory. Both the mystery religions and the Hebrew Kabbalah teach mainly from allegory.

10. The redemption of man to forgive sins (salvation)

11. Deliverance from demons

12. Blessings according to one's faith

13. Having visions of things divine

14. Partaking of sacraments for salvation

15. "Be of good cheer..." for salvation is imminent

16. Stirring of the emotions in order to learn

17. "The Spirit quickeneth..." etc.

18. The main issues: life and death

19. It's a personal religion open to all through religious rebirth

20. It produced saints, ascetics, and martyrs. Martyrdom for one's religion was part of the mystery religions long before Christianity came into vogue.

21. God was called, "The Most High," "The Beginning and the End"

22. "Only the pure in heart can see God"

23. No one can approach unless he is innocent (as a child)

24. Baptism (the Seal of the Son of God) is an important initiation rite for rebirth. As the Emperor Julian said of Christian baptism: *"Baptism cannot rid one of diseases but it is supposed to be a means of cleansing and purification. It does though, take away all manner of horrendous behaviors committed prior."*

25. Baptism of Water, Fire, and Spirit are required for the highest initiation

26. Church contributions taken

27. There are mysteries, things that will not be understood

28. The revealed (channeled) word is greater than the written word

29. Being born again, twice born, having a spiritual birthday

30. No one is saved without being reborn; a renewing of the mind

31. The Holy Spirit breathes within; being possessed by God

32. "I am in you and you in me"

33. A divine begetting to become sons of God

34. "Is it not written... 'Thou art gods?'"; the spirit of God dwells in you

35. God addressed as the bridegroom

36. The mystical marriage with God

37. Believers are soldiers of God

38. The consuming of the god in a sacramental meal

39. Man can ascend to heaven

40. All who are initiated are saved

41. The demand for self-sacrifice

42. The resurrection of the dead

43. The salvation of the individual soul is most important

44. The doctrine of divine grace

45. All of the initiates are brothers and sisters

46. The doctrine of Original Sin

47. Everyone sins

48. The dualism of the flesh and the spirit; the animal and human natures in man

49. Becoming as much like God as possible through righteousness and holiness

50. The body is the weight of the soul

51. The gods were saviors or redeemers

52. Man fell from grace

53. The god was the Light of the Life of man

54. The aim is worshiping a pure God, living a pure life, and cultivating the spirit of brotherhood.

55. The mother of the god is the "mother of sorrows"

56. Prayer is talking to God
57. Justification is by faith
58. God is born in the form of man; god incognito or god disguised as man
59. The heavens are seen as a "mansion"
60. If one does not meet retribution for evil deeds in this life, he will meet it in the next
61. The most important virtue to God is charity
62. God's kingdom is eternal
63. "Seek and ye shall find"
64. All know God according to their capacity to understand him
65. Sunday is the "Lord's Day"
66. The idea of a spiritual salvation
67. The idea of the one true religion (from the Persian Mysteries)
68. The idea of "being in Christ"
69. God is love and God loves you and the world

As you can see, there are entirely too many concepts and ideas taken from the mystery religions to be coincidental. All of this goes to prove again that there is really *no* uniqueness in Christianity and that it does not have any Divine origins. Further, even the Greek term musterion which is the term used in the Christian Scriptures for mystery or mysteries actually means secret. The mystery is through the idea of silence which was dictated by the initiation into religious service. Consequently, the idea of original Christianity being a mystery religion or being taken or modeled after the mystery religions begins to make a lot more sense. With this being a very strong possibility, the idea that it was founded by God is totally unfounded.

Alexander S. Holub, Ph.D.

The Gospel Story and the Mystery Play

O foolish Galatians, who hath bewitched you, that you should not obey the truth of Jesus Christ crucified that has been depicted before your eyes.

Galatians 3:1

The Gospel stories of Jesus have many aspects of more ancient mystery plays in them. Again, this cannot be mere coincidence. The story of Jesus' birth, his miracles, and his death and resurrection are filled with allusion and time sequencing common in ancient mystery rites. You will find things discussed in the Gospel stories which were witnessed by no one but are taken as factual events. Besides those already mentioned (the tempting in the desert and the "agony in the garden") you can also add the three Magi and their conversation with Herod as well as the details of Jesus' birth, Jesus' conversation with Pilate, and statements made by Jesus on the cross that no one heard. The focus here will be on the crucifixion as a mystery play.

The Last Supper, the agony in the garden, the betrayal of Judas, the crucifixion itself, and the resurrection are all parts of a mystery play from ancient Palestine. In fact Eusebius stated that the Resurrection was a *"mystery."* This came from the ancient Semitic annual rite of the victim known as "Joshua (Jesus), the Son of the Father" being sacrificed and ceremonially eaten. At first it was either the king or the king's first-born or only son that was sacrificed. Later this was modified to be a criminal, a captive, or an animal (the lamb or goat).

It was a custom among the early Hebrews to sacrifice the first fruits of one's labors whether it was grains, fruits, first-born animals...or the first-born child (Ex. 13:2, 12, 13; 22:29). Historically, the Hebrews/Israelites were one of the *last* cultures to give up blood and human sacrifice.[85]

---

85   Egypt, on the other hand, was one of the first to give up *blood* sacrifice of all kinds.

In the rival cults, especially those associated with the legendary Joshua, are seen the basic ideas and practices that gave rise to Christianity. The name Jesus was itself a variant of the name Joshua (Yeshu), an ancient god who later was reduced to human status. The Judeans of the Hellenistic period regarded Joshua as the actual founder of the rite of circumcision. According to the tradition, Joshua began his work of deliverance on the day fixed for the choosing of the Paschal lamb and ended at the Passover. Furthermore, the name of Jesus was revered in some quarters of Palestine and played much the same part in the Judean liturgy for the ecclesiastical New Year as the Judean Jesus in the Apocalypse on the Day of Judgement.

The Messianic idea seems to have come into the Judean religion during the Babylonian Captivity. Most likely it came from two sources: 1) the old Babylonian myth of the return of Hammurabi who declared himself to be Savior-Shepherd and the King of Righteousness (titles given to the Babylonian sun-god Tammuz and, prior to that, to the Sumerian god Dumuzi, also consider the meaning of the name Melchizedek mentioned in the Epistles and Hebrew Scriptures); and 2) from the Mazdean (Persian) doctrine that at the end of time Saoshyant, the Savior, the yet unborn son of Zoroaster, would raise the dead and destroy Angra Mainyu (Ahriman), the Evil One.

There is ***not*** a conception associated with Jesus that is not common to some or all Saviors (sun-gods) of antiquity: 1) They are all called Savior; 2) They take away the sins of the world; 3) They judge the dead at the last judgement; 4) They are called the "Soul of the World"; 5) They have all proclaimed the easy "yoke"; 6) They are called "the True Vine" and work the miracle of water into wine; 7) They all suffered, died, and rose again; 8) They take the symbolic keys of heaven and hell; 9) They are all mediators with the Father; 10) They are all destroyers of the Evil One; 11) They are all one of a Trinity; 12) They are all called the "Logos" or the "Word" or teacher of righteousness; 13) They are all associated with a Holy Family and a Holy Spirit; and 14) They are all called the Son of God. Hence, Christianity is nothing more than Paganism reshaped.

Seen in the crucifixion story are aspects of an ancient Babylonian feast called Sacaea in which a mock-king is given a mock-crowning, scourging, and death. In this feast are seen: 1) a mourning for the victim (See Ezekiel 8:14); 2) his alleged divinity and titles of Son of God and Son of Man; 3) his participation in a sacramental meal in which his flesh is mystically eaten; 4) his execution between two criminals; 5) his resurrection; and 6) his subsequent status as Messiah or Christos.[86] In fact, as late as the 19th century in the province of Orissa in India an aboriginal hill tribe known as the Khonds sacrificed a victim through crucifixion retelling the ancient story *exactly* as was seen in the Christian Scriptures and the Babylonian feast of Sacaea.

If you will look closely at the Pauline Epistles you will see Paul speaking of a crucified Jesus in terms of a slain and resurrected god or demi-god, rather than a teacher and wonder-worker. Miracles are conspicuously absent from the Epistles. As far as the idea that the Gospel story of the crucifixion was part of a mystery play, in the verse at the beginning of this section the author indicates that the Galatians were privy to a play or ceremony of some sort because it was a *portrayal* of a crucifixion and a death not an actual event.

There are also some major problems in the passion story itself, least of all is the sign placed on the cross above Jesus' head. Here are the primary problems:

1. A night trial was illegal in both Judea and the Roman Empire.

2. The basis for the charge of blasphemy against Jesus was unclear. This was necessary in order to prosecute according to Judean law.

3. The witnesses against Jesus did not agree and accordingly a mis-trial must be declared.

4. The Sanhedrin did not have the right to condemn anyone to death at this time.

---

86 There were some early Christian Gnostic sects who saw Jesus becoming Christ *upon* his death, not before.

5. A crucifixion would ***never*** have taken place at Passover.

6. Jesus' anticipation of his death as a covenant sacrifice is out of Greek mythology, not history.

7. If the disciples knew what was coming up, why did they fall asleep in the garden? This, as we have seen, is part of an ancient mystery play.

8. Pilate did not have a good reason to execute Jesus as "King of the Judeans."

9. Again, there was only ***one*** high priest. There were no high priest*s*.

10. There was no such thing as the high priest(s) joining in on the mocking of a prisoner while the prisoner is being punished.

11. There was no such custom in Judea as releasing a prisoner at Passover.

12. Prisoners condemned to crucifixion would carry the ***crossbar***, not the whole cross.

13. There was no such place as Golgotha at that time.

14. Jesus, or anyone else, would not be known as "Christ, the King of Israel." The Messiah concept was a completely different idea.

15. Crucifixion was used ***only*** for seditionists and insurrectionists, not for religious reasons or "blasphemy." Rome would ***never*** have approved of using crucifixion for punishment for local lawbreakers, only for those who were out to overthrow the Empire. Judean religious law was very specific as far as punishment for blasphemy. The punishment for blasphemy was stoning to death and the hanging of the body by the neck from a tree or impaling it on a stake.

Given the culture and the time period, many craved the teaching god, while the multitude still pursued the sacrificed god or messiah. A cult which combined both into one deity, while still retaining the cosmic Creator-god and adding the attractive appeal of the Mother-goddess, has a maximum chance of survival. Such a religion cannot be founded on a physical person; it must develop from personalized abstractions. The only real reason for believing that Jesus was a real person is the presumption that religious movements begin in this way. Whenever tradition tells of a founder of doctrines, or mysteries, a critical search actually finds mythological foundations. Mystery plays are nothing more than a reenactment of a mythical tale and only become a physical thing when the ignorant, at the urging of priests who obviously have a lot to lose if the people do not believe them, intermingle mythology with a small amount of history making it all seem to be an actual occurrence with actual people. The priests know that very, very few of the followers will ever consider to research and find out the truth. So, they have nothing to worry about.

The Historical Jesus and the Christian Movement

> *Think not that I am come to destroy the law, or the prophets: I am not come to destroy, but to fulfill.*

Matthew 5:17

For centuries researchers have been attempting to find the authentic Jesus in history. This has proven to be quite a difficult task. The major texts that everyone has had to go by are the Gospels and they recount no more than about *18 hours* of the life of an individual and even much of that can be disputed. Even many of the words which were attributed to Jesus are being contested by reliable and reputable scholars. So, what you have left is some highly unreliable material which may have been in bits and pieces for many decades until it was compiled much later. The compilations were then edited, changed, and otherwise modified with the originals being destroyed until you have an *extremely* watered-down series of unconnected and disunified texts. Consequently, you need to look at the writings of the historians and philosophers and other records of the times.

There are only *two* historical references to Jesus. One is in the writings of Flavius Josephus and is only *one* paragraph which is totally out of context, does not even mention anyone's name and is not even in Josephus' writing style. Hence, many scholars and historians feel that this paragraph was added *after* Josephus' death. The fact is that Josephus did mention John the Baptist but nowhere did he actually mention Jesus. Further, the first mention of this paragraph was by Eusebius about 324 CE. It's a very strong possibility that Eusebius himself was the author of this paragraph because Tertullian did a search of Josephus' works in the latter part of the 2nd and the beginning of the 3rd century and never mentioned this paragraph. In the 3rd century Origen alludes to a *version* of Josephus which *denied* Jesus' messiahship. Finally, in an old Russian edition of Josephus, apparently from the Middle Ages, Jesus was described as a "king who did not reign" and was said to have "a line in the middle of his head in the manner of the Nazoreans." Consequently, it appears that Josephus' work was being edited and changed probably from several decades after his death.

155

The only other writer to mention anything concerning Jesus was Tacitus about 112 CE. The only thing Tacitus mentioned was that the Christians were followers of a "Chrestus" who was put to death as a criminal by Pilate. The only problem is that it is known that this material *did not* exist *prior* to the 15th century for none of the early Christian fathers, including Eusebius, even mentioned or alluded to it even though they searched diligently for proof of Jesus' existence. Further, even if the statement was authentic, by 112 the idea that Jesus was put to death by Pilate would have been an accepted fact. Remember, all Paul said was that Jesus lived and died during Pilate's stint in Judea.

None of the writers and historians of the first few centuries of this era had a single word to say about a miracle worker in Judea named Jesus. These writers included: Plutarch, both Plinys (the elder and the younger), Juvenal, Epicletus, Celsus, Plotinus, Porphyry, Tacitus, Philo, Seneca, Justus of Tiberias, and Martial. Some did make note of the early Christians and all that they said was that they were followers of a fanatical superstition both corrupt and absurd. As mentioned before, Christianity was called blasphemous and atheistic by both Judean and Pagan alike for it invented its own god. In fact, the Emperor Julian stated, *"If God wished that none should be worshiped but himself, why do Christians adore this spurious son ascribed to him?"*

The reign of Pontius Pilate in Judea ended about 37 CE. His removal had **nothing** to do with the supposed crucifixion of a Jesus of "Nazareth," as tradition and Church history states, but to his intervention in the affairs of the people of Judea. Pilate's job was to oversee the affairs of the Empire, not to make decisions that would involve the Empire. Those decisions had to come from Rome.

Pilate, it seems was apparently an extremely cruel and stubborn man and despised being in Judea. He made mention in his writings how the place and its people stunk and how it was infested with flies and vermin. Somehow Pilate may have inadvertently aided the early Christians. For he and his wife were respected and revered enough by them to have feast days dedicated to them both. Even today several of the smaller rites of the Catholic Church still have a feast day for Pilate and his wife. On June 25th the Coptic Church (one of the oldest rites) of both Egypt and Ethiopia hold a holiday dedicated to Pilate and the Greek Orthodox Church has one dedicated to Claudia Procia, Pilate's wife. In one of the supposed Pauline Epistles the idea that Jesus died during Pilate's reign was promoted. Paul was familiar with several Judean traditions. One of these traditions spoke of the deaths of 800 Pharisees that died during the reign of Alexander Jannaeus (103-76 B.C.E.) and of Joshua ben-Pantera (also called ben-Sedata), a messianic pretender who lived about that same time and who was stoned to death and hung by his neck on a tree according to Judean law. Paul needed to make sure that *his* Jesus was not associated with any of these so he made him live and die during Pilate's reign. You will recall that the early Christians were called "followers of the hanged man" by that time. This is an obvious reference to ben-Pantera.

When the war between the Judeans and Romans began about 66 CE, Christianity went underground and emerged totally different around 80 CE. This latter form of Christianity was condemned by virtually *all* of the writers of their time.

Prior to this time, Christianity had mainly been a part of the Judean religion, a somewhat disruptive "Gnostic" form, but still a part of it. It was not until Christianity went out to the Gentiles that it had changed. It must be remembered that the Gentiles were all familiar with Pagan philosophies and mythologies and Jesus had to be equal or better than all of the other gods. Nothing was actually known of Jesus' true life: when he actually lived—*if* he ever lived; or what he taught. Hence, something had to be given to the Gentiles, the Pagans, to attract them to this new philosophy so that they would be willing followers of the new cult. So, Jesus was given a life replete with a miraculous birth, a period of teaching and teachings, a death, a resurrection, and an ascension back to godhead. All of these things, as you have seen, were part of the myths of the more ancient sun-gods of practically every culture.

Remember also that the Gnostics were the first to proselytize Christianity. Consequently, as the Gnostics began to convert the pagans the myths of the gods became mixed up with the teachings of Christianity and Jesus became god incarnate. It is entirely possible that the stories of the life of Jesus were invented in order to pass down the Christian teachings and it is equally likely that the

Gnostics were the ones who invented the life of Jesus. With the information you have seen so far, it is more than just a possibility.

If you look at the teachings of Jesus, you will notice that they are all in allegory and parable, the main teaching method of the Gnostics. Further, it must be remembered that Jesus (assuming his existence) was a Judean and according to Judean tradition (something totally forgotten by modern Christians) the mystical system from Egypt known as Merkovah or The Chariot (which later became a major part of Kabbalah) could only be taught through allegory, parable, and allusion—never directly.

Very early in Christianity there was a schism. This was the problem, as noted in the Epistles, between Peter and Paul. The argument was if Christianity should remain among the Judeans or go out into the Gentiles. Paul was adamant that it should be taught throughout the Roman Empire and had already begun doing so before the schism. Peter, on the other hand, felt that it was important to keep it Judean and to hold on to its *true* roots. This was in spite of the fact that it was making no headway in Judea. If it went out to the Gentiles it would have to be changed to fit the populace and the original message would be lost.[87]

Paul and his followers saw things differently. They saw Jesus more as a *Divine* messiah and something to be taught to the whole world. It was assumed that the Gentiles would be able to understand the true message of Jesus.[88]

The Judean Christians saw things differently. The Christ, the Messiah, was *not* Divine and his teachings and message would be misunderstood by the Gentiles. The Messiah was part of the Judean tradition and because of this all Christians would be subject to Judean Law. The Gentiles would not understand this nor would they accept many of the traditional Judean laws.

The differences between Peter and Paul were so great and heated that instructions were given by Paul that *his* words and no one else's were to be observed (Galatians 1:6-9). If you assume that both Peter and Paul existed, Paul is instructing the Christians to listen to no one but him, someone who *never* knew Jesus, and not the

---

87 Peter was right!

88 Boy, was he wrong!

words of someone who apparently did know him (Peter). It also states in the Epistles that Paul claims that the revealed word holds more validity than any received in person or written.

The early orthodox Christians were a fanatical group. They were a thorn in the side of both the Romans and the Judeans alike. The Judeans, in fact, called these early Christians "Edomites" and "idioti" for being such fanatical followers of a myth. The earliest Christians were very poor, lower class Judeans who gave up their religion, sold their birthright as far as the Judeans were concerned, in order to follow a myth. Consequently, Christianity was termed the "Kingdom of Edom" and the Christians were Edomites.

The term "idioti" means exactly as it appears: idiots or stupid persons. This term was applied to the Christians because they never considered the effects of their reactions. These early Christians blindly and stupidly followed and did what they were told without thinking (something several centuries later Constantine used to his advantage). Since the early Christians were from, literally, the dregs of the Empire any philosophy which gave them a feeling of superiority or power over others would be followed blindly.

The early orthodox Christians were out to over-throw any government in power. For their god was returning at any instant to take claim to all of the governments of the earth and enthrone the "kingdom of God." Hence, they felt that they were above the law and could do as they pleased. There was obviously no "Render to Caesar the things that are Caesar's and to God the things that are God's" in their philosophy, nor was there a "Do unto others as you would have them do unto you."

The fact is that these early Christians were so much trouble that the Emperor Claudius wrote to the Judeans of Alexandria and warned them not to become involved with any itinerant Judeans (remember that early Christianity was part of the Judean religion) from the province of Syria, of which Judea was a part, if they did not wish to be known as abettors of a group which threatens the Empire. In fact, in 50 CE Judeans and Christians rioted in Rome and Claudius had to expel them from the city.

Actually, the Roman government tolerated any cult as long as it did not practice or encourage sedition or weaken morality (remember the discussion of the Dionysian cult). The Pagans, it seems, were an extremely moral group of people. The immorality that you have been told about was the exception and not the rule. History verifies that Christian Rome was much *more* decadent and murderous than Pagan Rome.

The early Christians could not even get along with each other. Consequently, the statement by Tertullian, *"See how these Christians love one another,"* could not be taken literally.[89] We must remember that Tertullian himself was a Christian so his reporting would obviously be biased. What Tertullian was doing was stating what was a common joke of the time. The Christians had continually disagreed among themselves almost since before they went out into the Gentiles. First, it was the Paulist Christians against the Judean Christians, then it was the orthodox Christians against the Gnostic Christians, then it was the orthodox Christians against other orthodox Christians.[90] Historically, there were huge Christian riots in the 2nd, 3rd, and 4th centuries. In the 3rd and 4th century civil authorities had to be called in constantly to stop quarrels. In some places of the Empire there was a death penalty for celebrating Easter on the "wrong" day. Eusebius noted that several councils were convened in the 2nd and 3rd centuries to decide on a date for Easter.

The early Christians did not follow the astronomical movements of the stars, moon, or sun for their festivals. But due to the arguments councils had to decide when the festivals would occur. The date of Easter was finally settled on in the 4th century. No one knew when Jesus "rose from the dead" because no records were kept of such an "important" event. Not even tradition dictated the actual time of the "resurrection" nor did any of the early Church fathers state the time of this supposed occurrence. All that the Christians did was to believe blindly. Early Christian tradition did not place it around the Hebrew Passover. Church councils did that.

---

89 Unless he was talking about the Gnostics and not the orthodox. Due to his being an orthodox Christian, this is highly unlikely. Interestingly, this comment by Tertullian was made facitiously. He was commenting on the fact that the Christians would physically abuse and even murder another Christian who did not believe *exactly* the same way.

90 Not too different than today. There are almost *30,000 different sects* of Christianity in the United States alone and they all say that they are right and the other 29,999 are wrong.

The Church Councils

**Neither shall they say, Lo here! or, lo there! for, behold, the
kingdom of God is within you.**

Luke 17:21; Galatians 2:20

*Virtually everything that Christians profess to believe about
Jesus was decided upon by councils of the Catholic Church!* Very
little was brought in from tradition and literally **nothing** came from
historical data. The stories of the Gospels were written long after
the supposed events and no one knows who wrote them. It is sure
that the apostles (assuming their existence as well) had nothing to
do with them and, as you have seen, the Gospels were tampered
with, modified, and otherwise reconstructed for purposes decided
upon initially by the writers then later by the councils of the
Church. God had **nothing** to do with them.

As you have seen, early Christianity had no dogma. It's major
beliefs were that Jesus was born, like anyone else, he lived, he
taught, and he died — some say by crucifixion,[91] — and the resurrection[92] *of the body.* It was not until later that Origen began to
write that the early **symbols** of Christianity: heaven, hell, resurrection, and the second coming were to be taken literally.

The first major council of the Church was the Council of Nicea.
It was convened by the Emperor Constantine on May 20, 325. Its
purposes were fourfold: 1) To organize all of Christianity into one
philosophy for there were still many factions at that time; 2) To
heal the growing rift between the eastern and western Christians in
the early Christian Church; 3) To reorganize the Roman Empire for
it was beginning to break into different sections; and 4) To organ-

---

91   You will recall that Paul mentioned Christianity taught Christ *crucified* and
      that they *believed* Jesus rose from the dead, not that they *knew* it for a fact
      (see 1 Corinthians 15:14, 17).

92   Romans 1:4 states: "...by *the* (italics mine) resurrection from the dead:"
      Notice that it doesn't say "...by *his* resurrection from the dead:" This could
      refer to Jesus' resurrection or the idea of all righteous Christians being res-
      urrected from the dead at the end of times.

ize the books of the Scriptures into a basic canon. You will notice that from these purposes the Christian Church was a politico-religious institution. This is how it started and this is how it stayed.

Before the council had adjourned some three months later, on the 25th of August in 325, there were many heated discussions. Many of them dealt with "articles of faith": what the "true" pious Christian *must* believe. For, since Christianity was fractionated so were its beliefs. By creating a dogma Christianity could be given a single direction and purpose and, as Constantine well knew, its fanatic adherents could be manipulated easily.

For the council, Constantine brought in 2048 bishops from all over the Empire. An attendee, Sabinis of Heracles, described them as, *"...a set of illiterate, simple creatures who understood nothing."* One of the main philosophical problems encountered was that of who to worship. It was not known whether the worship should be of a god like the Hindu Krishna or the Druidic Hesus, or both under the united title of Hesus Krishna. With the voting came the startling results that 1730 bishops opposed the union and 318 were for it. Being that the union was Constantine's brainstorm the army was brought in and those opposing the union were forcibly removed. So, the name Jesus Christ became the one to be used in the chosen books of the Christian Scriptures. Before this time Jesus and Christ were usually separated for there were many different Christs. Recall that Christ was nothing more than a title. Hence, Jesus was invariably referred to as "the Christ." The early Christians were followers of a particular philosophy called Christianity more so than of a particular man. In fact, Eusebius called the Essenes Christians. Remember that early Christian fathers had searched all of the historical material available to them to find any evidence of Jesus' existence and found *nothing.*[93]

In the earliest Christianity there was no such thing as a man being nailed to and dying on a cross. One of the main reasons for this was that the Christians were hard-pressed to prove that Jesus *was* crucified. This and his resurrection, were to be taken on faith

---

93 The information concerning the proceedings of the Council of Nicea was validated by a letter from Sabinus, Bishop of Heracles to a friend of his.

alone, as it is today. Depicted on the cross, at that time, was a lamb This lamb represented the slain god or savior. The lamb represents Aries, the first sign of the Zodiac as well as the season of Spring when *life* is resurrected from its winter death. It is also a fact that the lamb was one of the representative symbols for the sun-god. In Egypt it was Ra or Horus, in Greece it was Dionysus, and virtually every culture had their lamb/sun-god representation. The title given to the sun-gods was the "lamb of God." This title was also given to the Essene Teacher of Righteousness.

The crucified lamb was used to represent the Christ until 692. Then at the 5th Council of Constantinople (the "Quinisext Synod") a man was placed on the cross and the lamb removed. This was a signal that the end of the Pagan mystical traditions, Gnosticism, and the Mystery Religions was at hand. Gnosticism was nearly obliterated by this time through the burning of tens of thousands of volumes of work. John Chrysostom in the 5th century wrote of some of these burnings. It is known that even into the 13th and 14th centuries the works of Hebrew mystics were confiscated and destroyed. Nothing should be left to stand in opposition to the "Prince of Peace."

Some of the other declarations of the other Church councils were:

1. ***The Council of Elvira (315)***
   The laying-on-of-hands would suffice for salvation of non-believers.

2. ***The Council of Nicea (325)***
   a) The Trinity concept was inducted into Christianity as a primary teaching. Prior to this time the Trinity was considered a Pagan concept by most Christians.

   b) Jesus was declared to be a god, and not a mortal prophet. As a god he could be associated with Sol Invictus, Constantine's sun-god and Mithra. It was also stated that Jesus, as the Son of God, is "begotten, not made" and "of the same substance as the Father."

   It was at this council that Christianity got its official god. This god, though had to go through official channels with senate approval and the approval of the Emperor being the final say.

3. ***The Council of Antioch (341)***
Christ's kingdom shall have no end.

4. ***The First Council of Constantinople (381)***
   a) The Holy Spirit is a distinct individual within the Trinity and part of the Godhead and was to be worshiped along with the Father and Son.

   b) The Son is begotten of the Father and the Holy Spirit proceeds from the Father.

   c) The laying-on-of-hands would suffice for the salvation of non-believers.

   d) Jesus was fully Divine.

5. ***The Council of Hippo (393)***
The first ratification of the books used in the Christian Scriptures.

6. ***The Council of Carthage (397)***
The second ratification of the books used in the Christian Scriptures.

7. ***The Council of Ephesis (431 and 433)***
   a) Jesus was declared to be both God and man; having two distinct natures united within a single person.

   b) Mary was the "Mother of God."
   Before this time the early Church considered the Egyptian goddess Isis the mother of god. St. Augustine, unlike what Church tradition states, actually dedicated himself to Isis, not Mary.

8. ***The Council of Chalcedon (451)***
   a) Jesus was *perfect* God and *perfect* man, of one substance with the Father in his Godhead and with us in his manhood.

    b)   Jesus was made known in *two* natures without confusion, change, division, or separation.

    c)   The difference between the two natures is in no sense abolished by the union.

    d)   The properties of each nature were preserved intact, and both came together to form one person and one existence.

    e)   Jesus constituted a distinct and operative reality or "nature" after the incarnation of the Word.

9.   **The Second Council of Constantinople (553)**
Emphasized the centrality of Jesus' Divine nature.

10.   **The Third Council of Constantinople (563)**
Allowed the use of images to worship a transcendent god. This was condemned in 726 and 754 and reestablished in 787 and 842.

11.   **The Fifth Council of Constantinople (692)**

    a)   The lamb was taken from the cross and a crucified man was to be placed on it. This action took the Pagan origins of Christianity away.

    b)   Jesus was definitely crucified and made the sin offering.

With just a little more research it can easily be found that virtually everything all Christians believe about Jesus is a product of the councils of the Church. There is, of course, tradition but this tradition has essentially no facts to support it. In other words, The Catholic Church created Christianity, so whatever they say about it is correct!

Constantine

Be not deceived; God is not mocked: for whatsoever a man soweth that shall he reap. For he that soweth to his flesh shall of the flesh reap corruption; but he that soweth to the Spirit shall of the Spirit reap life everlasting.

Galatians 6:7-8

Christians revere Constantine as the Emperor who made Christianity the "official" religion of the Roman Empire. So honored is he that the Church declared him to be a "saint."[94] Constantine is pictured as a "pious and holy emperor" who was a Pagan and "saw the light" prior to a major battle thus becoming a Christian and worshipping the "true God." He is seen as a Divinely inspired ruler whose one objective was to promote love, Christianity, and Jesus. He is seen as a noble representative of the highest ideals and power of Christianity. But is this true?

Probably the man most responsible for the spread of Christianity throughout the Roman Empire was the Emperor Constantine. But what the Church says about him and his reasons for the spreading of Christianity and what actually occurred are *very* different things.

The Church had Constantine declared a saint. The fact is that the Roman Empire had *rarely* experienced a more blood-thirsty, violent, self-serving emperor than Constantine. They show a painting of Constantine being baptized on his deathbed with a "holy light" shining about him and the dove of the Holy Spirit over his head. This partially is true. Constantine was baptized on his deathbed. This was after years of countless *murders* of people in order to hold on to his throne. The following is a small list of his victims and the years of their murder:

---

94 His mother, Catherine who, for no other reason than she supposedly found the "true" cross, was likewise made a saint.

Maximian, his wife's father in 310
Bassianus, his sister's husband in 314
Licinius, his *11-year old* nephew in 319
Fausta, his wife in 320
Sopater, his *former friend* in 321
Licinius, his sister's 2nd husband in 325
Crispus, his own son in 326

Constantine had several reasons for his tolerance of Christianity and *none* of them had anything to do with his finding the "true way." The first reason is that there was over *5-million* Christians in the Empire at the time. That was a full one-fourth of the whole population of the Empire. Hence, that is a large political block that he could use and manipulate to his advantage. Remember, these fanatic Christians will do whatever they were told by their bishops. The fact is that Jesus was unimportant to Constantine. What was important was the political advantage that the 5-million Christians afforded him. Faith, to Constantine, was a matter of politics.

Second, the Christian priests told him that upon baptism he could be forgiven for *all* of his sins by Jesus. It seems that the Pagan priests told him that he was responsible for his deeds and would have to make up for them in the next life or through reincarnating back here into this life. Consequently, he figured that all he would have to do is to kill off anyone who stood in his way and be baptized on his deathbed and he would be sure that he would go to heaven when he died.

The fact of the matter is, Constantine *never* totally embraced Christianity. The vision that the Church claimed Constantine saw of Jesus and the chi and rho ☧ (See Christian Symbols #10, pg. 225) was that of the sun-god of a mystery religion named "Sol Invictus"[95] of which he was an initiated member *and,* continued to be, a high priest. Constantine *never* stopped sacrificing to Sol Invictus throughout his life. Consequently, the victory he suppos-

---

95 Mithra was himself called the "unconquered sun" or Sol Invictus. Constantine belonged to the Sol Invictus and probably the Mythrian mystery religions all his life.

edly had in the name of Jesus was actually under Sol Invictus. Constantine saw Christianity simply as another sun-worshipping cult and Jesus was the earthly manifestation of Sol Invictus.

We have been told that Constantine made Christianity the "official" religion of the Roman Empire. This is definitely *not* true. Christianity was just given the right to practice openly for sun-worshipping was *still* the state religion of Rome. Constantine's Edict of Milan (313) granted the Christians toleration but not any more toleration than the Emperor Gallienus (c. 260) granted them. The Edict of Milan was a purely political move. The fact is that Constantine had obviously felt some guilt about his murderous life for he gave toleration to any religion which could afford him and the Empire Divine favor and restricted those which did not. He figured it would be wise not to anger anyone's god.

Constantine also had a rather unique way of converting people to Christianity. His methods were simple: he would either pay them, give them political favors, or threaten them with physical harm or death. Consequently, the more people he could have on his side the greater would be his political advantage in the Empire.

Constantine further saw the need for a single head of the Church. This was when *he* declared the Bishop of Rome to be the "Vicar of Christ." In other words, Constantine initiated the Papacy! Prior to that time the Bishop of Rome was just one of more than 2800 bishops throughout the Empire. Any lineage back to Peter and Jesus cannot be verified. The statement in the Christian Scriptures (Matthew 16:18) that Peter was "the rock" upon which Jesus would build his church is a later addition by the Church to make the Papacy seem to be an ancient tradition.[96] You will also remember that there was no mention of a "church" until *after* the beginning of the 2nd century so the addition had to have come at that time. Since Constantine also controlled the rewriting of the Scriptures, the chances are that this was added during Constantine's time.

If anyone declared to be a saint deserves to be disenfranchised,

---

96   The Pope officially assumed the title of "Pontifex Maximus," which was a title of the Roman Emperor, in 378 CE when Demasus, the Bishop of Rome was elected Pope. The title "pope" was given to the Phyrigian god Attis.

it is Constantine. The only reason that he is given such credence by the Church is for his efforts at forcing Christianity upon everyone in the Empire. He even went so far as to force the Pagans to pay for Christian churches. In fact, he even gave the Christians Pagan temples for their use and took state money out for their refurbishing. It is quite obvious that Constantine knew the value of the 5-million Christians in the Empire and he played to them in order to keep his advantage. Recall that Christians were, and still are, fanatical followers who could easily be manipulated for another's profit.

Other Facts

And ye shall know the truth, and the truth shall make you free.

John 8:32

1. Constantine had commissioned and financed the writing of *new* copies of the Christian Scriptures all to his satisfaction. All of the original books of the Scriptures that he could find were destroyed. The 1st century originals were most likely written in Hebrew and Aramaic and all that is found is Greek and these date from much later. In 1516 Erasmus of Basel, Spain sloppily assembled the texts of the Christian Scriptures from poor manuscripts and used little or no critical care. From 1633 onward these were the accepted texts by both Protestants *and* Catholics. Any corrections were forbidden. Later, King James I of England (c. 1603) emulating Constantine gathered 47 "scholars" together to translate the whole Bible into English. What he did was a revision of the Bishop's Bible which was a revision of the Great Bible, which was based on the Matthew, Coverdale and Tyndale Bibles. All of which are later English translations of the translations of Erasmus of Basel's translations. With every chapter the "scholar" would come to King James and *the king* would either approve or disapprove the translation and James would make the appropriate changes. The editor of the completed text was Francis Bacon.

2. There are *no* complete books of the Christian Scriptures found that are *older* than the 4th century. This is known to be true because in 303 Diocletian took to destroying *all* Christian writings he could find and in 331 Constantine did his rewriting of the Scriptures and the hasty destruction of the available texts. Hence, with these new versions of the writings the orthodox writers were free to revise, edit, rewrite, add, remove, and otherwise change the material as they saw fit. Prior to the 4th century there were about 5000 different manuscripts of Christian Scriptures. So, the Christian

Scriptures with which you are familiar are a product of the 4th century Catholic Church. The completed texts, though, are only about 500 years old.

3. In the Dead Sea Scrolls (authenticated to have been written between 200 BCE and 80 CE) are many ideas and teachings found in the Gospels and Epistles. In fact, there are almost 200 direct quotations and parallels in the initially published scrolls. There were over 200 scrolls found but until recently only about 20-percent have been translated and published. At the present time in the newest translations of the formerly unpublished scrolls are statements which put the Gospel stories into a new light. It appears that the writers of the scrolls were the forerunners of the orthodox Christians and that the Gospel stories, which may have come from the scrolls, were written to incite the overthrow of the controlling government. It shows the writers as a militant, violent, aggressive group who were readying themselves for an apocalyptic war against evil.

    As was pointed out by John Allegro (Dead Sea Scrolls); *"The Dead Sea Scrolls give added ground for believing that many incidents (in the Christian Scriptures) are merely projections into Jesus' own history of what is <u>expected</u> of the Messiah."* Also, there are books older than the Christian Scriptures that cast significant and even controversial light on the accepted accounts of Jesus' life (i.e. the Gnostic and Apocrypha texts).

4. The Jesus of the Christian Scriptures, according to tradition, was an Essene. But the Essenes were a breakaway group from the Sadducees and many of the teachings attributed to Jesus were not Sadducee but Pharisee. The Essenes were a well-known group of Judean ascetics who were performers of "miracles," magicians, and healers. They were apparently known to the Greeks and Egyptians as Therapeutae. They considered themselves as the carriers of the true Judean religious tradition and supposed by some as the carriers of the Kabbalah mystical system. In fact, in the most recent transla-

tions of the Dead Sea Scrolls is mystical material similar to that in the Kabbalah. But the Sadducees did not believe in a mystical tradition. This may be another of the many reasons that the Essenes broke from the Sadducees. The Sadducees were literalists in Biblical interpretation. It was the Pharisees who believed in a mystical tradition. Hence, it was they who would have carried the Kabbalah. Tracing the handing down of Kabbalah through tradition we see that: Abraham gave it to Isaac (in Biblical terms, the word "beget" refers to the passing on of the teaching), who gave it to (beget) Jacob, and so forth until it was "lost" for a period of time during the "Egyptian Captivity." Then it was given to Moses on Mt. Sinai, who gave it to Joshua, who gave it to Judges, who gave it to the Sanhedrin, who gave it to the Tonain, who gave it to the Pharisees. It is an interesting note that the Pharisaic branch of the Judean religion and the Essenes developed at about the same time and this is why it is believed that the Essenes developed into the Phariasiac tradition. But we must remember that tradition and history rarely, if ever, coincide.

5. In early Christianity Jesus **did not** die by crucifixion. It was Paul that promoted this idea. It was known that a century before the assumed birth of Jesus, a well-known magician and exorcist name Joshua ben-P'rahia, an Essene, lived. His name was invoked in Judean rites of exorcism up into the 6th century CE. He had a disciple named Jesus (real name, Jacob) of "Nazareth," or rather, the Nazorean or Nazarite[97] who was called "the heretic." His surname was ben-Pantera. This was during the time of Alexander Jannaeus (103-76 B.C.E.). He was stoned and hung according to the Mosaic law dealing with heretics.[98] Paul was familiar with this tradi-

---

97 A Nazarite is an ascetic. The term literally means, "one with a mission."

98 The Mosaic law stated that a heretic was to be stoned to death and his body hung by the neck on a tree or impaled on a stake outside of the city. With the body hung in this manner, it was believed that the soul would wonder indefinitely on the earth and not enter Paradise.

tion. It was also known that Jannaeus crucified 800 Pharisees (referred to as "righteous men") and that this left a powerful impression on the Judean world. The early Christians were called "the followers of the hanged man" by the Judean religion. Further, if Jesus was either of these two men, then Paul may have also belonged to an earlier period.

6.   The most famous teacher and magician of the 1st century was Apollonius of Tyana. He studied philosophy and mystical arts in Greece, Egypt, India, Tibet, and Babylon. These are many of the same places where some believe that Jesus studied— and he studied at the same time that Jesus was supposed to have studied. There is also some evidence that it was Apollonius who may have brought back what later became the Gospels from India and translated them into his native tongue—Aramaic. Unfortunately, Constantine and the Church saw to it that the more than 60 volumes of work that Apollonius wrote was completely destroyed.

7.   There is *no* evidence of a town, city, village, or even an area named Nazareth in Judea or Galilee during the first couple of centuries of this era. If it did exist it was probably nothing more than a few houses. If it was a few houses, the name would indicate the occupants, not the name of an area. The first historical evidence of the place was in a letter that Constantine wrote to one of his generals in Palestine probably officially founding it, and this was just a brief mention. The first Judean mention is that of a 6th century poem. We must remember that by the time of Constantine the Christian pilgrims had established a place that eventually became Nazareth. Further, there was also *no* barren hillside outside of Jerusalem named Golgotha until it was decided upon as to where it was. Remember that John (who claimed to have been an eye witness) said that near to where Jesus was crucified was a garden. The name of the garden was Gen Nassaret, which was a holding of the Hasmonean kings of Judea. The word Nazareth comes from the Hebrew root which means a

"crown or diadem" or "to be consecrated." It refers to having knowledge of the Torah.

8. According to Indian legends, even though the Buddha and Krishna were princes, they were born in a stable while shepherds kept watch. Their births were heralded by heavenly voices and song. Also, as soon as the local king found out about the birth, he had ordered his soldiers to kill every male child under the age of 12. This legend was well-known around the 1st century as Indian Buddhists were the first to proselytize their religion.

9. Mithra, the Persian sun-god, was also born in a stable while shepherds kept watch. Traditionally, Mithra's place of birth was Bethlehem. His birth was likewise heralded by heavenly voices and he was visited by three Magi (Persian priests and magicians). He was also condemned to die by a man similar to the Pilate of the story. He was scourged and ridiculed the same way and finally crucified between two criminals. Mithra, too, rose from the dead.

10. Mithra was born on December 25th of a virgin birth. *All* of the sun-gods of *every culture* of mankind were born of a virgin on or about the winter solstice.

11. Many of the ancient sun-gods had the ram, lamb, or horned animal as their main symbol. The main symbol for the Holy Spirit, an idea which is not even Christian, has often been the white dove. In the Judean tradition, ruach ha-qadesh (the holy spirit), is a state of consciousness, *not* a white dove, or flame of fire from above, or a part of a triune godhead.

12. The title "Christos" was one of the titles given to the Greek god Dionysus, as well as Bacchus, the horned-god of wine and vegetation. This title was sometimes given to the Greek god Pan, who turned up later to be the model for the Christian devil. This title was also given to the Essene Teacher of Righteousness.

13. According to ancient Hebrew tradition, a star appears in the east with the birth of a prophet. A star in the east heralded the birth of Confucius 500 years earlier, and Buddha before that, and almost every one of the mythical sun-gods. Further, the Star of Bethlehem was a local name for a Middle Eastern flower.

14. Crucifixions were used by the Romans and Roman appointees *only*. Crucifixion was reserved *only* for those who were convicted of sedition and insurrection and *never* under Judean law for any reason whatsoever (See #5). The Mosaic Law was quite specific as to what is to be done to a heretic. The Judeans considered crucifixion barbaric. Records of those executed in this manner were well-kept by the Romans and each governor was required to keep these records. There is *no* record of a man by the name of Jesus (Joshua or Yashu) of Nazareth being crucified during the time of Pilate in the manner described in the Scriptures. Pilate's records had been searched long ago and found to be conspicuously lacking this information. In fact, in the writings of Iranaeus (c. 180) he stated that: *"The Lord did not die on the cross and that those who claim that he did do him a great disservice: they rob him from the honor of teaching in his old age."* It must be remembered that even the early Christian fathers had only heresay to go by. There are several sources which claim that the crucifixion was a fraud: the Gnostics Basilides and Mani, The Koran, and the Acts of Thomas each state that Simon of Cyrene was crucified as a substitute. In Matthew 27:32 and Luke 23:26 it is said that Simon of Cyrene carried the cross to the crucifixion. Basilides claimed Simon let himself be crucified. According to an ancient tradition, a substitute could take the place of the condemned person. Carrying the cross implied being the substitute for the condemned. Also, according to Roman law after one is condemned to crucifixion there is a 40 day waiting period to allow anyone to come forward to present evidence that the person should not be crucified. There was no such thing as being condemned and crucified the same day. Also, according to Roman law a person or their body could be redeemed with enough money. Recall, Joseph of Aramathea with Pilate.

15. From its earliest inception, orthodox Christianity has had a reputation for violence and intolerance. This still holds true 2000 years later.

16. The Stations of the Cross, as practiced by the Catholic Church during the Lenten season, came from the Elysian Mysteries of the Stations of the Sufferings of Demeter who searched the underworld for her daughter, Persephone. In fact, much of the Catholic Church's ritual is Egyptian and Greek in origin.

17. There were at least four Christs worshiped by the early Christians. The major ones were: Jesus, Serapis,[99] Seth,[100] Hibil, a savior-god, and even Simon Magus were all considered Christs. The Seth worship seemed to die out rather early but the Serapis worship proper continued on into the 4th century when it was obliterated by the Council of Nicea. Serapis, though, became the image that the Christians have of Jesus so Christians are essentially *still* worshipping Serapis but they do not know it. In the Koran and the Gnostic texts, Jesus is described as short in stature with bowed legs and one eyebrow connecting over a large hook nose. It is said that God wanted him this way so people will be attracted to his teachings, not to his appearance. The appearance we have today is just the opposite, almost WASPish: the image of Serapis.

18. The early Christians were well-known forgers and falsifiers of documents. The Catholic Encyclopedia states, "In all these departments forgery and interpolation as well as ignorance wrought all manner of mischief on a grand scale." Pope Stephen III went so far as to write a letter and sign St. Peter's name to it. In fact, down into the 15th century forgery contin-

---

99 This is verified by a letter from the emperor Hadrian to Serranius in 134 and in the Gnostic texts.

100 Also found in the Gnostic texts.

ued. An excellent example is that of verses 9 through 20 in the last chapter of the Gospel of Mark. These verses did not exist in the canon prior to that time. They did, though, exist in one of the Gnostic writings.[101]

19. The Jesus worshiped by Christianity apparently developed out of the Essene Teacher of Righteousness, whose name was never mentioned. Christianity seemed to develop from the Essene philosophy and the Christian system of government virtually mimicked the Essene government. This is verified by the writings of Epiphanus and Eusebius both early Christian fathers, *the Dead Sea Scrolls* and was later collaborated by St. Augustine.

20. The Silvanus mentioned in the Epistles of Peter and Thessalonians most likely is the same Silvanus mentioned in the Nag Hammadi Texts. He was apparently a very esteemed person or he would not have had texts attributed to him. Since nothing else is mentioned of him in the Epistles he may well have become, or had been, a Gnostic.

21. The Essenes called themselves the "New Covenant" or the "New Testament," the "Sons of Light," the "Elect," the "Poor," and the "Saints." To the Judeans of the time the term

---

101 The Shroud of Turin is a well-known Medieval forgery. Even though the cloth has been found to not be older than the 10th or 11th century (by carbon dating and recent statements by the Church). There are still people who want to believe otherwise. Some have gone so far as to say that the carbon dating was purposely mishandled or that the fire which scorched parts of it confounded the dating thus giving the wrong date. Several things that these "believers" do not take into account is that the coins on the eyes are *Roman coins,* not Judean or Judean Temple coins or that the image is over six feet tall and his arms are way out of proportion to the body. Any faithful member of the Judean religion, especially an Essene, would make sure that he went into the next life with the correct coins. Also, it is assumed that ancient history was not known around the time of the creation of the Shroud. If some knowledge of ancient history didn't exist, how could the Church forge so many documents that appeared valid? With all of this, when the Shroud first appeared the Church did state that it was a fraud but they kept it because it was (and still is) an "article of faith."

New Covenant meant a reiteration of the *Old* Covenant in the hearts of God's people.[102] The word saint meant nothing more than a believer.

22. The Essenes used the term Christ as a general title to denote the united offices of Priest-Messiah and King-Messiah in one individual. This was their last Teacher of Righteousness who supposedly was put to death, probably through crucifixion, about 68 BCE by the Roman Government for sedition under the rulership of Hyrcanus II.

23. The belief that God the father as the Son suffered and died on a cross was considered *heresy* by the early orthodox Christians. This doctrine was known as Patripassionism and its chief proponents were Noetus and Praxeas, Gnostics who taught about 200 CE.

24. Those who think that Jesus studied eastern mystical practices are completely unaware that the eastern mystical practices were *outlawed* by the Judean religion around 200 BCE and *no* member of the Judean religion would ever consider studying them—especially an Essene! The Essenes, you will recall, considered themselves the "true dispensation" of the Law. That is what we would refer to as a *true* Jew today. You will remember that Jesus stated that he had "...come to fulfill the law, not destroy it." Further, the Gnostics were the first Christians to proselytize. They had, in fact, gone as far as India, China, and Tibet. Their influence was even seen in the Bhagavad Gita, which did not get compiled until the 6th century CE. Consequently, any of the stories of a "St. Issu" from the west most obviously are restatements of tales that they recounted in their proselytizing.

25. The fundamentalist hatred for the Catholic Church is quite well known. But they *totally* and without question accept the

---

102   See Jeremiah 32:31-35; Ezekiel 11:19-20.

Catholic Church's **version** of the history of Christianity as well as **all** of the Christian beliefs all of which came from councils of the Catholic Church. They also teach basic medieval Catholic Christianity, and without question accept the Catholic Church council's dictates, doctrines, and dogma as being true Christian teachings. As was previously mentioned, if one would take the time to search the history of the proceedings of the Church councils it will be found that all of the beliefs of Christianity came from these councils, not from fact, and very little from tradition.

26. John 3:16 states that Jesus was the **only** Son of God while in Exodus 4:22 **God** states that Israel (Jacob) is his Son. The Greek word John uses is monogenes and this is mistranslated as "only begotten." It actually means "one of a kind" or "unique son." The term "Son of God" meant nothing more than someone who had a special relationship with God: (i.e. a prophet). This was the title of many of the kings of the time. Kings were not Divine nor were they the actual "sons of God."

27. Matthew 13:39; Mark 4:11, 15:9; Luke 24:25; Galatians 4:22-26, 29 all give instructions against a literal interpretation of the Scriptures.

28. Josephus reported that a hoax was perpetrated during the reign of Pilate. Someone professing to be a deliverer (Messiah) rallied crowds around himself preaching his own philosophy and promising to reveal where the treasure from the First Temple was hidden. In the Copper Scroll from the Dead Sea Scrolls is directions to a hidden treasure. It is believed that this scroll may have been part of that hoax.

29. The Persians used the name Jesus to allude to the sun and, hence, allude to the sun-god or Mithra. The Judeans used the name Jesus to allude to the Messiah. It was **not** the name of the Messiah. In India the name **Issu** was a name used to allude to the sun (see #24).

30. If you translate the name Jesus Christ into its actual meaning of anointed savior or anointed redeemer and place that in the Christian Scripture instead of the name of Jesus, this sheds a whole different light on the Scriptures. They begin to sound more like the Essene documents of the Teacher of Righteousness. The Gospel stories then become more of an idea of how the messiah would act, not of the "life" of the messiah.

31. The following is a list of the slain and risen gods/saviors from around the world:

Crucified and Risen	Slain and Risen
Jesus - Israel	Hercules - Greece
Krishna - India	Adonis - Greece
Sakia - India	Sahazios - Phrygia
Perusia - India	Zagreus - Crete
Iva - Nepal	Dionysus - Greece
Indra - Tibet	Osiris - Egypt
Mithra - Persia	Apollo - Greece
Tammuz - Babylon	Iacchus - Greece
Criti - Chaldea	Bacchus - Greece
Attis - Phrygia	Serapis - Greco-Egyptian
Baili - Orissa	Cora - Greek goddess
Thules - Egypt	Inanna - Sumerian goddess
Witoba - Telingonese	Bel - Babylon
Odin - Scandinavia	Alcestis - Pherae
Hesus - Drudic	Quirinius - Roman
Quetzolcoatl - Mayan/Aztec	
Prometheus - Greece	
Orpheus – Greece	

32. Concerning the mythological correspondences in the Christian Scriptures, Gerald Massey found 137 similarities

between Jesus and the Egyptian god Horus and literally hundreds between Christ and the Hindu Krishna. There are many strong correspondences between the lives and teachings of Buddha[103] and Jesus as well as those of Jesus and the Persian sun-god, Mithra.[104]

33. Around 180 CE Irenaeus stated that there were actually hundreds of gospels. What exists are only Four Gospels and some other writings. The Nag Hammadi texts, most of which date from the 2nd and 3rd centuries CE, contain no less than 45 different Epistles and Gospels. As you have seen, Irenaeus was the first to compile a set of Scriptures for the orthodox Christians and it was not until the 4th century CE that this compilation was approved. By the 4th century CE it was noted that there were around 5000 Gospels.

34. *All* of the mentions and references to the cross in the Christian Scriptures come from the Greek word stauros meaning a pole or a cross. The term actually refers to the process of self-denial. The term translated as crucify is actually the Greek term stauroo which means to impale. Besides crucifixion the Romans would also impale those who were seditionists. The term stauros actually refers to the subduing or extinguishing of passions or selfishness.[105]

---

103 Tradition says that Jesus was the son of a poor carpenter but in 2 Corinthians 8:9 it states that Jesus was born rich but became poor. This follows the life of the Buddha for the Buddha was born a prince but gave it all up for a life of contemplation.

104 They all were born of a virgin, died and rose from the dead, performed miracles, had followers, and promised to return again.

105 See Matthew 26:2; 27:22, 23, 26, 35, 38, 44; Mark 15:15, 24, 25; 16:6; Luke 23:23, 38; 24:7, 20; John 19:16, 18, 20, 23, 41; Acts 2:28, 36; 1 Corinthians 1:13, 23; 2:2, 8; 2 Corinthians 13:4; 3:1; 5:24; 6:14; Revelations 11:8.

35. The early Christian hierarchy was divided into seven posi-
tions. These were: the Apostles, the Prophets, the Evangelists
or Teachers, the Pastors or Miracle Workers, the Healers, the
Helpers or Deacons, and the Elders or Bishops. This was
exactly the same set-up that the Essenes had. The Mithraic
Mysteries had seven levels of initiation as well. They were:
Crow, Nymphus, Soldier, Lion, Persian, Heliodromus or Sun-
runner, and Father. Seven levels of initiation were a part of
just about every mystery religion.

36. In the Mediterranean world there was an ancient festival
called *Adonia.* This festival was held in honor of the death of
the god Adonis.[106] It was held mainly in Greece, Rome, and
Phoenicia. This occurred right after the harvest. The celebra-
tion of the resurrection and ascension of Adonis into the
heavens occurred later in the year.

37. In Luke 24:51, the verse states that Jesus was "...carried up
into heaven." Christians take this to mean that Jesus' physical
body was taken up into the skies. The Greek term for heaven
here is ouranos which means elevation/the sky, heaven as the
abode of God. The implication of the term is happiness,
power, eternity, air, heaven or heavenly, and sky. If any of
these words are substituted for the word heaven in this verse
another possible meaning emerges. That is, that Jesus *died!* If
Jesus had not died on the cross but was drugged in order to
appear to be dead, as some writers feel, and he was attended
to by Essene doctors during the three days in the tomb, he
could have easily died later of the wounds he received during
the crucifixion (i.e. loss of blood, shock, etc.). His resurrection would have literally been *"in spirit."*

---

106 The name Adonis, you will recall, means "Lord" and is the root for the
appellation for Yahweh, Adonai. It comes into the Hebrew from the
Phoenician term *adoni,* which likewise means "lord."

38. There were two methods that the Romans used for crucifixion. The fast method was to *tie* the individual to the cross so that he was supported by his feet on a small stand. Then after a period of time the legs would be broken and the individual would suffocate because he could not support his weight. The slow method was to nail the person to the cross. In this method he would be placed on a small seat with both of his feet being nailed through the ankles. This method was designed to have the person suffer. It usually took several days to a week to die using this method. There were records of people who did survive being nailed to a cross. They were then referred to as being "raised from the dead." This meant that the person had cheated death.

39. In the ancient Judean religion, the Holy Spirit was a state of consciousness, not part of the Godhead or of a Trinity or something like a bird that would come down and settle on your head. It was a state prior to that of Prophecy. In essence, there were three states of consciousness: chiah or animal life; ruach ha-qadesh or the Holy Spirit; and navi or Prophecy. There was no white dove or tongues of fire appearing over the head of the individual when in the state of ruach ha-qadesh.

40. The upper echelon of the Essene organization consisted of three priests or elders and twelve laymen who assisted. The Christian Scriptures continually refer to Jesus, the Father, and the Holy Spirit and the twelve apostles.

41. In the Gospels, Jesus is referred to several times with the title "rabbi." During that time, that title was given to the Pharisees, not to just any teacher. The Pharisees were those who taught in the synagogues, the priests and High Priest were Sadducees who controlled the Temple in Jerusalem.

42. The idea of a "kingdom of God" had nothing to do with a place in the skies. It would be the time when the "wrath of

God", dispensed through the armies led by the Messiah, would free Israel from oppression ultimately ushering in a period of peace and bliss where Yahweh's theocracy would rule the earth and all evil would be banished. The Messiah ordained by Yahweh, according to the tradition, would be a military leader and definitely *not* be Divine. This is seen in the most recent translations of the Dead Sea Scrolls.

43. A common belief in the Middle East was that at some unspecified time in the past the savior-god had lived and died and rose from the dead. The whole process was a nature rite related to the death and rebirth in nature. After many centuries the mythology was believed as reality and the god actually did exist. That is, ritual persists long after the original purpose of it has been forgotten. Quite often the myths became attached to a real person (e.g. Gilgamesh) and the rituals supposedly explained his life experiences.

AFTERWORD

[For in the beginning] God created man. [But now men] create God. That is the way it is in the world—men make gods and worship their creation. It would be fitting for the gods to worship men.

The Gospel of Philip
71:34-35; 72:1-4
Nag Hammadi Texts

As you have seen, there are only *two* things that make The Bible the "Word of God:" 1) tradition, which is essentially someone told someone who told someone else, who told someone else and so on and everyone buying into it; and 2) The Bible itself says that it is the "Word of God."[1] Both of these are hardly reliable sources. Tradition is based on mythology, legends, and possibly a smattering of historical data. It is what people would *like* to believe happened and not what actually did happen. Further, the stories in the original Bible were initially transmitted by word of mouth for centuries. When they were written down it was long after any of the supposed events were assumed to have transpired. It is true that archeologists are finding objects which seem to verify some of what the Hebrew Scriptures describe. In the last months of the 20th

---

1   Albert Ellis, Ph.D., the developer of Rational-Emotive Behavior Therapy, in his pamphlet **The Case Against Religiosity** states: *"...religiosity is, on almost every conceivable count, opposed to the normal goals of mental health. Instead, it encourages masochism, other-directedness, social withdrawal, intolerance, refusal to accept ambiguity and uncertainty, unscientific thinking, needless inhibition, lack of self-acceptance, and reluctance to acknowledge and deal with reality."*

century and the beginning months of the 21st century articles have appeared in *U.S. News and World Report*, *The Chronicle of Higher Education*, *Reader's Digest* and other magazines detailing some of the recent findings in the Middle East. The difference between interpretations of the findings by academic archeologists and "Biblical" archeologists is easily seen. The Biblical archeologists immediately interpret the findings as "proving" the Bible. The academic archeologists interpret the findings historically and wait to see what else is found. The Bible does describe objects which were familiar to a culture and which essentially have not changed in centuries and archeologists have found some things which collaborate some of those descriptions. An excellent example of archeologists wanting to prove the actuality of the Bible is the James ossuary; the bone box which the Biblical archeologists immediately claimed to be the box that held the bones of Jesus' brother James. This turned out to be a major fraud.

It does not matter what findings may be uncovered it does not mean that the events occurred *as described* and it especially ***does not*** mean that there was Divine intervention in any of the events. What the writers of The Bible did was simply place known events into a context that the people understood using their own cultural heroes and involving their god in order to give an appearance of Divine intervention. All mythologies are done in the same manner. After all, the gods of all of the other cultures and religions intervened with the lives of their believers why not this one as well?

The earliest religious beliefs of humankind were set up in order to attempt to explain the elements of nature that early humans could not understand. What causes the rain and lightning? How is it that the sun can replenish and destroy? Why does one person die young when another lives on? Since plants die and are reborn, does this happen to us? Everything seems to be here for a reason. Do humans have a reason to be? Questions like these can cause people who have no access to scientific knowledge and information to assume that nature has a mysterious ***Divine*** source and direction; that the sun, the moon, the wind, the storm, and so on must be the focal points of this source. So, they must be ***gods***. Since they are gods and since gods can heal and destroy they must be placated, worshiped, and adored (more appropriately, satiated) so that they will smile down and grant favors. Therefore, if a sacrifice is accepted by the gods there is prosperity. With no acceptance, there is war, famine, pestilence, and disease and more sacrifices need to be performed until the gods become satisfied. The most common of the ultimate sacrifices to appease the gods was human sacrifice. "Surely," was the constant reasoning, "(the) god(s) will be more pleased with this immense (human) sacrifice than with any other." Historically, the peoples of Judea/Israel were one of the *last* to give up human sacrifice. You can find many references to human sacrifice throughout the Hebrew Scriptures. The whole basis of the Christian Scriptures is that of the use of human sacrifice. If you are to use the reasoning for the use of sacrifice with the sacrifice of God's own "son" you will find that God must *not* have been pleased with it. For when a god is pleased with a sacrifice there is prosperity, happiness, and peace. In the past two thousand years this has not been the case. There have been more wars (the bloodiest being based on that sacrifice), more intolerance of others, and less cooperation than in all previous millennia, to say nothing about evil being still alive and well.

Both tradition and religious beliefs are based on superstitious behavior. Psychologically, superstitious behavior occurs when someone *assumes* that a specific preceding event caused a particular subsequent occurrence. The idea of walking under a ladder being the cause of bad luck is an example. If someone walks under a ladder and several hours later or even days later has an accident, the attribution of the accident is to the act of walking under the ladder, not with a lack of personal responsibility or to not paying attention to what he was doing. Religious superstition goes something like this: Someone prays to a deity and whatever he is praying for happens. It is then *assumed* that the deity permitted that thing to occur or had granted it. Hence, a series of beliefs become built up by a group around that deity in the form of a tradition. After some years other things are *assumed* to occur in spite of the fact that the focus, effect of, and the concept of the deity has changed. In the face of all of these assumed occurrences, what is not considered is that there have been a *myriad* of prayers that were *never* answered. Specific powers still become attributed to that deity.

These powers are related to the believers in the form of stories, dogma, and tradition. The stories are called myths and it is these myths which are passed down either orally or written. Either way, there are always changes made with each individual telling or writing the stories because the stories are based on the period of time that the stories were being told and the effect that the teller of tales wants from the followers. These stories are, in essence, made to fit the group, its time, and its particular problems. Consequently, you can see that tradition is hardly a reliable source for factual information.

Religions are replete with superstitions. The idea of gods and goddesses, demigods, angels and demons all to try to explain the elements of nature and the reason that people become ill or die, or well after being ill, or why people make the choices that they do, or why some people are "blessed" by good fortune, and so on, all indicating a belief in something **outside** of the individual being the cause. Western religions continually promote the idea that human beings are at the mercy, so to speak, of the whims of the gods. Even though religious tradition says humans have free will the dogma promotes a rather different idea. Even our sciences reflect the religious ideas. Classical physics is based on an idea that the universe moves along and everything in it simply follows. In contrast, Quantum physics sees the perceiver as the controller of the direction of the universe.

Take a look at how the concept of God has changed. In the beginning in the book of Genesis God is spoken of as a creator. Then, as the text goes on, that same god becomes a destroyer. It is this same destroyer-god that brings both good and evil (e.g. if you do not do what you are told it is *you* who becomes the destroyed). Later on that same God becomes the benevolent father and the evil is brought about by another deity (Satan). It is also interesting how even that concept of Satan changes from one similar to that of the Egyptian god Set (the accuser of the righteous in the underworld) to the enemy of the benevolent Father-God and of humanity. All of these ideas are based on superstitious thinking, not on reality.

If tradition is not a very reliable source for factual information, the book which was written on that tradition is just as unreliable. It is, as you have seen, a well-known fact that The Bible has had words, phrases, stories, and even whole books changed, deleted, and manipulated in spite of the directive that it invalidates the book by doing so. Consequently, to assume that The Bible, *as we have it*, is factual or exactly the same as the original just because The Bible itself says so, is ludicrous. This is like saying that the film, *"Plan Nine from Outer Space"* is the truth on the basis of the statement made at the end of the film by Criswell[2]: "Who is to say that this didn't happen?" The fact of the matter is that The Bible was written *by men* for their own particular purposes and reasons and these men were *hardly* inspired by any deity. Their reasons were mainly political and manipulative. They had no desire to become disenfranchised as priests if the people turned toward the gods of their neighbors or conquerors or toward other priests or other religions. Consequently, The Bible was written *by priests* with a specific purpose in mind and there was *no* Divine involvement in its writing at all, just as there was no Divine involvement in the myths of any other cultures of the world. Even if there was Divine involvement in the original texts of The Bible, they have been translated and rewritten, and retranslated and rewritten, and retranslated and rewritten so many times that the original Divine intent (assuming there ever was one) has been long-lost completely. Besides, it is quite obvious that there has *never* been any Divine inspiration in any of the translations, retranslations, and rewritings of the more than *two hundred fifty different versions* of The Bible...or in those doing the translations or rewritings.

The teachings of The Bible are quite simple. They are summed up very nicely in a story about Rabbi Hillel (c. 30 BCE):

---

2   Criswell was a popular prognosticator who had a program on television in the 1950s called *Criswell Predicts*. In it he would make predictions, many of which seemed ridiculous at the time, but eventually came to happen. His prediction rate was *higher* than the celebrated *psychics*.

The rabbi was confronted by a student who thought that he could trick him. The student said to the rabbi that if he could recite the whole of the Torah while standing on one foot he would study hard and become a scholar.

The rabbi took hold of one foot and said: *"Whatever you find hateful to yourself, do not do to your fellow-man. That is the whole of the Torah: the rest is all commentary. Now, go and study."*

All of the teachings of The Bible, and any other Scriptures for that matter, can be summed up in this simple injunction: love God and love your neighbor (Deuteronomy 7:5; Leviticus 19:18; Matthew 7:12; Matthew 22:37, 39; Mark 12:30-31). This is completely forgotten, especially by fundamentalist Christians. To them the law is: *"Impose yourself on everyone. Use any means possible to instill confusion* (1 Corinthians 14:33 states that God does not author confusion) *in order to induce fear* (2 Timothy 1:7 states that God has not given the spirit of fear), *ignorance* (1 Corinthians 1:17-18 states that Christianity is for the ignorant), *and superstition. Don't allow anyone to think, reason, and understand.[3] Blind faith* (which is not faith at all) *and adherence to dogma and the manipulated word as well as the control of the masses and their wallets is most important."*

There are many today who have set themselves up as "God's Official Interpreter" of The Bible. They quote verses *out of context* (even though nowhere in the Bible does it say that the "true believers" are to memorize verses and quote them out of context), read things into the verses which are not there, never were there nor were intended to be there, and talk down *at* people making them feel stupid and ignorant for not seeing things which are not there while building up their own already over-inflated egos to an

---

3   This is interesting for you are to love God with your whole mind. If you cannot think, reason, and understand you cannot completely love God with your whole mind. Without having the freedom to search you cannot be transformed by renewing your mind if you cannot think to renew it. (Romans 12:2)

unholy degree. The belief of the writers of The Bible states: ***"He who translates a verse literally is a liar; he who adds to it is a blasphemer."***[4] Unfortunately, not even today's Jews have anything even approximating an actual original copy of their Scriptures. Further, no one knows what changes were put in by some rather zealous scribe as he was copying.

The Bible, as we know it, is *less* that two-thousand years old. The canon itself was decided upon *by men* in a rather arbitrary fashion. The complete Hebrew Scriptures are only about 1600 years old. The Christian Scriptures, depending on the version, can be from 1600 to 500 years.

The Bible has also been looked at as an historical reference source. As you have already seen, it cannot be relied upon for much accurate history. Many of the times are inaccurate, and many of the people cannot be proven to have existed and most of the events never occurred. What Biblical archeologists do is find some*thing* in one of the digs which was described in some text in The Bible. They then assume that since it was described in a particular book of The Bible, in a certain chapter and in this verse that everything and everyone discussed existed and certain events occurred. It is unfortunate that so much history is placed in the time line of The Bible when the reverse should be done. Remember, the history that is there was *not* written at the time it was going on but handed down orally until it was written some centuries later. Then, when it was written down, it included those teachings and restated myths and folk tales and heroes of the time in order to promote a particular view point.

The Bible has helped historians to get information on some of the Middle Eastern cultures of 2000 to 3000 years ago. It has also shown some of the religious practices of the time and area and it has assisted in separating some of the many different cultures living during the period of around 1000 to 400 BCE. It is *not* a history book nor was it designed to be one. It is, though, a book of *rewritten mythology*. It is filled with mythological tales from the

---

4   See Deuteronomy 4:2 and Revelations 22:19. If not one word is to be changed or it invalidates the whole book, then translations, which change *every* word are the ultimate invalidation.

ancient Semitic Middle East, Egypt, Persia, and Greece. Other mythological counterparts are too numerous to have been simply coincidence. These tales are, in many instances, word-for-word but with names changed to suit the Judeans/Israelites of the times. Hence, The Bible is a cultural mythology of a specific Semitic peoples. These peoples were constantly being conquered by other more powerful empires. So, they were continually looking for someone to save them from the fate that had befallen them (apparently some groups thought that Yahweh was not doing too well even though it states that Yahweh *is* the savior). Finally, at one point some of them fabricated a physical savior, a messiah who would take care of their enemies and bring them into the forefront of **world domination**. Consequently, several different traditions developed around that idea. That is why there are *several* messiahs described in the Judean tradition.

According to the Messianic beliefs, the Messiah is to usher in a period of peace and love among *all* humankind. In the past two-thousand years Christianity has brought anything but peace. It's main fruits have been hatred instead of respect, intolerance instead of understanding, bigotry instead of acceptance, ignorance instead of wisdom, bondage instead of freedom, and fear and superstition instead of peace of mind. It can easily be seen with Jesus' own teachings that he talked of discord in families, wars, and the murder of his enemies (Matthew 10:34-35; Luke 12:39-43; 19:27, etc.). There are more than thirty verses reputedly spoken by Jesus denoting violence and intolerance. How can Jesus be a man/god of love and peace and still speak of violence? How can one who professes love of his neighbor and forgiveness make any statements of intolerance and brutality? Either the words were put into his mouth or he was **not** the Messiah. If the words were put into his mouth then there is actually no *true* record of anything that he said.

It is a fact that the Epistles were written before the Gospels. It is also a fact that in the Epistles, Jesus is **never** quoted. Paul (or rather, the writer) is the ultimate authority. All that is mentioned about Jesus' life is that he was born according to the flesh. It is implied that he lived a rather obscure life and that he rose to prominence during Pilate's stint in Judea. Then he died during that same period, and rose again *in spirit.* Otherwise, nothing else is said. You will notice that none of the Epistles mentions any of the Gospels in any way at all. This is a direct indication that the Epistles were written earlier than the Gospels and that the writers of the Epistles had no knowledge of the Gospels (which is the current view), or that the Gospels do not give an accurate account of Jesus' life...or both. Remember also that the Gospels describe no more than about *18 hours* of a person's life. If you took the best 18 hours of anyone's life it wouldn't be too far fetched to attribute Divine inspiration to that person. The fact of the matter is that there may have been someone who had gained a following at some particular time during or around that era. Members of his following became insistent that this person *was* some sort of Messiah and began teaching this idea. This is a very strong possibility because at the turn of the current era (c. 100 BCE to c. 150 CE) messiahs by the score were preaching and gathering followers in Judea/Israel. There is no reliable historical evidence of a teacher/healer named Jesus (Joshua) around 30 CE. Historians, philosophers, and rabbis of the time knew of no one who fit the Biblical description.

There is the book of Q from the Galilee area. It is assumed that the oral tradition of Q came from around 20 to 30 CE, possibly earlier. The sayings listed in the book of Q were from a Cynic-like teacher—who in all probability was *not* Judean but of *Greek* descent (Paul?). No one knows for sure.

If you look at Judean history to try to find Jesus you have several possibilities. First is Joshua ben-Pantera (called "Jesus of Nazareth"or the Nazirite) a.k.a. Joshua ben-Sedata and his teacher Joshua (Jacob) ben-P'rahia who lived around 100 BCE. Later there was an unnamed individual who lived around the time of Pilate who claimed to know where the treasure from the 1st Temple was buried. Remember there was *no* rabbi, writer, or historian who was a contemporary at Jesus' time having any idea who this Jesus was or any recollection of his existence. If he did exist at the time specified, he had to have led an extremely insignificant life. If he did exist at all the Gospel stories have *nothing* to do with him or his life for they came about *decades* after his assumed death. Later the followers used these stories as a means of conveying the teachings and points of wisdom that this unknown teacher expressed. Later on, the stories got mixed up with some of the messianic tales (most likely the Essene Teacher of Righteousness and one or more of the Joshua [Jesus] groups of the time) and they became the actions that a deific messiah would do and the points of wisdom he would teach. The vast majority of the sayings attributed to Jesus in the Gospels are from other writings: Judean wisdom literature, Pagan and Greek philosophical teachings, and moralistic beliefs of the time. Hence, no one knows what Jesus taught, who he was, or *if* he was.

It must be remembered that the teachings of the Christ called Jesus were in parable (Matthew 13:34) and in secret (Matthew 10:27; Mark 4:11; John 16:12; 1 Corinthians 2:6). We must also not forget that (as Galatians 4:22-26 states) the two testaments are allegorical. They are not to be taken literally. Hence, it becomes a personal and individual search to find meaning in your own life. This does not mean that what you found has any meaning for anyone else. It may. Just not to the degree that it has meaning for you. It is *not* the *complete truth*. Truth, like the whole universe, is constantly changing and is only relative. No organization, book, or individual can tell you how to find what you feel you are searching for. It is an inner journey. Looking to the outside only attaches you to the objects of the sense world and to things on the outside: churches, teachers, philosophies, and dogmas.

It is true that the existence of God cannot be proven beyond any doubt. Many believers use some of the physicists comments about God to mean that physicists believe in the existence of a God. This is not entirely true. When a physicist talks about God he is referring to what he does not understand—at the time. God, to most physicists, is like the x in algebra. It is not some being somewhere in the æther who watches over this little speck of dust in the galaxy or even watches over the whole universe. Most scientists tend to be more agnostic in their beliefs about God. They are not saying either way.

Since God cannot be proven beyond any doubt, it is in this area of doubt where faith and belief are placed. If you *have to believe* and *have faith* in the existence of God then you really do not know. This makes you agnostic. But, what is faith? Many people equate belief and faith together as essentially the same thing. This is not so. Belief is something other than faith. Faith can be defined as confidence that something will happen or that it exists. A better definition of faith is the ***acceptance of expectation***. This means that you are simply *assuming* that what is imagined to occur or to exist actually does. From this assumption expectations about the imagined concept are formed. Consequently, you would simply accept the expectations as reality.

As you have probably guessed, this is nothing more than superstitious behavior. Due to the transitory nature of both belief and faith religions have created "articles of faith" and placed them in front of believers in order to promote continued allegiance. These articles of faith include anything from bones, slivers of wood, well-fed, cared for and constantly handled snakes which bite rarely or other "sacred" animals, meteorites, "unexplainable" pieces of art work, unverifiable stories, the very few prayers which were answered (while the innumerable ones which were not are relegated to, "God in his infinite wisdom knows what's good for us" or that one of God's greatest blessings is unanswered prayer), and so on. Belief and faith are transitory because if something is not done to close the mind in order to maintain the belief and faith they will eventually fade. A good example is the fact that in ancient Palestine the Judeans and Israelites were constantly turning to the gods of their neighbors because Yahweh did not reveal himself in deed. The gods of their neighbors obviously were stronger by leading and protecting the conquering armies and so on. Yahweh, you will recall, was not even represented by a single statue (that archeologists have been able to find thus far)! The other gods were. These representations made it easier to assume an empowerment to the deity: that is, the statues were articles of faith!

Beliefs are generalizations that are taken to be all-pervasive. They are inferred from some, usually, singular aspect of the environment. Consequently, since there is an assumption from experience, you will operate ***as if*** the beliefs are universally factual. This makes beliefs idealizations of experience. An example of a generalization is the statement, "I can't do *anything* right." Whenever you make this statement you are usually referring to some particular thing. Unfortunately, since it is such a general statement it ends up enveloping your whole life.

Beliefs are based on *opinions* and *convictions*. Beliefs most often are *not* based on facts. If a belief is based on any facts the facts are usually incomplete, misconstrued, and/or misinterpreted. The truth of something is not in whether you are convinced of its possibility but in its *actual and provable existence* in reality. In other words, beliefs are taken on faith (expectation) *alone.* They cannot be substantiated by direct proof. Once a belief system is formed, in order to support that belief system, you tend to delete everything to the contrary. Look at the statement in the previous paragraph ("I can't do *anything* right"). Once you have made that statement anything that you have successfully done is forgotten.

Beliefs are sets of expectations about how things should be or how things should operate. In other words, when you hold on to a belief you see *only* what you want or *expect* to see or to happen thus preventing what *can* happen or *can* become from actually occurring.

Faith is the acceptance of an expectation. If things do not happen according to your belief you react in some way that will reinforce that belief. After all, you would surely hate to find out that something that you have made a part of your life, something with which you have identified yourself so strongly, is not true. So, you will insure its reality by refusing to deal with facts. What you will end up doing is arguing intensely for your unsubstantiated beliefs.

The main component of belief is *faith.* Faith, likewise, is not based on proof but, as you have seen, on expectation. This expectation is based on what you are told while you simply assume that what you are told is true—or even truthful. This expectancy comes from the assumption that what you have been told is factual and that the individual imparting the information is knowledgeable, honest, truthful, and aware.

Beliefs and objective reality are not the same things. Beliefs are essentially what you would like to see—not what is. Beliefs are nothing more than *opinions* acted upon *as if they are real*. Alfred

Korzybski, the founder of General Semantics, put it this way: *"People build beliefs when they do not know what's real."* So, beliefs are built upon unexplored *assumptions* and the *assumptions* are used for evidence for the beliefs. There is a difference between assuming something to be and knowing that it is. Consequently, a separation between the two would create in you frustration, anger, and an acting-out toward those who do not hold the same beliefs—or even an acting out toward those who hold the same beliefs, but in a different way.

There is a major distinction between belief and knowledge: a belief assumes that something exists or occurs and knowledge is actual proof that it does. You do not believe that the sun will "rise" in the morning. This is a statement of fact as long as the Earth continues to turn on its axis. You may believe that there is such a thing as an "Ethereal Tube,"[5] for example, because it is only an assumption. It cannot be proven. You can believe that the color blue inspires you. Knowledge of the color blue, on the other hand, places it in the electromagnetic spectrum at a specific frequency and so forth. Consequently, knowledge is very different from belief. The atom and its construction was only a theory (based on mathematical models) until it was seen by researchers.

The argument always proceeds: "Just because *you* don't believe in it, doesn't mean that it doesn't exist." The true test of a belief is if it can be made an object of the senses. This would prove the efficacy of the belief and the actuality of its being. That is, once the belief becomes reality, it is then knowledge. Argumentation and philosophical dissertations have been proposed and promoted concerning beliefs of all sorts but have not proven anything. The problem is that the tools being used, words, are meta-symbols: that is, symbols of symbols. The beliefs are symbols and the tools of the arguments, the words, are also symbols. Consequently, the use of symbols to explain symbols is ludicrous. This is no different than using a word to define itself (e.g. happiness means that you're happy). It just does not prove anything except that one arguer is more effective than the other with the use of his/her particular set

---

5   This is another "New Age" buzz-word.

of symbols. The problem with argumentation is that as soon as a statement of argumentation is made it is *assumed* to be factual. Hence, the argument for or against the existence of God automatically *assumes* that a God exists. If you are arguing against, then as the old adage in war goes: "The attacker must totally destroy; the defender need only overcome." This is why anecdotal "evidence" generally does better than actual facts in many philosophical arguments. Anecdotal "evidence" most generally has emotions attached to it. Emotional arguments tend to attract more supporters than factual arguments. This, unfortunately, is the rule rather than the exception.

Conversely, just because you may professes a belief in something does not mean that it exists. The existence or non-existence of something is not found through belief and argumentation but through direct testing; proofs and personal and physical experience with the object of the belief. An example are hallucinations. Hallucinations are seen only by the hallucinator. This does not make them a complete object of the senses available to the experience of others. Even if the proofs are convincing it is still not to be taken without question for *"The truths of one era are found to be the myths of the next."* Hence, there is a relativity to belief, truth, and knowledge. Beliefs are relative to the individual. Knowledge, even though it is relative to the time, the culture and to the experience can usually be progressed into future times without having to go through much change.

It is interesting to note that many ancient philosophers and mystics felt that all that is perceived is illusion or "maya." They felt that the human perceptual apparatuses could easily be deceived, so, they did not rely on their senses unquestionably. Hence, the belief that what is being experienced with the senses as well as the experience of the senses themselves as being absolute reality is untenable.

Knowledge does not require belief. Knowledge refers to something which can be supported by and experienced as an actual object of the senses. It is based on your verifiable experience of the physical reality. It is not based on what you would *like* to exist but on what *actually* exists. It is something that cannot be disputed. If something's existence or processes cannot be directly measured then its existence or its processes are taken on faith and not on fact.

This same approach can be seen in the difference between actual scientific study and those that disguise themselves as a science looking for respectability.[6] A science is any ***study*** and ***experimental system*** based upon that study which seeks to understand some aspect of nature or natural processes. It is founded upon ***direct observation*** of nature or natural processes and it initially builds hypotheses and theories established upon these observations. After the hypotheses and theories are set up experiments are performed in order to find out how well the hypotheses and theories hold up. From this point, the theories will be brought together into a coherent system that can be proposed in an attempt to illustrate that aspect of nature or the natural process observed. One of the marks of a true science is that it is ***amenable to change***. That is, a science can propose a theory that, at the time of its proposal, is correct. Later, after more experimentation and measurement new information may be found that may prove it to be incorrect or incomplete. Science will then change its theories to accommodate new data. In this context it means that knowledge and science are amenable to change. As Einstein put it so well, ***"Science is conditional truth."***

To sum up, direct knowledge of the existence of God is impossible because God, by definition, is beyond comprehension and cannot be defined.[7] No book, person, or organization can tell you what to do, what to look for and what to see, or even what to feel in order to get in touch with what is undefinable. Hundreds of millions of people blindly follow some book, person, or organization that claims to know what cannot be known. They also want to force others to follow these same convictions. They do not want to be bothered with the facts. They do not want to know the truth.

---

6   This includes the pseudo-sciences such as phrenology, many of the "alternative sciences," and "creation science." One commonality that all of these ideas have is their stubborn refusal to accommodate any sort of change as well as the fact that there is literally ***no*** experimentation done on their theories.

7   Buckminster Fuller said, ***"God is a verb, not a noun."*** This goes along with the ancient teachings that God is always becoming and never is...until humans stake their claims on ***it***.

No human being can possibly know everything. This is true because knowledge is constantly changing. The whole of nature, including the human brain, is changing as well. With change being the only true constant throughout all of nature as well as the rest of the whole universe and since God *is* considered omnipresent, then God like all of nature is constantly changing. If all nature is constantly changing and God is changing then it is impossible to even have the slightest knowledge of God because God is constantly changing. Since you cannot possibly know God because God is constantly changing can God even know itself? Since knowledge is constantly changing God cannot possibly know itself because what is changing can only experience and know change. So, the only thing that God can actually know is change. Now, this is interesting because, in essence, that is all that human beings can know as well. In order for God to know itself God must stop changing and *become something* instead of being in a constant state of *becoming*. Since God is constant change and knowledge is constantly changing as well, change is all that exists. If God is change then all that God knows is change, not constancy. It is the human mind that knows constancy only because the human brain *creates* that constancy in order to make human existence seem more stable. Hence, it may be that God, assuming there is a God as *we humans* have defined it, needs entities that are capable of knowing constancy and that may be why sentient beings evolved and continue to evolve. In order to begin to understand the Unknown you need to understand change. To oppose this by following *one* point of view is in opposition to nature: in essence it is in opposition to God! This opposition creates the ego: the "I am" and constancy. Remember that God does not exist above and outside of nature but is *all* nature and all things visible and invisible (i.e. energy). What God has created, God is. It is man that creates religions and religious philosophies and attributes them to God.[8] It is the person(s) who developed the religion and its philosophy who claim Divine Guidance, Special Knowledge and Revelation.

---

8   To paraphrase Richard Bandler, co-founder of Neuro-Linguistic Programming who paraphrased Carl Jung: ***"When one person says he talks to God and sees angels and demons, they lock him up. When a whole group of people make the same claim, it's called a religion."***

Once you acquire a belief you tend to hold on to that belief in spite of factual information and proofs to the contrary. Hence, beliefs are structured in such a way that opposing viewpoints are ignored and even disregarded. This makes them and their proponents unresponsive to information and to change.

Beliefs are associated with particular states of consciousness. They are characterized by an intense focus of attention[9] which would limit your experience and responsibility. In essence, you would be "hypnotized" or "entranced" by the belief. While in the belief state you could be manipulated, controlled, and otherwise directed by anyone who was adept at producing and controlling the particular state.

Beliefs perform the function of being a filtration system for experience. That is, they limit your ability to perceive, analyze and thus respond appropriately to your environment. They set up predispositions or assumptions which are difficult to get around. Consequently, they tend to determine what you pay attention to and how you model and experience your world. In essence, what you believe limits the sort of information that you get and the responses and distinctions you make as you are reacting to your world.

Your value system is tied to your beliefs, and your judgments of "right" and "wrong" are based on this value system. It is these values that you bring into your interaction with your environment and with others. As soon as you decide what is right or wrong, good or bad you have made a judgement about it. You must remember, these judgements are based on what *you have* decided is or is not appropriate in any given situation. It does not matter what your decision is. It is tied to your beliefs about its inherent worth, benefit, or outcome and importance to you.

Beliefs tend to be built-up when you don't know the facts. Beliefs are not based on what you know about a particular thing. They tend to be based only upon your ***opinion*** of it and opinions

---

9   Carl Jung called this intense focus of attention a ***complex***. Once one has a complex that person's behavior and experience revolves about the complex. A complex is essentially a concept with a series of behaviors supporting it.

and beliefs do not need to be supported by facts. They are only a brief abstract of the experience and not the experience itself. Your support or opposition to a belief is based upon how well that belief seems to hold up in *your* experience. Since beliefs are trance states they will tend to be relied upon strongly when induced thus actively deleting opposing and contrary information. The value of holding on to a belief is based on two things. First, are the ***consequences*** of having or not having the belief. Second is the self-identification assumed and afforded by the acceptance of the belief. People will die and kill to preserve their beliefs even though no truth exists to those beliefs. One of the main reasons for holding on to the beliefs is that of personal identification. With western religion, fear is the great inducer of belief. Fear will lead you to accept a belief without question. With the assumption of the belief you will identify yourself with it and assume that there will be positive gains received from having the belief and punishments from not having or rejecting it. Beliefs invariably have emotions attached to them thus causing you to make identifications with them ("I am..."). In effect, you ***are*** the belief. It is not something that you have chosen to accept. Identification of the self with the belief likewise does not automatically make it factual. It is this identification of the self with the belief that causes a person to strike-out in some way. Giving up the belief, in essence, means giving up part of yourself. The belief makes you somebody and gives you a reason to be. Without it you are nothing. So, holding on to the belief becomes an absolute necessity.

Beliefs are acquired the same way as any other habit. This includes the conditioning processes especially imitation and modeling, reward and punishment, and superstitious behavior. They are, as you have seen, generalizations. Generalizations help you to make some sense out of the world and to give the world some sort of stability. So, beliefs help to make the world a bit more predictable. This predictability produces expectations. It is these expectations that you mistake for the actualization of your beliefs. These expectations are based on faith, not reality. The predictability producing expectations is based not on what exists but upon what you ***expect*** or ***want to have*** or feel ***should*** happen. Consequently, beliefs, expectations and faith are the products of immense biases causing you to make incorrect interpretations and decisions concerning your environment.

After beliefs have been internalized they operate unconsciously. Beliefs are filters and cause the omission, the misrepresentation and the misinterpretation of information. You do not realize that you have acquired the beliefs nor do you realize that you are acting upon them. Hence, whenever you have acquired beliefs they tend to govern your behavior unconsciously, the same as any emotional and trance state. It is in the motivational aspect of beliefs where you have problems. Since you will be acting in a certain way, perceiving in a certain way, and thinking in a certain way you will not be open to other possibilities. So, you will not explore any of your potential because of erroneously perceiving your experience. Your whole existence will be based on a highly biased and limited experience both internally and externally. Beliefs are self-fulfilling prophecies because of their biases. In them you have little or no way to experience anything outside of the opinions holding your beliefs in place.

The driving and motivating force for the placebo effect is belief. A placebo is an inactive substance or process which has no natural value itself and that produces a change physically and/or psychologically. It is due to the ***belief*** or ***expectation*** of the individual that causes the improvement in some condition. A placebo can be *any* revitalizing strategy (or element of any remedial strategy) which is given or performed intentionally to have an effect, or unknowingly has an effect on an individual's physical body or life. The placebo effect is the outcome of the use of a placebo. It may be done with or without the conscious knowledge that the procedure is a placebo. It may be an ***active placebo*** (non-inert), or an ***non-active placebo*** (inert) substance or *approach.* This would include all medical strategies no matter how specific, prayers, affirmations, meditations, visual imageries, and psychotherapeutic procedures. Even though they act at a presently unknown mechanism, it does not make their effects any less specific. Placebos also include non-specific factors such as the elements of a therapist's or doctor's method which are secondary to his theories about a treatment but which have therapeutic value. The therapeutic situation itself can also produce effects. These are called *nocebo effects*. These are changes due to non-specific factors of the therapy which are negative rather than positive. So, even the *approach* of giving therapy can be part of the reaction to a placebo. Consequently, the actual incidence of change occurring outside of scientific knowledge and understanding is extremely low – less than chance occurrence.

The *setting* in which the placebos are dispensed is important in regulating their effects. The most important aspect in the use of the placebo is how the particular circumstances influence the beliefs and expectations concerning the outcome. The apparent success of healing methods, is based on all sorts of convictions (e.g. your *beliefs*, *faith,* and *expectations*). The methods used bring about the conclusion that *the power of faith resides in the individual's state of mind (a state of expectancy) and not in the significance of the object, person, strategy, or concept incorporated in the process*.

The placebo's effect in physical healing is not confined to simple ailments, or to illnesses attacking a single organ system, or only to pain, as has been their general use. Placebos have been seen to affect the cardiovascular system, heart disorders, cancer, rheumatoid and degenerative arthritis, gastrointestinal disorders, migraine headaches, allergies, radiation sickness, hay fever and coughs, acne, multiple sclerosis, diabetes, organic brain disorders, psychiatric syndromes, psychomotor abilities, and psychophysical processes such as reaction time, grip strength, pulse rate, blood pressure, short-term rote memory, and self-perception of relaxation and activation. Just as psychological components can weaken or amplify physiological outcomes of an active drug with some psychological effects patients can notice with a placebo they may be able to activate a stronger psychological response and govern a more formidable healing resistance. The pattern of responses to a given placebo can parallel the pattern of responses to active drugs given for the same purposes. The carry-over effects (side effects) of placebos, among other properties, *mimic* those of active drugs. Placebos can produce toxic reactions the same as undesirable side effects of other drugs. What this all means is that *in virtually every instance of change attributed to God it is the individual's own belief system (personal convictions) in action.* Prayer, meditation, affirmation, visual imagery and so on are all techniques which activate the belief system. The individual then assumes it is God answering prayer. Whether God is seen inside or outside doesn't matter. It is actually the individual himself answering his own prayer.

No religion that has ever been devised by human beings has ever really worked for the benefit of humanity. If it did there would be no need for police forces, governments, armed forces, laws, and so on. If what Christianity is teaching is true by nature, human beings would have an innate predilection to that philosophy. It would be readily acceptable by any and all human beings and would be a natural way of life easily gleaned from the laws of nature. But this is not the case. Historically, Christianity, this philosophy of peace (?), was forced upon individuals through manipulation of the mind and/or threats of physical, emotional, and/or eternal harm. Nowhere in the world will you find that the Christian philosophy was accepted without some sort of struggle from the people of the culture.[10] Hence, Christianity, especially fundamentalist Christianity, is based not on any natural way of existence but on contrived, misunderstood statements supposedly attributed to an individual or individuals who presumably had some sort of connection with an Unknowable deity.[11]

Two-thousand years ago it was stated that God created man but that men create gods and worship what they create. Humans *do* create their gods – their religions – and make-up the laws that their gods supposedly rule by. We claim that our creations can take *all* of humanity back to the Source from which we came and that it is only through this practice or that practice where this is achieved. It is interesting to look into the history of the religions that we have

---

10   Throughout the world Christianity had been *forced* on the culture with threats of death. A perfect example is what was done by the Spanish in Mexico and Central and South America. It was simply, convert or die. Also look at the fact that the slaves in the U.S. had Christianity forced upon them at the end of a whip and the butt of a rifle.

11   How can anyone write about or discuss something that they do not and cannot possibly know or understand?

created to find if it has really enlightened **anyone** who has followed its tenets and dogma. What you will consistently find is that in order to become enlightened or to achieve the internal peace and freedom that man-made religions profess to bring, it is necessary to go **outside** religions and their dogma. The religious philosophy which is conspicuously absent of any enlightened persons is evangelical Christianity.[12] In the two-thousand years of Christianity itself there is an absence of truly evolved persons. There are a few well-known philosophers, writers, and "saints" but very few highly evolved individuals. This should be an indicator of its potential. What Christianity has shown is not personal evolution at all but mental and psychological control, manipulation, and restriction. It has constantly promoted ignorance, intolerance, fear, greed, hatred, bigotry, murder, and all sorts of other social and personal vices that it purports to be against. Belief in this "Prince of Peace" has caused the bloodiest wars that mankind has ever known. First, they were among the Christians themselves with constant riots, to the Inquisition which included a war against other European Christians (Catholics against the Protestants and Cathar and Alberginian Gnostics then Protestants against Catholics and other Protestants), to the Crusades which was war against Islam (another branch of Christianity).

It has been said that the reason that Christianity has not worked is because it has never really been tried.[13] This is not true. The tenets and beliefs of Christianity have been turned every which way and *imposed* on the believers but have proven to be ineffective in assisting personal evolution and impotent in social and self-governance. As long as a religion controls and restricts the freedom to think, to reason, to search, to find, and to be, the individual pos-

---

12 You can find a lot of "hell-fire and brimstone" preachers, intolerant and fearful people, and especially quite a few extremely wealthy televangelests and ministers. Nowhere down through the history of fundamentalism is there one single enlightened individual. Memorizing texts out of context and parroting them back ad nauseum is not a spiritual practice.

13 If by this statement it is meant that no one knows what original Christianity taught, then it is true.

sibilities and potential of that religion are nullified. It is impossible to find potential[14] of any sort when ignorance is prized and promoted. Ignorance is slavery and fear is its driving force. By adhering to an extremely limited view of life you restrict your capacity for finding anything outside of that limited view. This means nothing more than a restricted ability to find God. A finite god, then, is what you eventually find. A god within the range of human understanding is **not** God at all. Consequently, by giving God a name, an existence, and human faculties you have *created* a god within human realms. In order to even begin to search for an **in**finite God you need to have a mind that is unencumbered by laws, dogma, rules, regulations, ceremonies and so on with which the religions bombard you. You need to be able to experience as much of **life** as you can because in that experience, with God being omnipresent, aspects of God can be found. To bury your nose in a book or give yourself over to a religious perspective does not help you to get in touch with the portion of God within you (assuming that god existed and is omnipresent). In order to find God you need to begin to experience life and to begin to experience life you need to begin to understand that all life is change. In order to begin to understand change the mind must be free to think and to reason and to search throughout life, otherwise, there is only restriction.

Take a look at the difference between your objective and subjective experiences. The objective experience is one which is verifiable by concrete methods; the subjective experience is not. The subjective experience tends to be dependent upon the beliefs, prejudices, attitudes, wants, needs, and desires which are part of your learned traits and are inferred from internal states. The objective experiences are based upon the experience of the senses. You tend to assume more from the subjective experiences because they are biased by your personal *interpretation* of what is going on inside of you and your identifications not by what exists in actuality. Consequently, subjective experience is unverifiable and is judgmental and its interpretation is highly colored by your beliefs, traits, attitudes, physical and psychological desires and needs, and

---

14   Change is potential.

other internal states. Subjective experience is also susceptible to a lot of unfortunate mislabeling. Due to the fact that you were taught which emotions were appropriate, in what situations they are appropriate, and in what quantities and qualities they are appropriate you actually have no idea what your true emotional experiences are. Actually, more often than not you hide your true emotions even from yourself. This is where the mislabeling comes in. Since there is so much emotion attached to your beliefs, especially the beliefs that you hold on to tenaciously, and since you have no idea what emotions you are truly experiencing the beliefs attached to those emotions are mislabeled and subject to error and your experiences are misread.

All of your internal experience is made up of biochemical reactions. There is literally *no* experience that you have which is not a product of chemical reactions in the nerve cells of the brain and body. From the feeling of the fur on your cat or dog as you stroke it to seeing a magnificent sunset or listening to the subtle nuances of the music of Mozart, Haydn, or Debussy to the dreams that you have as you sleep all of these experiences are nothing more than chemical reactions that the *brain* has *perceived* and *interpreted.* So, your *total* experience, objective and subjective, are biochemical reactions that you interpret from previous *similar* events, training, and so on. Not only are your objective experiences based on chemical reactions, but likewise is your subjective experience. Consequently, whenever you feel some sort of emotion, all that occurs is a chemical reaction. You *interpret* that chemical reaction, for example, as love. This not only goes for all of your emotional experiences but also for psychological changes you may experience (i.e. the "peak experience" of the Humanistic psychologist) or anything that you may interpret as a *"spiritual"* experience, or the experience of God. In other words, what you may interpret as the experience of God or a transcendental experience is a matter of biochemicals. Since the chances are quite good that you do not have a solid handle on your real emotions, a manipulated trance or emotional state can be easily mistaken for a "spiritual" experience.

Hypnotic or trance states and the emotional states associated with them are quite easy to induce and manipulate. These states can lead you to believe that you have undergone a transcendental experience when this, in fact, has not occurred. There is, though, a difference between an actual transcendental or spiritual experience and one that is based upon emotional and trance state manipulation. The difference is one of the impact you feel *after* the experience. There are test questions that can be asked in order to find out if the experience was truly a transcendent experience or one that was controlled and manipulated by a group or individual:

1. *Did the experience lead to sound, decent, and virtuous values, to humanitarian, altruistic and beneficial behaviors and attitudes?* Do your behaviors contribute to your total experience of the world and to all of the people and things in it or is your contribution specifically for the group, a philosophy, or an individual? Are you being told that your contribution to the group is a contribution to the whole world? Are you being told what to experience, even in the vaguest of terms? If so, your experience is being manipulated and controlled by others.

2. *Is what you are learning in accordance with the most penetrating and wisest of human experience as has been seen consistently down through the ages.* Are you being taught only *one* point of view and told that *only* this group or philosophy has all the answers and that the experience that you have is a "true" mystical experience? Is the love that the group promotes biased and with ulterior motives? That is, does the love actually extend to those outside of the group or are you given "freedoms" with those who will not accept the groups philosophy? Do you have to promote a particular philosophy by proselytizing, selling sessions, or promoting the group and being made to think it's your choice?

3. *Does the experience that you are having feel deeply, intuitively "right"—and does it continue to feel right as time goes on or are you just being told that it is right?* Do you have the *slightest* doubts that there may be something wrong with it? Are your doubts being allayed by "pat answers"

and/or groups of followers inundating you with "love" and verbal barrages?

4. ***Does what you are experiencing and learning allow for the freedom to think, to question, to grow, and expand beyond the present point free from attachments to previous, and even present, institutions, philosophies, beliefs, and so on?*** Are you allowed to criticize, to research, and to find out for yourself on your own without castigation, disenfranchisement, disbarring, or any other sort of ostracizing?

5. ***Do you continually have to return in order to have your "mystical" experience again and again, or to come back for "reinforcement" or other lessons, treatments, new findings, etc?*** Constantly having to go back only fortifies and strengthens the tenets, dogma, and teachings that were installed. If you do not grow beyond the initial experience *on your own* you will not grow.

6. ***Has your life been changed in such a way that your viewing of yourself and others is changed in a positive way?*** Do you find yourself with a deep sense of peace and a deep concern for others without wanting to change or impose your views on them? Do you find yourself more accepting of your own failings and those of others? Do you find it unnecessary to attach yourself to any group or individual? Do you find yourself with a sense of curiosity to learn about life and a drive to find things out for yourself? Do you feel a renewed vigor for life and a connection to all existence?

A true transcendental experience is beyond the common emotions found in most religious practices that are being passed off as the "experience of God" or some aspect of God. Many people are seeking something that *they feel* is lacking or lost from their lives. So they turn to religious movements and expect the religions to provide it for them. All that the religions provide for them is a highly controlled dogmatic environment which limits their experience. It tells them what and when to think, what to say and when to say it, what to read and when to read it, and *who they are.* There is no transcendent growth in an environment such as this. Transcendental growth comes from personal experience and constant reinterpretation of the environment free from any constraints or controls. It is through a wide and varied range of experiences that changes in perception, attitude, behavior, and, eventually, biochemistry occur. Research has shown that a restrictive environment restricts growth on *all* levels—including in the brain itself.

Human beings have a great capacity for pseudo-love. This pseudo-love can be directed toward one who is new and almost unknown: an adoration of someone or something in fantasy such as the love of your automobile, your country, a dead hero, a food, or a *god.* It is not a true form of loving. If something is performing according to our *believed* expectations or assumptions, a pseudo-love can develop. Further, if you assume there is a love coming to you, an idealized type of love, then you can develop a pseudo-love. For true love to develop, there *must* be a feedback-loop that continually sustains itself with *actual behavioral activities* (physical proofs). Without this feedback-loop real love cannot possibly develop and survive. You will notice that with pseudo-love this feedback-loop does not even exist thus eliminating the possibility for any real love to develop. Claims of loving God are only *assumptions* because for a true love to develop it is necessary that a *verifiable behavioral relationship* exist prior to its occurrence. A verifiable behavioral relationship is one where there is an actual *physical interaction* between the lover and the loved. There needs to be real give and take, real verbal and non-verbal communications, and even physical touching. Being that God is unknowable and its existence cannot be proven, any claims of "love" coming from that source are only *assumptions*. Since God is "invisible" then the behavioral activities are assumptions and in actuality nonexistent. The term "love" is in fact a symbol for specific behavioral activities. Without actual behavioral activities, love does not, and cannot exist. *Love is known through actions, not in words*: Love is what is *done*, not what is said or assumed. Consequently, any claims of love either to or from God are assumptions based on what you would like to have happen and not what actually is happening. The *assumption* made that this deity "loves" this person, this group, this race, and so on become "proof" of the deity's existence and of that love. Proof, you will recall, is an extension of knowledge and to have actual knowledge of love means that there has to be *actual* and *verifiable* physical evidence of its existence. This means that there needs to be observable behavioral actions proceeding from the source of the love, not conjecture and assumptions. The idea that the answering of prayer by a particular deity is proof of that deity's existence and love is also an assumption which is based on belief and conjecture alone.

One thing that is never considered when discussing the idea of God answering prayer is that there are literally *billions* of prayers said per day to God. Out of those billions of prayers only an immensely *minute* number seem to be answered. Even in the parapsychological laboratory it is assumed that if a person scores 17% on the testing there is the possibility of something happening. Truly answered prayer rates less than 1%. With ratings this low it is only chance occurrences which are providing the "proof" that God answers prayer. The argument that God knows what is good for a person and that is why the prayer is not answered or that unanswered prayer is a gift is a cop-out. If you want to know exactly what kind of person you are dealing with, if you really want to teach a lesson, the best thing to do is to give that person what she or he wants. If there is responsible and honorable actions with the gift you then will know that he or she will act the same way with whatever else is given. Refusing to give someone something because you "know what is good for them" is an arrogant ego-trip. It is not in the best interests of proving that person to be responsible and loving. The loving individual wants to teach a lesson through experience. Restriction does not teach. It causes resentment, or worse, giving up on life.

There is also the argument that Jesus "loved" you so much that he sacrificed his life for you in order to remove your sins. You may recall that in the Gospels Jesus was to have said that he did not want to be worshiped (Matt. 15:9, Mk. 7:7). If Jesus sacrificed himself for mankind's sins without question and without reservation did he not know that this action would lead to him being worshiped? If he did not know this then he was not God. If he did know it then the sacrifice was not altruistic (without question and without reservation wanting nothing in return), as Christians assume, for he knew the ultimate outcome. In essence, the "sacrifice" of "love" was not for mankind at all but a self-centered indulgence designed to bring about a postmortem worship, not to prove his "love." Again that sacrifice was to usher in a period of peace and love for all of mankind where evil and death would be conquered. This unequivocally did not happen. Hence, we have the reiteration of the idea that men make up the rules by which the gods live.

The current western religions have done an excellent job of convincing people that it is only through them that they can find or experience God. None of them has successfully proven that they can do this. Remember, that proof of beliefs is in the manifesting of those beliefs into physical form, not in the quoting of verses out of context, or the laws, dogma and tenets devised by councils, or the amount of money taken in, the people duped into following, and so forth.

Western religions have made unsubstantiated claims of being the "savior of mankind." History, though, shows a different image. As you have seen, western religions have caused more problems than they have solved. They have produced all sorts of emotional and psychological aberrations and more social evils than ever before imagined. Your personal experience shows that ***humans need to have personal controls over social controls***. Western religions teach that all controls in life are outside. In essence, humans are at the mercy of God and the devil. The free will humans are supposed to have only pertains to not acting on temptation, nothing more. With such a limited perspective, no wonder the experience of God is so unreachable. Carl Jung put it so eloquently when he stated:

Religion is a defense against mystical (or religious) experience.

It is a fact of nature that the neurons of the brain grow through experience and learning from the environment. The more experience that you have relating to your environment, the larger the brain becomes and the more connections are created in the brain. Nature (God) has designed your brain for learning, creating new and different possibilities, and passing on all that you learn. Any philosophy, group, or institution that restricts the potential growth and the learning experiences that you can have by controlling your life and thinking is directly anti-nature and, hence, anti-God.

There are more people in mental institutions due to religion than any other reason. This is a fact. It is not a belief. Western religious movements have created more fears, anxieties, and neuroses while contributing to more psychoses than anything—including nature itself. Not only does this go for traditional (orthodox) religious movements but for non-traditional (cults and pseudo-religious) movements as well.

How does this happen?

As a member of any western religion you are subject to constant pressures to conform, to fears of the unknown (known as anxiety), and are kept in a constant state of apprehension afraid that whatever you may do may displease the deity, the group, or some "favored" individual. The vast majority of these pressures are unconscious. Consequently, they are not perceived directly. It then seems that what you are doing is of your own "free will" when it is actually highly controlled.

Once you have accepted the tenets of a particular religion you **must** also live by their rules and laws. Hence, it is necessary to do, think, and be as everyone else. Any ideas, thoughts, or feelings other than those which are prescribed by the religion are not permitted and you are coerced into repressing them. After all, these thoughts are "evil." Remember, repressed thoughts and emotions restrict your potential to experience life thus limiting your possibility for a true transcendental experience. Some of the most repressed of these thoughts are erotic, aggressive, doubting, and curious in nature. The anxiety comes from an increase in the likelihood that some of these thoughts might break through into consciousness. If they do, you might act on them or even enjoy them (e.g. the erotic thought) and commit a "sin" thus, in your own mind anyway, separating yourself from the deity or the group. This would then arouse guilt and fear of retribution from either the deity

214

or the group. The most common retribution in religions and pseu
do-religious cults is that of the loss of love. Humans have a need
to feel loved and cared for. Self-esteem is based on this need. Most
people will do just about anything to supply that need. In religious
movements, acting on or enjoying totally natural thoughts brings
about the fear that you will lose that love.[15] This fear of the loss of
love causes more anxiety, fear, and guilt thus forcing you to repress
your feelings and thoughts even deeper. You then have a fear of the
fear and guilt about feeling guilty and you're anxious about your
anxiety. So, you involve yourself even more in the practices of the
religion assuming that these practices are actually eliminating the
natural inclinations that you have when in reality the practices are
doing nothing more than pushing these emotions deeper into the
unconscious (called repression and repression is the main component of neuroses). It gets to the point that it is necessary to act in
specific ways and to do **specific** things (ritualistic or compulsive
behaviors) in order to not experience the anxieties, fears, and guilt
that are repressed and which may surface at any time. You will then
be willing to give up your self in order to become a member of the
group. Therefore, an already unstable personality becomes even
more unstable and sees "...the speck in his brother's eye while fail-
ing to see the log in his own": projecting your own failings and
fears on to others. From this you become self-righteous, indignant,
arrogant, and egoistical in your approach to others.[16]

The manipulation of fears of the unknown is one of the greatest
controllers of humanity. It does not matter if it is a government
(e.g. "It's a *threat* to our [national security or national interests]")

---

15 Francis of Assisi used to have erotic dreams and would chastise himself with a
    whip in an attempt to control these dreams. Finally, after he learned that they
    were natural responses to his personal experiences he wrote, "Too late have I
    whipped my brother" referring to the beatings he would give his body.

16 There is an old maxim: *God may forgive your sins, but your nervous sys-*
    tem won't. This indicates that whenever you feel that you have made some
    sort of transgression you will continue to act *as if* that transgression is ongo-
    ing. If you are indoctrinated with some sort of "sinner's consciousness," the
    generated fear and its accompanying guilt will be used to manipulate and
    control your behavior.

or a philosophical or religious movement which produces it. Fear can effectively control another's behavior. Just about every cult that has gained wide support has used fear in one way or another. What, in essence, is happening is that the members of the group are being conditioned like Pavlov's dogs. Due to believing that positive gains are occurring, when you are involved you will perform whenever your buttons are pushed.[17]

Literally every cult or religious movement has commonalities. These include:

1. They *all* think that they *own* the "Truth" or God. Only that group is right and everyone else is wrong and are all doomed. Only this group has a Divine purpose and this group takes precedence over the individual in the group or any outside teaching.

2. They *all* make a lot of statements that can easily be agreed to by just about everyone ("yes sets"). Then, after enough "yes sets" they bring in one of their tenets. When enough agreements have been established the statement of their own philosophy appears to naturally follow. Then they will begin to skillfully manipulate information inducing a confusion state and installing their programming. In what is called "loading the language" a whole new vocabulary is invented and many familiar words are given new definitions. This effectively seals the mind of the member from outside influences. This process is a way to give insecure personalities a feeling of superiority.

3. *Only* they have *all* of the answers and *only* they are the "saviors of the world." It is *only* through them that you can achieve true liberation. Through their rites and rituals you will be "saved" or taught to "think clearly" or be your "true self." Of course, these are all on-going and you never completely evolve.

---

17 Recall in H.G. Well's ***The Time Machine*** when the whistles blew the Eloi would walk in a trance into the bunkers where the Morlock lived in order to be the victims of the Morlock feast.

4.   They all create an emergency that *only* they can solve (the end of the world, political disaster, technology, the government, etc.). With this emergency comes a scapegoat (the devil, liberals, science, the IRS, the nefarious "they," secular humanists, science, etc.). Cults will *always* have a scapegoat, whether real or imaginary. This is a necessity because there has to be an outward direction for the repressed energy in their expressed hostility.

5.   They *all* create a depersonalization, a dissociation of you from your body and yourself. There is a distance created from you and your emotions as well as from your experience of your world. Consistently being depersonalized is a sign of mental illness and this occurs with frightening regularity to many cult members as well as to many in mainstream religious movements. This depersonalization prevents you from the experience of the truly mystical in your life. Hence, it's *not* a transcendental experience but a sign of psychic deterioration.

6.   They impose their own brand of morality on to the members of the cult claiming that they are morally and ethically right and pure. Hence, anything that you may do to someone from the outside is "absolved." In this way the more violent members of the group have an outlet for their violence and a way to expiate their guilt ("I was only following orders"). They even want to impose their brand of morality on everyone else and actively seek ways of doing just that such as manipulating elected officials to legislate laws.

7.   Much of their information is based on half-truths,[18] verbal manipulations (i.e. "buzz-words," "..."s, special vocabularies, and contrived logic) and misquotes of material. They are experts at this type of programming. This all helps to effectively close the mind to any real thinking processes. (See below)

---

18   There's an old Yiddish proverb: "A half truth is a whole lie."

8. They use the "carrot-on-the-stick" ploy to keep the members within the organization. It is always "the pie-in-the-sky" or in the next lesson or group of experiences, or the next life, etc.

9. They **all** promise **personal** and **spiritual** freedom but bind you to the organization, its tenets, and its philosophy. True freedom does not bind.

10. They are quick to point out the evils in the society and in everyone else but do not see any in themselves. This is part of the scapegoat process. It is through this that an emergency is created, fears induced, money collected, and their messiahship is reinforced, and someone or something else is the problem that only they can cure.

11. They **all** promise some sort of "transcendental" experience, quick road to enlightenment or God, access to power, or clarity of thought. The group's dogma is the only logical system and must be obeyed. This is always done through specific programming that the group sets up, induces, and manipulates.

The way that the vast majority of western religions are set up is on the same lines as the cults.[19] Today's cults are using an extreme form of religious indoctrination. There have been many instances where cult religious movements have ended up as orthodox religions (e.g. Christianity and Islam). All cults have offered some sort of relief from the problems of the world (e.g. the world to come or the appearance of the Kingdom of God), or an idea of a Utopia, and this is what attracts followers.

As you get a better understanding of what cults do, you will see that what they do is not much different than what is expected of the followers of just about any religion. In order to be a member of a

---

19 A cult is defined as: a unique system of religious worship especially involving rites and ceremonies; a group that is bound together by the devotion to or veneration of the same thing, person, ideal, concept, etc.

religion and assume the title of membership it is necessary to follow the tenets and practices of that religion. These practices are designed to control the creative and mental direction, the emotional responses, and the leisure time of the participants. They are **not** designed to instill change and freedom of choice but just the opposite. In order to be a follower of any western religion it is necessary that you **not** be allowed to change – except in the approved areas – and not be free to make choices. Neither of these behaviors can be tolerated otherwise you will be ostracized and will not have the "love" of the group and/or the deity and may even be condemned to an eternity of pain and suffering.

One of the basic necessities of cults and of most western religion is ignorance. It is this ignorance which helps them to gain and control masses of followers. The ignorance is often upgraded to "wisdom" by the group. You are told that you are gaining in wisdom and awareness as you go through the indoctrination programming while others not in the group are wallowing in ignorance. Ignorance follows two paths. The first path is that of **restricted ignorance**. In this path, either by virtue of not having the mental capacities for some physical reason or not having access to information you are ignorant. This is ignorance due to circumstance. The second path is that of **chosen ignorance**. This is the path where an individual out of *conscious choice* and/or *fear* refuses to research, to listen to other points of view, and find the facts. This second path has caused the death, destruction, and torture of untold millions of people throughout history; more so in the past two thousand years than ever before. This path involves all kinds of fundamentalism: religious, political, scientific, and ethnic/racial to name a few. Those who choose to be ignorant do so out of the fear of seeing some part of themselves that they prefer to keep hidden. They will continue on that path imposing themselves on others while using their own ignorance as an excuse and wearing it like an honored prize. Then they will claim righteousness because they were "only following orders" or were "chosen" and "doing God's (or Allah's) work."

There are literally tens of millions of people today who are involved in mind-controlling pseudo-religious cults and do not even realize it. The vast majority of these cults go under the guise of mainstream religious movements. These people follow blindly the tenets of some self-appointed "messiah," "mystic," leader, or "expert" on some kind of scripture or writings. They claim belief in some form of a deity or great teacher without question and will proselytize for their professed belief no matter how much of an imposition they are on others.

How can you be involved in a cult without knowing it? Do cults not "brainwash" their members?

Unlike the "brainwashing" that was encountered and researched during the 1950s, the cults are different. Initially cults require you to voluntarily join. From the outset, the control of your life and your mind is secured not by direct force, as was done in the 1950s, but through the subtle coercion and the exploitation of information and indirect manipulation of emotions. They are experts at the use of deceptive and distorted language, half-truths, skillfully designed hypnotic suggestions, the manipulation of confusion states, and intensive emotional experiences. Add to this that the use of mentally crippling routines designed to intensify physical exhaustion, and isolation upon the initial entry into the group. This is all designed to break down your mind and will making you much more receptive to indoctrination and control.

Groups will use subtle coercive devices such as the manipulation of your emotions, especially fears, a constant barrage by other group members for the purpose of pressuring the new recruit, and so on. Whether it is direct or indirect, the main purpose is to break your will in order to make you pliable for indoctrination.

All religious movements make their way of life look very attractive. They offer easy paths to enlightenment, personal encounters with God, Jesus, the group's personal savior, or the freedoms that their training is supposed to bring.

Once you are hooked, there is generally a single moment of "conversion." This is nothing more than a masterfully controlled emotionally intense experience. It is brought about by a series of hypnotic inductions and suggestions expertly engineered through a precise manipulation of both information and the environment. After this, the indoctrination is stepped up because receptivity is increased. This is also the time when specific suggestions are imbedded in the mind. These suggestions involve the: turning off of the "Satanic" (or "Reactive") mind; "surrendering" to the group, the leader, to Jesus, or God; or letting things "float." All of these are nothing more than hypnotic suggestions designed to induce a more permanent trance state making you easier to be controlled.

After an ongoing trance state has been induced, in order to continue it is necessary to perform different ritualistic behaviors which will reinforce the state. Some of these include: fund raising drives; recruitments and proselytizing; mind-stilling chanting, prayer sessions and/or singing sessions several times per day while in group housing or several times per week if at your personal residence; testimonials, witnessing, and other confessionals in front of the group; and attendance at required lectures, seminars, workshops, get-togethers, or study groups.

Through their simple self-hypnotic rituals two main responses are produced: First, your mind is closed to doubts, questions, and puzzling memories of your family, friends, and the outside world[20]. This is done in several ways. There are question and answer sessions where "pat" answers are given to questions about their own particular point of view, studies, writings, and rituals. Opposing points of view are not considered and most generally are ridiculed or in some way considered anathema. With this your mind is subtly closed and all freedom of thought and reason is cut off. Second, There is a sort of an "empty excitement" which is a kind of numbed, mindless high that is seen as the achievement of the group's "ultimate spiritual goal." This is achieved through the expert use of hypnotic patterns and language, the use of "ringers" and cohorts, and the manipulation of the environment and the experience. This is the reason that cult members and religious zealots have this vacuous look in their glassy eyes. This is obviously ***not*** the result of a valid mystical experience.

---

20 Many groups, cults especially, label outsiders, devils, demons, Satan worshippers, or something else. Through this process, non-members' humanity is removed and any feelings of guilt that may be associated with taking advantage or hurting another are removed. This contributes to the "anything goes" and the "ends justifies the means" attitude toward outsiders. Hence, it doesn't matter what a group member does to one outside the group, especially if the outsider refuses to join.

You usually cannot tell that you are hooked until its too late. By that time you are rationalizing your reasons for being involved and you have begun to accept your "fate." So, you go about doing as you are told and try to convince others that what you have is *the* right way. There is a convincer-loop promoted here: the more people that you convince of your point of view, the more convinced you become of it. Conversely, the more people who become hostile toward you and your point of view, the more convinced you become that the group is correct. This is because you have been told that you will encounter that sort of reaction "doing God's work" or from those possessed by "demons," from subversives, etc.

You know that you are hooked when you: 1) have to attend meetings and group gatherings at least three times per week or have some particular processes done; 2) chant or pray at least twice a day; 3) read or study *only* the group's materials consistently and if you do read opposing viewpoints it is with a specific mind-set looking at and for specific things; 4) accuse detractors of reading the "wrong" materials; 5) find yourself unable to relate in *any* intimate way or not at all with those outside of the group as well as having a fear of outsiders; 6) *refusing* to listen to other points of view whether it is by getting away from that person or creating a "wall of listener hostility" that blanks out what is being said; 7) constantly repeating group dogma and thinking; 8) wearing the group's own particular style and type of clothing, wearing your hair the particular way as defined by the group, and doing everything to look like the "perfect representative" as described by the organization; and 9) handing over your bank account and property to the group or leaving it to the group in your will.

If you find yourself: 1) anxious outside of the group or with those not of the group; 2) unable to communicate in *any* realistic way with people outside of the group; 3) acting too nice in order to be the "perfect" representative of the group or to forcibly repress erotic, aggressive, or curious and questioning thoughts and impulses such as those encountered when *having* to deal with persons who are not members; 4) having to repress earlier unpleasant events of life that are coming to surface consciousness; 5) having guilt or fear of retribution for your transgressions; and 6) having

222

your emotional needs being manipulated and/or threatened by the group, then you are involved in a mind-controlling cult. Most often these behaviors are not directly impressed or coerced. They are just subtle pressures to conform and the rest can all be up to you after the indoctrination.

More than seventy-five percent of the direct mind-controlling cults today are fundamentalist Christian, Evangelical, and Christian oriented. This is so because the statements in The Bible are so easily manipulated and interpreted and many *want to believe* that The Bible is what it claims to be. The fact of the matter is that virtually *every* Christian sect uses *one* main verse from the Scriptures to prove that *they* are the correct Christianity. The Church of God (Pasadena, CA based) uses 1 Timothy 3:5 as their Scriptural "proof." The Catholic Church uses Matthew 16:18 as their "proof." The Jehovah's Witnesses base their "correctness" on Isaiah 43:10. These are just a few of the verses which "prove" only three of the nearly *30,000* different sects of Christianity "correct." If you take a ride through any of the cities in the U.S. you will see these "store-front churches." On the majority of the signs hanging above the door you will see below the name a Biblical verse either quoted or given in book, chapter, and verse which "proves" they are the "true" Christianity and are interpreting The Bible as God wants it interpreted. It is interesting that each of those sects claims to be *the* correct one and *all* of the others are wrong.[21]

God did not give us the spirit of fear but of power and of love, and of a sound mind.

2 Timothy 1:7

---

21 If any group should know the "truth" about Christianity, it would be the Catholic Church. They created it and virtually everything that Christians believe about Christianity is a product of the Councils of the Church. As Pope Leo X (1513-1521) put it, *"It is well known the gains we have made through this fable of Christ."*

Allow yourself the freedom to think, to reason, and to find who you are without the restrictions placed on you by some religious dogma or tenets for it is only without these restrictions that a sound mind is reached, fear is overcome and power and love are expressed. It is only through the experience of life and nature that you can begin to find who you are and where you came from. And it is only through knowledge of yourself do you begin to know God because knowing God begins from within. From within you will begin to see God everywhere: in a flower, in a sunset, in a cloud, in a tree, in the eyes of another human being. It is then that you will find *your* God—if you choose to believe.

CHRISTIAN SYMBOLS

THE SWASTIKA found in the catacombs, the swastika is a symbol of the Four Elements of Earth, Water, Air, and Fire in constant motion and is seen in cultures as widely diverse as the Hopi and Egyptian. (Figure 3)

(3)

THE CROSS represents all of the crucified and risen sun-gods throughout the world. It was a very important symbol to the Egyptians. (Figure 4)

(4)

THE CRUX ANSATA/THE MALTESE CROSS were both symbols of the Egyptian god, Osiris (Ausar) and both were adopted by the Early Christians. (Figure 5)

(5)

THE CROSS OF SAINT ANTHONY is a symbol that both Egyptian and Greek soldiers wore into battle for protection from harm and success in battle. (Figure 6)

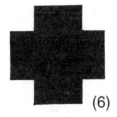

(6)

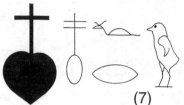

THE CRUX IN CORDE is the Egyptian hieroglyph for goodness. It was also seen in Etruscan works. It was adopted as the Sacred Heart by the Christians. (Figure 7)

(7)

THE CELTIC/DRUIDIC CROSS was adopted by the Christians from England. The Druids used it to represent their sun-god Hesus. (Figure 8)

(8)

THE CROSS OF QUETZALCOATL was adapted in the 17th century from the Mexican Aztec Indians. (Figure 9)

(9)

THE CHI AND RHO was called The Signature of Osiris the Egyptian god before the Christians adopted it. It was also referred to as The Monogram of the Sun. It is the vision that Constantine saw. There are several versions of it. (Figure 10)

(10)

IN HOC SIGNOS is known as The Monogram of Bacchus the Greek god of wine and the enjoyment of life who was given the title of **Christos** or **Christ** (Figure 11)

(11)

226

THE TRIANGLE is a cross-cultural symbol of the Heavenly Trinity of gods of every culture. (Figure 12)

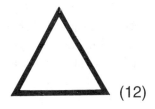

(12)

THE FISH is the symbol of the Babylonian Oannes, the Phoenician Dagan, the Hindu Vishnu and just about a dozen other of the world's savior gods.
It also represents the Zodiacal sign of Pisces, the current astrological era. (Figure 13)

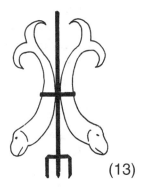

(13)

THE PENTAGRAM was described by Rennet, bishop of Peterborough thusly: ***"When it is delineated on the body of a man it points out the five places wherein the Savior was wounded, and, therefore the devils are afraid of it."*** The early Greek Christians used it at the heading of their manuscripts and at the beginning of books for good luck. It was believed by Christianity that no evil spirit could pass where it was displayed and spirits of darkness have no power over the person who has this symbol on their person. In the Middle Ages it was a symbol of immense power, and was worn for health and safety, both spiritually and physically. It became a negative symbol toward the end of The Inquisition at the insistence of The Church. (Figure 14)

(14)

227

THE CRUCIFIED MAN (sun-god) was a standard which the Roman army carried into battle. The early Christians criticized the Romans for their worship of this icon. (Figure 15)

(15)

THE FISH in this form; but standing on its tail it was the symbol of many goddesses including the Syrian goddess Atargatis before the Christians adopted it. In this form it was a representation of the external female genitalia or yoni (the vesica piscis) and is called "the Pearly Gate." (Figure 16)

(16)

PRINCIPLES OF CRITICAL THINKING

1. Knowledge is acquired only through thinking, reasoning, and questioning. Knowledge is based on facts.
    a. Belief is not knowledge. Beliefs are *opinions* acted upon *as if* they were facts.
    b. Opinions are not based on facts, knowledge, or reasoning.
    c. Critical thinking is an *active* process based on applying analysis, the synthesis of data, and your ability to assess the information being received.

2. It is only from learning *how* to think that you learn *what* to think.
    a. The unquestioning acceptance of what another says as fact is not learning nor is it part of the skill of thinking critically. It, in fact, inhibits any learning from taking place
    b. Learning *how* to think does not involve rote memorization.
    c. To become educated you need to learn how to gather, analyze, synthesize, assess, and apply data for yourself.

3. Critical thinking is an organized and systematic process used to judge the effectiveness of an argument.
    a. It is void of emotional constrictions and is, consequently, unbiased.
    b. In order to be most effective as a critical thinker you must have data and facts available for a rebuttal of an argument.
    c. Effective argumentation is based on empirical evidence.

4. Critical thinking is a search for meaning.
    a. The meaning is for yourself in what an author or speaker says, implies, and insinuates.
    b. It is a way of making sense out of what you are reading or hearing in order to find the validity of the data being presented.

5. Critical thinking is a skill that can be learned.
    a. It is based on active, logical reasoning, on facts and evidence, and a desire to learn.
    b. Your attitude toward learning is all-important in being a critical thinker. It is important that a high value be placed on learning in order for learning to be useful.
    c. The skill of critical thinking is learned by doing and by an interchange of information and ideas with others who are assessing the same things. In this way one's ideas and arguments can be presented and evaluated.
    d. You must be actively involved in exchanging thoughts and ideas in order to become a critical thinker. Sitting passively by is not how any skill is learned.

BIBLIOGRAPHY

Allegro, John
The Dead Sea Scrolls

Angus, S.
The Mystery Religions

Asimov, Isaac
Asimov's Guide to the Bible

Barnstone, W. (Ed.)
The Other Bible

Barthel, Manfred
What the Bible Really Says

Baigent, M; Leigh, R. and Lincoln, H.
Holy Blood, Holy Grail

Bloom, Harold and Rosenberg, David
The Book of J

Bottger, T. Brett
Bible Origins Research Institute Findings Report: The Hexateuch

Bromage, Bernard
Occult Arts in Ancient Egypt

Bushby, Tony
The Bible Fraud

Chadwick, Henry
The Early Church

Charlot, John
New Testament Disunity

D'Alviella, Goblet
The Mysteries of Eleusis

Darmesteter, James (Trans.)
The Zend Avesta (Parts I & II)

Doane, Thomas
Bible Myths and Their Parallels in Other Religions...

Eisebius (G.A. Williamson, Trans.)
The History of The Church From Christ to Constantine

Farrington, Benjamin
The Faith of Epicurus

Finegan, Jack
Archaeological History of the Ancient Middle East

Freedman, Benjamin H.
facts are facts

Friedman, Richard Elliot
Who Wrote The Bible?

Friedrich, Johannes
Extinct Languages

Gaster, Theodore
The Dead Sea Scriptures

Graham, Lloyd
Deceptions and Myths of The Bible

Hall, Manley P.
Secret Teachings of All Ages

Heidel, Alexander
The Gilgamesh Epic and Old Testament Parallels

Higgins, Frank C.
Hermetic Masonry

Jonas, Hans
The Gnostic Religion

Joyce, Donavan
The Jesus Scroll

Kaplan, Aryeh
Meditation and The Bible

Kaus, Mulla Firus Bin (Trans.)
The Desatir: or the Sacred Writings of the Ancient Persian Prophets

Leedom, Tim C. (Ed.)
The Book your Church Doesn't Want You To Read

Maccoby, Hyam
The Mythmaker, Paul and the Invention of Christianity

Mack, Burton, L.
Who Wrote the New Testament? The Making of the Christian Myth

The Lost Gospel, The Book of Q & Christian Origins

Massey, Gerald
Egyptian Book of the Dead and the Mysteries of Amenta

MacMullen, Ramsay
Christianizing the Roman Empire, AD 100-400

Meyer, Marvin W.
The Ancient Mysteries, A Sourcebook

Mills, L.H. (Trans.)
The Zend Avesta (Part III)

Pagels, Elaine
The Gnostic Gospels

Palumbo, A.E., Jr.
The Secret of the Dead Sea Scrolls

Patai, Raphael
The Messiah Texts

Pavitt, William
The Book of Talismans, Amulets and Zodiacal Gems

Potter, Charles F.
Is That in The Bible?

Pritchard, James B. (Ed.)
The Ancient Near East (Vols. I and II)

Pryse, James
Restored New Testament

Robertson, J.M.
Pagan Christs

Robinson, James (Ed.)
The Nag Hammadi Library

Schiller, Ronald
The Biblical Exodus: Fact or Fiction
Reader's Digest, May 1983, P. 133-138

Schonfield, Hugh J.
The Passover Plot

Sheler, Jeffery L.
Is the Bible True?
Reader's Digest, June 2000, P. 186-193

Shenkman, Richard
Legends, Lies & Cherished Myths of American History

Legends, Lies & Cherished Myths of World History

Staniforth, Maxwell (Trans.)
Early Christian Writings, The Apostolic Fathers

Stone, Merlin
When God Was a Woman

Stuart, Gene S.
America's Ancient Cities

Taylor, Thomas (Trans.)
The Arguments of the Emperor Julian Against the Christians

Thomas, Winton D. (Ed.)
Documents from Old Testament Times

Thompson, Thomas L.
The Mythic Past: Biblical Archeology and the Myth of Israel

Ulansey, David
The Origins of the Mithraic Mysteries

Walker, Benjamin
Gnosticism: Its History and Influence

Wells, G.A.
The Historical Evidence for Jesus

Did Jesus Exist?

Wilson, Ian
Exodus: The True Story Behind the Biblical Account

REFERENCE WORKS

Ben-Yehuda, Ehud
Ben-Yehuda's Hebrew/English Dictionary

Brown, Francis; Driver, S.R., Briggs, Charles A.
A Hebrew and English Lexicon of the Old Testament

Eliade, Mircea (Ed.)
The Encyclopedia of Religion (Vols. 1-15)

Jastrow, Marcus
Dictionary of Targumim, Talmud Babli, Verushalmi and Midrashic Literature

Strong, James
Strong's Exhaustive Concordance

BIBLES:

Authorized King James *Version*

Holy Bible from the Ancient Eastern Text (George Lamsa, Trans.)

The New American Standard Bible

The Holy Scriptures According to the Masoretic Texts (Vol. I & 2)

Another title available by Alexander S. Holub, Ph.D.

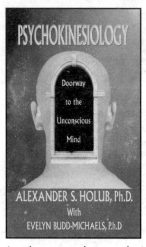